Heinemann IGCSE

English –
First Language

Peter Inson

www.pearsonis.com

Free online support
Useful weblinks
24 hour online ordering

Heinemann

Part of Pearson

Heinemann is an imprint of Pearson Education Limited, a company incorporated in England and Wales, having its registered office at Edinburgh Gate, Harlow, Essex, CM20 2JE. Registered company number: 872828.

www.pearsonschoolsandfecolleges.co.uk

Heinemann is a registered trademark of Pearson Education Limited

Text © Pearson Education Limited 2011

First published 2011

15 14 13 12 11
10 9 8 7 6 5 4 3 2 1

British Library Cataloguing in Publication Data
A catalogue record for this book is available from the British Library

ISBN 978-0-435991-18-0

Edited by Christine McCafferty
Designed by Tech-Set Ltd, Gateshead
Typeset by Tech-Set Ltd, Gateshead
Original illustrations © Pearson Education Limited 2011
Illustrated by Tech-Set Ltd, Gateshead
Cover design by Creative Monkey
Picture research by Joanne Forrest Smith
Cover photo/illustration © Photodisc.Steve Cole
Index by Indexing Specialists (UK) Ltd
Printed in the UK by Scotprint

Websites
The websites used in this book were correct and up-to-date at the time of publication. It is essential for tutors to preview each website before using it in class so as to ensure that the URL is still accurate, relevant and appropriate. We suggest that tutors bookmark useful websites and consider enabling students to access them through the school/college intranet.

Acknowledgements
We are grateful to the following for permission to reproduce copyright material:
Jo Edkins, Celtic Knots for extract and images from 'How to make a Reef Knot' http://gwydir.demon.co.uk/jo/knots/reef.htm, copyright © Jo Edkins. Reproduced with permission; The Strait Times for an extract from 'Portable blood pressure device' by Judith Tan *The Straits Times* 13 October 2009, copyright © Singapore Press Holdings Limited. Reproduced with permission; Expatica for an extract from "My first Fête Nationale Suisse", 10 August 2009, www.expatica.com, copyright © Expatica, 2009; The Buenos Aires Herald for an extract from 'Brazilian floods claim 39 dead', *Buenos Aires Herald*, 28 October 2009. Copyright © Buenos Aires Herald; Canwest Digital Media for an extract from 'Urban sprawls take toll on children: study' by Laura Stone, *The Ottawa Citizen*, 28 October 2009 Stone, Canwest News Service www.canada.com. Material reprinted with the express permission of CANWEST NEWS SERVICE, a CanWest Partnership; The Courts Service for an extract from the Judgement in "D.P.P.-v- Mark Doran", 31 July 2009, citation [2009] IECCA 113, Court of Criminal Appeal, as published on http://www.courts.ie/Judgments.nsf/09859e7a3f34669680256ef3004a27de/7ef428a29c3ca5b88025764f0052c1fc?OpenDocument copyright © Court of Criminal Appeal; The Southland Times for an extract adapted from 'Focus on Police Competence - The Trevor Franklin Police Botchup', *Southland Times* 25 October 2001, copyright © The Southland Times, Invercargill, NZ; United Agents for an extract from *The First Rumpole Omnibus* by John Mortimer, published by Penguin Books, 1978. Reprinted by permission of United Agents on behalf of The Estate of Sir John Mortimer; David Higham Associates Ltd for an extract from *The Case for the Defence* by Graham Greene published in *Complete Short Stories*, Penguin 2005. Reproduced by permission of David Higham Associates Ltd; Guardian News and Media Ltd for an extract from 'The First Resort' by Benji Lanyado *The Guardian*, 14 March 2009, copyright © Guardian News & Media Ltd 2009; UN High Commission Refugee Council for the poster "Refugees are so lucky", copyright © UNHCR; Karen Hegmann for "Telling the Story: The Impact of Art, Science and Technology on Brand Communications and Marketing", by Karen Hegmann, 30 July 2007 published on http://karenhegmann.typepad.com/tellingthestory/advertising/, reproduced with permission; Patrick Scissons, Creative Director, BBDO for a 2007 quotation concerning refugees, reproduced with permission of Patrick Scissons, Creative Director; Sheil Land Associates for an extract from *I'm the King of the Castle* by Susan Hill, published by Penguin. Copyright © Susan Hill 1970, 1988. Reproduced by permission of Sheil Land Associates Ltd; Serpent's Tail for an extract from *From Boy A* by Jonathan Trigell, published by Serpent's Tail, 2007. Reproduced by permission of Serpent's Tail; David Higham Associates Ltd and Pollinger Ltd for an extract from *The Day of the Triffids* by John Wyndham, pp.37-38, first published by Michael Joseph 1951. Reproduced by permission of David Higham Associates Ltd, Pollinger Limited and Wyndham Case Pty Limited as

Contents

Introduction

This book has many features that will help you during the course. These features are described below.

Colour coding

The book is divided into five sections. The sections have colour-coded page numbers to help you navigate through the book easily.

Section One: Basics

→ Looks at the importance of communicating accurately and responding appropriately to texts, as well as examining the way language works and how to check the use of it.

Section Two: Narrative

→ A closer look at storytelling and the choosing and arranging of words to develop a plot and storyline.

Section Three: Descriptive

→ You'll practise describing things and events, including other people's feelings, using comparisons and word pictures.

Section Four: Opinions and ideas

→ You'll look at how pondering, persuading, reasoning and explaining are handled in verbal discussions and written work.

Section Five: Ready for the exam

→ We'll look at a sample of each paper and at the coursework closely. There are several routes through the examination which are set out here.

Hint boxes

Helpful comments and hints feature throughout the book and key words are explained.

> The narrator is the person who tells the story. The narrator can be a character in the story or they can be outside the story (a third person narrator). Some longer stories and books have more than one narrator.

Activities

The book contains useful activities that you can undertake in class. Most of these activities are suitable for paired and group work.

ACTIVITY 1

Work in groups or pairs.

(a) List very briefly the essential events of the story. A simple numbered list would be ideal.

Exercises

The book provides ample opportunities for you to practise what you have learned. Most of the exercises are suitable for independent work.

The answers to selected Activities and Exercises can be found in the Exam Café CD.

EXERCISE 2

You are going to plan and write a short story for young children. The theme of your story, that is the idea which drives it, could be the need to warn young children about something or to encourage them to try something out. You want them to remember something important. You might, for example, belong to a successful young people's organisation and want children to consider joining when they are old enough. Once your story has been marked, again, be prepared to read it in class or to allow someone else to read it.

The challenge exercises and activities are of a level that students of the Extended course should be able to do but which students of Core should also consider trying.

Accuracy in speaking and writing

Getting started

In **Section One**, we are going to start by looking at the importance of communicating accurately and responding appropriately to what we read. We are also going to examine the way language works and consider how we can check the way that we use it.

Most of the time we use the spoken form of English, easily, fluently and without giving it much thought. With the written form, however, things are very different. We have to be clearer in our thinking and more precise in expressing ourselves.

There are some things that we do with little thought and doing them can seem very easy. Examples are combing our hair or spreading a slice of bread. If someone asked you whether you can send a mobile phone text message, for example, you would probably answer yes straight away. However, if you were asked to set out written instructions for doing this, you might find it more difficult than you expect.

Learning to write clearly

It is easy to express things in the wrong way when we write them down or for readers to misunderstand what we mean. Here are some examples to illustrate this.

Do not attempt to stop chain with your hands.

On a chainsaw

Do not iron clothes on body.

On packaging for an iron

Do not drive car or operate machinery.

On children's cough medicine

Do not turn upside down.

On the bottom of a pot of tiramisu dessert

For indoor or outdoor use only.

On a string of Christmas lights

Not to be used for the other use.

On a food processor

Instructions: Open packet. Eat nuts.

On a packet of nuts distributed by an air steward

Do not increase volume past threshold of pain.

On a pair of headphones

ACTIVITY 1

Work in pairs or groups.

(a) Discuss what is at fault with each of the instructions above. Make a brief note for each example.

(b) Think of some more nonsensical instructions that could be included in the list above.

EXERCISE 1

For each faulty instruction discussed in Activity 1, write a paragraph in which you analyse the fault and explain what should have been written.

Which was easier, talking about the faults or writing about them?

Clearly, it was the talking. It is usually much more difficult to write clearly than just to say what you mean. This is especially true if you are trying to explain something or give instructions. Nonsense is more easily written than spoken.

We usually speak to an audience, either an individual or a group of people. Alongside our words, we use our body language and facial expressions to help make what we are saying more clear. If what we say makes no sense then our audience will usually tell us quickly and easily. Written material, on the other hand, is usually intended to be read in the absence of the writer. An instant response is unlikely. Writers therefore have to be much more careful than speakers to ensure that what they are trying to convey is expressed clearly. Readers can rarely ask the writer for clarification so this must be provided, before it is asked for, by the writer. This truth is at the heart of this book.

ACTIVITY 2

(a) The aim of these activities is to practise giving clear instructions. You can work in groups, or as a class. Two volunteers are needed, One and Two. One will need to be able to tie a tie or lace shoes. One stands to one side, looking away from the group. Two stands in front of the group. One tells Two how to tie a tie or lace up shoes and Two carries out One's instructions.

◀ Tying a shoelace – easier done than said!

(b) The rest of the group must judge how clear the instructions that One gave were. When the task is complete, or when the group judge that the attempt has failed, make a list of what was helpful about the instructions that were given, and what was not. Decide how the instructions could have been made more helpful.

(c) Working in pairs, write a sequence of instructions for tying a tie or lacing shoes and then try out the instructions on others. Next, try reading other pairs' instructions to others. With this experience, as a class, make a list of points to remember when you are writing instructions.

It will help you to consider answers to these questions as you do this:

Did One find it difficult to decide how fast to give his or her instructions?

How difficult was it for One because Two's actions could not be seen or followed?

Did One want to use his or her hands to demonstrate?

Did Two try to ask any questions?

How easily was Two able to understand One?

EXERCISE 2

(a) Consider some other familiar activities, such as making tea or coffee, riding a bicycle, sewing on a button, downloading information onto a computer or saving a document onto a memory stick. Are some of these activities easier than others? Try and explain why. Write out instructions for one of these activities, or a similar activity. Ask someone else to check what you have written to see whether it makes sense.

(b) Look at the two sets of instructions for tying a reef knot that follow and decide which set you prefer. Try improving one of the sets of instructions. When you have done this, give your instructions to someone else to try out.

Instructions 1

Step by step instructions for tying a reef knot

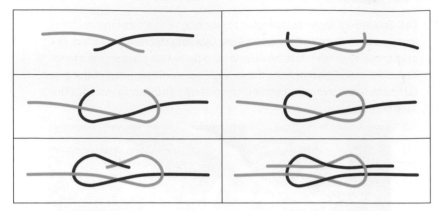

Holding one end of each rope in each hand, pass the left rope over the right, and tuck under. Then pass the same rope, now in the right hand, over the left rope, and tuck under.

Instructions 2

How to tie a reef knot (known as a square knot in America)

It is the best knot for tying string round something, like a parcel, as it lies flat, and is easy to undo. Both strings should be of equal size.

Hold one string in each hand. Twist the string on your left side round the one in your right, first over, then under, then over again.	Pull gently to tidy up.	Twist the string on your right side round the one on your left, first over, then under, then over again.	Pull gently to tidy up again.

The usual mistake is to make the same half knot twice. The top half in the illustration is a mirror image of the bottom half. Think of the string rather than your hands. The same string goes from left to right, over, under and over again. Then it returns from right to left, over, under and over again. (If you make the same half knot twice, you end up with a granny knot which is useless and dangerous!) You must also be careful when tightening the knot. Pull both strings equally, and not too hard, at first. If you pull one string much harder than the other, the knot will be pulled out of shape, and at worst will be merely a number of loops of one string round the other. When tying a parcel, you can make this knot much tighter by tightening the first half as much as possible, then persuading someone to put their finger on it while you tie the second half. Then tighten the top half, slipping it under their finger.

ACTIVITY 3

In this activity, we will think about how to set out instructions so that they are clear and easy to follow. Working in pairs, make a list of steps that should be taken when setting and laying out instructions. Try to think of different situations in which instructions are helpful or necessary. Examples are cooking, mending or adjusting machinery, programming electronic equipment, doing make-up, working with animals and doing first aid. Share your ideas with the class.

◀ Recipes are instructions for cooking.

EXERCISE 3

Using the list of steps created in Activity 3, write a full set of instructions for one of the examples, such as cooking or doing first aid. Remember to explain clearly what is to be done at each stage.

Learning to speak clearly

So far in this chapter you have needed to focus clearly on what you are reading and what you are writing. Now you are going to extend these skills to what other people are saying and to what you yourself are saying.

ACTIVITY 4

In this activity, you are going to play a game. You may have heard of the British Broadcasting Corporation (BBC) radio show called *Just a Minute*. In this panel game, contestants have to speak for 60 seconds on any topic that is given them, without any time to prepare in advance. While one contestant on the panel is speaking, the others have to interrupt them if they hesitate, repeat themselves or deviate from the topic that they have been given. A point is awarded to the person who interrupted them.

More information about the programme is available on this website:
www.bbc.co.uk/programmes/b006s5dp

(a) Set up a panel of four, with your teacher as the umpire or chairperson. One contestant has to try speaking for just 30 seconds on a topic provided by the chairperson, without hesitating, without deviating and without repetition. Obviously common words such as *the*, *a* and *I* will have to be repeated if the speakers are to make sense, but other words must not be repeated. Your topics might come from this list.

> My favourite meal
> Our pets
> Nightmare teachers
> Love at first sight
> Babysitting
> Lies I have told
> Living abroad
> Absentee parents
> What to do about homework
> A fantastic result
> My first date
> The best band in the world
> The neighbours
> Learning a new language
> Small brothers and sisters
> Grandparents

If another contestant on the panel interrupts the speaker because he or she has hesitated, repeated him or herself or has deviated from the topic, then that contestant wins a point and then begins to speak on the topic. If the chairperson decides that the challenge is not fair then the person who is speaking gains a point and continues with the topic. The person who is speaking at the end of the 30 seconds gains an extra point. You will need someone to keep the score.

(b) Now the whole class will take part in the game. There is one contestant but anyone in the class can interrupt if the contestant hesitates, repeats him or herself or deviates from the topic. Anyone in the class can try to earn points by interrupting for these reasons. You can use the topics suggested in **(a)** above or the class can decide on some new topics. Your teacher or a member of the class can umpire the game and someone else should be appointed scorer.

Just a minute is not as easy as it sounds, but it's lots of fun. ▶

Making and using notes

In the game you just played, you had to make impromptu speeches which wasn't easy. Making notes will help you to remember what you need to say when you are giving a speech.

 ACTIVITY 5

(a) In this activity each member of the class is going to make a short prepared talk. The class is divided into groups of four or five. Each of you will prepare a short talk (five minutes is long enough) on one of the topics used in Activity 4. Take five to ten minutes for everyone to prepare some notes.

(b) Now each student in the group has a turn to give his or her speech. As each student speaks, the others in the group will consider their voice and ideas.

After each speech, ask the other members of your group about your voice.

Volume: Were you loud enough, too loud or too quiet?

Pace: Were you too fast, too slow or just right?

Clarity: Were your words clear and distinct? Or did you mumble and not make your tongue and mouth parts work sufficiently hard?

Now ask the other members of your group about your ideas.

Did your ideas make sense?

Were all the points you made clear and understandable?

Did you give examples to help your audience understand what you wanted to say?

Were your points arranged in the most effective order? Did you finish with your strongest or funniest point?

(c) Discuss, were your notes helpful? Ask the other members of the group whether their notes were helpful? If not, why not? Discuss how one's notes can be improved.

Do not be shy about speaking to the rest of the class. Being able to speak out to an audience is very useful. It is a little like learning to ride a bike, frightening at first, but worthwhile and it gets easier with practice. No one regrets learning to ride a bike and, in the same way, once you get the hang of making speeches or speaking publicly you will feel more confident.

Having good notes is key to making a good speech. When you speak, try to look up rather than down. Looking down is natural when you feel shy or embarrassed, or if you are struggling to remember what to say next or if your notes are too detailed. Look up and away over the top of the group if you can. Imagine that you are speaking for the special benefit of the people at the back and then everyone is much more likely to hear you properly. It will also help to take a deep breath as you start and this extra air will help you to project your voice. Regard the audience as friends who want you to perform well. Look directly over your audience and count slowly to five before you start. Doing this will convey a sense of confidence and will help you to avoid fidgeting which can be a distraction from what matters, which is what you have decided to say to them.

Keeping your notes short and succinct will help you to present your speech better. If you have no reminder of your main points in front of you, you could easily forget to convey something important. However, if your notes are too long, you could end up merely reading the passage and looking down too much. In the next exercise we will work on making short but effective notes.

ACTIVITY 6

(a) Choose another topic. You have five minutes to plan what you are going to say and to make notes. Make your final notes on a piece of paper that is no larger than a post card. In your final notes, only write down the essential, key words upon which you will focus. You should aim for no more than six key words.

(b) In groups, give your talks. Evaluate each other's speeches. Did the person do better than in the last activity?

(c) Think through and note down what you have learnt about speaking to other people as a result of activities 4 to 6.

Remember that keeping your notes short will ensure that you look at your audience rather than the notes when you are speaking.

Summary

You started off by looking at things that we can all do and regard as very simple. However, when you tried to explain or set out instructions to do these simple things, you probably found that it was more difficult than you expected. Great care is required when we tell someone what to do. Before we give an instruction, we have to think about what the reader does or does not know about the topic and what is likely to happen when they try to follow our instructions. We also have to imagine how clearly other people will understand what we are telling them.

In the game, *Just a Minute*, you learnt about the need to listen very carefully to what others are saying and to think carefully and quickly before saying anything yourself. Then you learnt about the need to make brief notes when you are planning a speech.

Chapter 2

Communicating the most important points

Getting started

Note-making and summarising will help you to listen and read carefully so that you can better understand what is being said or written. To help with this you must learn to identify the main verb in a sentence, whether reading or listening. The main verb is the guide to what is most significant in a sentence.

In this chapter you are going to develop your ability to identify the main point of a sentence through a close reading of it. This will help you to select and organise information and then communicate it as economically as possible.

Identifying verbs

First, let's revise some grammar because to find the main point you need to know how to identify the verb in a sentence. You should be aware of the different kinds of words that we use and the different functions that they have; **nouns** name things, **adjectives** describe things and **adverbs** qualify action words (verbs). The most important of these types of words, however, are **verbs**. They are often called 'doing words'. Verbs indicate the action in a sentence. They are at the grammatical heart of a sentence and without them you cannot have a sentence.

Verbs are action words. It is obvious that action is involved in verbs such as *smash, stroke, shout* and *whisper.* These are physical actions that can be seen and heard. The action of other verbs such as *think, fear* and *calculate* reveal actions that we can detect, not with our senses, but with our understanding.

> Be aware that the verb *to be* (which appears in many different forms in the English language) is an exception. It does not tell us about an action but about identity, a sort of = sign. Examples are:
>
> John is the driver.
> Miriam is good.

ACTIVITY 1

(a) Discuss in class which of these groups of words are proper sentences, that is groups of words that make complete sense.
  [1] Wonderful people in rickshaws, taxis and on elephants, from all over the world.
  [2] Stop.
  [3] The cat sat on the mat.

    (1) Flowing gently through the tree-lined valley, the river at last.

    (2) Strawberry is my favourite.

    (3) Clicking his way through hundreds of web pages was the only way.

    (4) While the others held up the traffic and explained matters to the drivers, the student leaders called the police so that there would be no further trouble.

The answers are in the Exam Café CD.

Remember, however, that there are times when the main verb of a sentence is neither heard nor seen. An example is, *'Over here.'* A main verb is implied here. The main verb can be omitted from a sentence when the listener or reader knows the context or receives other signals, such as the waving of an arm. Then we know whether what is really meant is, *'Look over here'* or *'Come over here'* or *'Wait over here'*.

Sometimes verbs consist of more than one word, forming a phrase. Examples are *do remember*, *can be*, *can't stop, do need*, *is happening*, *has happened* and *will happen*. More than just a simple action is being used in these examples. *Do* is a verb in its own right. Remember, we *do* things.

When the word *do* is combined with a word that tells us who or what is doing the action, it forms a question. Think of *Do you swim?* Another example is *Can he swim?* This example uses a different verb, the verb *to be able* which forms *can*.

In the case of *has happened*, the additional verb is the verb *to have* which indicates a past tense, that is, an action that has taken place in the past.

These extra verbs are used as auxiliary verbs (*auxilia* is Latin for help or assistance). An auxiliary verb, combined with an ordinary verb, forms a compound verb. Examples of compound verbs are *was working*, *is trying* and *will succeed*.

EXERCISE 1

The last question here, (j) may well prove a puzzle. The reason is that the subject of the sentence, the band, is not the agent or the doer of the action, which is hearing. In this sort of construction, using the passive voice of the verb, the agent, the doer of the action does not have to be identified. The passive voice tells us to whom or to what the action is done. For example: *The ice cream was eaten*, or *cheats are despised* or *you will be rewarded*.

The answers are in the Exam Café CD.

Here are ten sentences with **compound verbs**. Identify the auxiliaries then write down what they tell us about the main verb.

(a) William was smiling.

(b) They don't smile here.

(c) He couldn't wait.

(d) She might have waited.

(e) Can it be?

(f) He would have left before ten o'clock.

(g) She will be waiting for her friends to arrive.

(h) The bus had arrived before they were ready.

(i) Just before dawn they were trying to light a fire.

(j) The band could be heard for miles.

Listening, note-making and writing reports

In this section you will practise listening, note-making and summarising. As you listen to the passages that follow, you will make notes. Later, when you read your notes, they should serve as an aide-mémoire. Your notes must make it easy for you to recall the important facts and ideas as quickly as possible. In this way you will be able to concentrate on writing fast and accurately. If you have to read over words and phrases that are not really necessary while you are trying to write, it will distract you from the business of writing well.

Also, if you spent too much time writing down unimportant words while you should have been listening, you might have missed some important facts.

Portable blood pressure device in *The Straits Times*

A HOMEGROWN company has come up with a portable home device to measure blood pressure from a person's aorta.

This reading is a better indicator of the risk of heart attacks and strokes than one taken the conventional way from the arm, say several studies worldwide.

The device, called the A-Pulse CASPal, yields two readings: One is the blood pressure from the artery in the arm, and the other, the aortic blood pressure, which is measured with a sensor resting just above the artery in the wrist. The latter is usually a lower reading.

The device offers a non-invasive way of getting a reading of the blood pressure from the aorta, the main vessel which carries oxygenated blood out of the heart to the rest of the body.

Until now, it has been possible to measure blood pressure from the aorta only in a hospital or clinic setting, in an invasive procedure involving the insertion of a pressure-sensor tip catheter into a blood vessel in the patient's groin.

Singapore company HealthStat International will launch the $490 device here this week. It uses the same technology as its predecessor, the BPro, a watch-like device loaded with software to read the blood pressure from the aorta.

ACTIVITY 2

The article above is from a Singapore-based newspaper, *The Straits Times*. As a class, look at the first sentence of the report. *Which are the key words? Which are the important ideas?* You might want to make notes like these.

'HOMEGROWN' — it's produced locally. A sense of pride may be involved or relief that a local company is performing well.

'Portable' — It's easy to carry around and convenient to use.

Now examine the first two paragraphs, deciding on the most important words in each sentence.

EXERCISE 2

(a) Make sure that you have a pen and paper to make brief notes. You are going to listen to your teacher, or a member of the class, read the article about the portable blood pressure device. As you listen, make very brief notes. Aim to write no more than four words for each point that is made.

(b) Using your notes, write a summary of what you have heard without looking at the passage.

(c) Now compare the summary that you wrote to the passage. Did you cover the main points?

Planning and checking your work can sometimes seem to get in the way of finishing a task but it is important, especially in examinations. If you are impatient then you should remember that it is even more tiresome to have to go back over and fix up a piece of work that has been rushed than to plan and check carefully in the first place.

If you are going to write a passage, planning what you will write beforehand will ensure that you cover the most important points, and present them in the best order. To practise this, in the next exercise you are going to plan and write a short topic of your own.

EXERCISE 3

(a) You are going to write a short report of about 150 words. First, choose a topic. You could choose your own topic or use one of these:

- An event that has recently been in the news
- Someone you have recently met or heard of for the first time
- A career that you are considering
- Local charities
- Facilities for young people in your area.

Doing some research for your passage for homework would be useful.

(b) Make a list of the key ideas that you have on the topic you have chosen. These should be expressed as key words. Next, consider whether your key words are in the best sequence in order to present your ideas in a way that makes sense and holds the attention of your reader.

Asking someone to check your list will be helpful.

(c) When you are satisfied with your list of key ideas, write out a first draft of your report. It is a good idea to use only alternate lines on the sheet of paper so that you have room to fill in alterations and improvements when you read it back to yourself. If you have to make a lot of alterations then you should write a second version which should be neater and easier to read.

(d) Finally, read your reports to each other. The listeners should say which points in each report they found clear and easy to follow. They should also suggest ways to improve each report.

Learning to identify the important points made by a writer is an important first step in improving our ability to read and absorb information and to understand what is central, and secondary, to the writer's purpose. This helps us to take in what really matters when we are reading. Similarly, knowing the most important points that we want to convey will make us better writers.

Summarising the key points

This section takes finding the most important points in a passage a step further. Imagine that you work in a huge organisation and that you are responsible for transmitting to all its employees important information that has to be extracted from long and complicated documents. It could involve employment law, health and safety requirements or arrangements for their pensions.

Selecting information to be communicated to others is of great importance in many aspects of practical and professional life. It is also a very important part of studying and of learning to acquire, analyse and present information. It must be done as economically as possible to save time and to keep yourself or your audience focussed on the most important information. If you can summarise ideas succinctly, you will save yourself and others a lot of unnecessary work. We will practise this skill in the activity that follows.

New York Daily News

Ralph Lauren model Filippa Hamilton: I was fired because I was too fat!

In this Ralph Lauren ad, which features Hamilton, her appearance was altered to make her look very thin.

Ralph Lauren's clothing company fired the model whose body looked emaciated in a touched-up ad because she weighed too much, the woman told the Daily News on Tuesday.

Filippa Hamilton – whose hips appeared slimmer than her head in the recent altered ad – said her contract was terminated in April because she was too heavy.

"They fired me because they said I was overweight and I couldn't fit in their clothes any more," she said.

The 5-foot-10, 120-pound stunner was amazed to see her body digitally distorted for Ralph Lauren Blue Label.

"I was shocked to see that super skinny girl with my face," she told the Daily News. "It's very sad, I think, that Ralph Lauren could do something like that."

Hamilton, 23, worked for Ralph Lauren since about 2002 and considered the company like a second family – until she was bounced.

Then out of nowhere last week, the altered ad – which appeared only in Japan – caused a sensation and drew the ire of critics who thought it appeared sickly and unrealistic.

Polo Ralph Lauren said in a statement Tuesday night that Filippa is a "beautiful and healthy" woman but their relationship ended "as a result of her inability to meet the obligations under her contract with us."

"The image in question was mistakenly released and used in a department store in Japan and was not the approved image which ran in the U.S. We take full responsibility," the statement said. "This error has absolutely no connection to our relationship with Filippa Hamilton."

Hamilton's lawyer, Geoffrey Menin, said the image is "gross distortion of how she really looks and which we fear will be extremely damaging to her."

Hamilton is concerned about its impact on the public.

"I think they owe American women an apology, a big apology," she said. "I'm very proud of what I look like, and I think a role model should look healthy."

(a) As a class, read the article from *The New York Daily News*.

(b) Take a few minutes to identify what you think are the two main concerns of the model and the two main concerns of the fashion house. Discuss these main points as a class or in groups.

(c) Now each student should make short notes on each main point. Remember to make your notes as brief as possible – a few words are sufficient for each point. By using a minimum number of words, you will focus much more closely on the things that really matter. Make sure that you do not simply report everything that the model and the fashion house spokesperson say, but only those things which they seem to feel most strongly about and which seem to be most important for them.

You will also need to write a brief introduction to your four points so that the reader can learn quickly about the context in which they occur. Aim to write three paragraphs: a single sentence introduction and two further paragraphs of about 40 words each. Do not write more than 150 words.

(d) When you have finished, read your work. Check that what you have written makes sense, and that it matches your purpose. Reading your work aloud will help you check this.

(e) Exchange your work with someone else so that you can read and comment on each other's work. Again, reading the work aloud will help you check the effectiveness of the way the passage is written.

EXERCISE 4

You are going to write an informative, but objective, passage about yourself, your friends or your family. Aim to write 400 words. Before you write, take note of these pointers.

(a) Discuss in class, or in smaller groups, what topic you should write about. As you do so, try to gauge what aspects of your topic others would be most interested in.

(b) Stick to the facts. Try to avoid the temptation to write about your opinions at this stage, especially if they are strong ones. You will have opportunities to do so later on in **Section Four**.

(c) Think clearly about what you are going to write. Even before you start to write, divide what you want to write into sections and decide in which order you will present the different sections.

(d) Also consider the manner in which you are going to write. Will your passage be very serious, light-hearted, humorous or simply matter-of-fact?

Once this passage has been returned to you, it would be a good idea to keep it safe. Later, you could develop and improve this item as a piece of coursework, so long as your teacher has only commented upon the piece but not marked it.

Summary

The aim of this chapter was getting you to understand and handle information as accurately and economically as possible. An important part of this is identifying the main verb of a sentence in order to understand better the sentence's main point. Being able to identify the most important points will help you to study any subject or topic. It will also prepare you to play a full role as an educated adult in a wide range of careers and occupations.

Chapter 3

Beneath the surface – reading and writing

Getting started

Reading a passage of good writing can require a great deal of attention from the readers. There is the basic narrative or 'story' of the passage, but then there can be deeper levels of meaning too. As readers we might, for example, need to be thinking about the feelings of the different characters in the passage or what they, or the writer, might be hiding from us.

Handling more complicated passages

The passage that follows is a good example of a one that requires some attention on the part of the reader to get fuller understanding, and enjoyment, out of it. It is the beginning of a short story entitled *The Lumber Room* by the author Saki.

The children were to be driven, as a special treat, to the sands at Jagborough. Nicholas was not to be of the party; he was in disgrace. Only that morning he had refused to eat his wholesome bread-and-milk on the seemingly frivolous ground that there was a frog in it. Older and wiser and better people had told him that there could not possibly be a frog in his bread-and-milk and that he was not to talk nonsense; he continued, nevertheless, to talk what seemed the veriest nonsense, and described with much detail the colouration and markings of the alleged frog. The dramatic part of the incident was that there really was a frog in Nicholas' basin of bread-and-milk; he had put it there himself, so he felt entitled to know something about it. The sin of taking a frog from the garden and putting it into a bowl of wholesome bread-and-milk was enlarged on at great length but the fact that stood out clearest in the whole affair, as it presented itself to the mind of Nicholas, was that the older, wiser and better people had been proved profoundly in error in matters about which they had expressed the utmost assurance.

"You said there couldn't possibly be a frog in my bread-and-milk; there WAS a frog in my bread-and-milk," he repeated with the insistence of a skilled tactician who does not intend to shift from favourable ground.

So his boy-cousin and his girl-cousin and his quite uninteresting younger brother were to be taken to Jagborough sands that afternoon and he was to stay at home. His cousins' aunt, who insisted, by an unwarranted stretch of imagination, in styling herself his aunt also, had hastily invented the Jagborough expedition in order to impress on Nicholas the delights that he had justly forfeited by his disgraceful conduct at the breakfast-table. It was her habit, whenever one of the children fell from grace, to improvise something of a festival nature from which the offender would be rigorously debarred; if all the children sinned collectively they were suddenly informed of a circus in a neighbouring town, a circus of unrivalled merit and uncounted elephants, to which, but for their depravity, they would have been taken that very day.

Nicholas' so-called aunt was devious. It is worth finding out what Nicholas does next so try to read the rest of the story. Another one of Saki's stories, which you might enjoy, is *Shredni Vashta*. Roald Dahl is another, more recent, author who understood what it is like for a child who is confronted by unpleasant adults.

In this passage there is a great deal to think about, for example, how Nicholas is feeling or what his aunt's motives are. Have you ever managed to play a trick on someone? Have you ever caught an adult cheating or lying or simply trying to mislead other people? It can be a source of some satisfaction for you when they realise that you understand what is going on. Learning that adults are not perfect is an important part of growing up. Later, we come to realise that we are not perfect either. Many of these issues are dealt with in this passage.

ACTIVITY 1

After you have read the passage aloud in class, consider carefully the answers to these questions. Discuss the questions in groups, or as a class, before writing down your answers. Try to limit your answers to one sentence each. When you have finished writing your answers, read them aloud to one another.

(a) What had Nicholas done to be in disgrace?

(b) Explain his so-called aunt's technique for dealing with children who were in disgrace.

(c) What do you think was Nicholas' view of the matter?

(d) Explain the effect of these words in the passage:

    (1) 'The dramatic part of the incident'

    (2) 'sin'

    (3) 'to shift from favourable ground'

    (4) 'had hastily invented the Jagborough expedition'.

The answers are in the Exam Café CD.

The difference between reading and writing

Have you ever thought about how long it takes you to read a passage? Now, think about how long it would take you to write a passage of the same length. You can guess which one requires more time and effort, but how much more?

ACTIVITY 2

(a) Look back at the extract from *The Lumber Room*. Time yourself re-reading the passage, silently, to yourself. This will probably take between one minute and one and a half minutes. Also, time yourself reading it aloud and see what happens to your reading speed.

Calculate your reading speed in words per minute. To do this, divide the number of words in the passage (378), by the number of minutes or fractions of a minute that you took to read it. For example, if reading this passage took you 1 minute 40 seconds, that is 1.7 minutes, then this is the calculation you need to complete:

$$\frac{378}{1.7}$$

The answer is 222 words per minute.

(b) Now you are going to time yourself writing. You will need to write a paragraph of about 100 words, which is approximately between six and ten sentences. You could write about:

> Something seen on television recently
> Social networking
> A new website that you have discovered
> Your plans for next weekend
> Keeping tidy
> Bossy people.

Otherwise, choose any topic that you feel strongly about. Make a note of the time when you start writing and when you finish. Count the number of words that you actually write. You need to calculate how long it would take you to write 100 words. For example, if you wrote 118 words in 25 minutes then your calculation would be:

$$\frac{25 \times 100}{118}$$

This equals 21 minutes.

(c) The last and crucial calculation is to work out roughly how long it would have taken you to write what you could read in one minute. Using the example above, we have 222 words read in one minute and a writing speed which requires 21 minutes to produce 100 words. The calculation would be:

$$\frac{21 \times 222}{100}$$

This equals 46.6 minutes.

In other words, you read approximately 46 times faster than you write. Or, to put it another very approximate way, what we can read in one minute would take us three quarters of an hour to write.

Examination questions for Cambridge International Examinations require you to write a certain number of sides. Beware of how much (how many words) you write on one page.

The first important point to note here is the length of time required to set things out in writing. When we read we can sometimes absorb information in the blink of an eye, however, to write things out so that this can happen is much more demanding. If written material is not carefully planned and accurately presented then reading it is much more difficult and, whatever its purpose, it will be less effective.

The next important point is to consider the sort of things which we might have to write about in our lives. Here, we are not just thinking about the writing that we do in the classroom, while we are at school, or later at college or university. We also need to consider our working and our personal lives.

The importance of literacy

In some ways, English is different from subjects like Geography or Business Studies which have clearly defined content. Instead, English is a skill which we will need in every other subject and throughout our adult lives. Literacy is what we call the ability to use letters and words properly. Educated adults are expected to be able to communicate effectively, in both speech and writing. Few of us have difficulties with speech as out of necessity we practise it all the time. Writing though is not that simple and we need to decide to develop our writing skills and work on them. Even clever people, adults with all sorts of skills and abilities, who cannot write effectively, will be at a disadvantage. This lack of skill can be very embarrassing and can be a serious barrier to progressing in our careers and personal lives. It can prevent us from fulfilling our potential. Remember also, that the more able a person is, the more aware that person will be of his or her lack of writing skills.

▲ Doctors need to write medical reports and letters of referral.

Literacy will continue to be important throughout our lives as we may be called upon to write for all sorts of purposes such as:

- to record a simple sequence of events in a statement for police or lawyers
- to describe the cuisine in a restaurant for a review
- to explain something that you have invented to potential investors
- to persuade someone to consider you for a job when you write a letter of application
- to write a letter to your child's teacher setting out concerns that you have
- to conduct an argument, setting out your views clearly and the reasons for them, on a blog or in a letter to a newspaper or the government
- to write a letter of complaint to a company

to entertain by writing a story or a script for a play or a film

to write poetry with its special ways of using language (more in **Section Four**) to give an informed response to the arts – be it film, drama, literature, music, dance, architecture, painting or sculpture

to ponder, reflect, philosophise and ask difficult questions.

Just think of that most important word in the English language, the word *why*. It is probably an important part of your repertoire of words. Why homework? Why bedtime? Why limits on pocket money? Why stay home?

Later in this course, you will have opportunities to try out many of the kinds of writing listed above.

Planning your writing

Learning how to write well will help you throughout your life. The key to writing well is to plan well. In this section we will work on the business of planning and thinking through what we want to communicate in writing.

EXERCISE 1

In this exercise you are going to plan and write a short passage (200 to 300 words) introducing a stranger to the area where you live. The information can be presented in a straightforward, angry, amusing, flippant or dismissive manner, depending on how you feel about the place.

(a) First list, as briefly as you can, the points that you want to make. Even if you feel that you don't need to do this for this passage, doing it will provide good practice for dealing with the more demanding writing that you will encounter later in this book, and later in life.

(b) Now write a plan for your passage. Try and reduce each of your points to one or two words. You have already seen the importance of brief notes in **Chapter 1**. Then consider how you might start the passage, and end it, allowing for new or modified ideas to emerge as you write. You could leave writing the introduction until you have finished the middle sections and even the final section. Note if there are any special requirements for any particularly important points. **Keep this plan safe as you will need it in the next activity.**

(c) Write each main point as a paragraph. Each paragraph may contain just one or several sentences, but keep the topic in mind as you write. Each new paragraph should introduce a new point, or a substantial development of a point.

(d) Now allow yourself time to write and check through your work. You might need to complete it for homework.

Remember, the place where you live has people, buildings, an atmosphere, a history and a geography.

What do you see as you approach it, as you set off from the place? What do you see from the windows: sky, buildings, fields or water? What do you hear: traffic, people, machinery, animals or birds? What have you found out about the place? Is it new or old? What have other people told you about it? Do they like the place? Are you planning to stay or to leave?

Remember, you are also part of it!

ACTIVITY 3

(a) In class, exchange passages so that you read someone else's work. Mark or highlight what you consider to be the main points. These essential parts might be individual words, phrases or sentences. Now compare the passage with the writer's original plan. Ask yourself:

Do they match?
Has the plan been followed?

(b) Discuss with the writer what might have been done to make the main points clearer and to improve the passage.

(c) Be prepared to read out passages in class and show how they relate, or do not relate, to the plans.

Writing and reading more complicated sentences

Working with complicated passages will help you to follow an involved story and difficult explanations, and write them. Look at the way this short sentence is expanded into a more complicated one:

The cat sat on the mat.

Second Stage

While it was raining outside, the cat sat on the mat.

Third Stage

Although it preferred to be out in the garden first thing, while it was raining outside the cat sat on the mat.

Fourth Stage

Although it preferred to be out in the garden first thing, while it was raining outside the cat sat on the mat which needed cleaning.

Final Stage

Although it preferred to be out in the garden first thing, while it was raining outside the cat sat on the mat, which needed cleaning, and read the newspaper.

At each stage, whatever else we are told, the cat still sits on the mat. As we progress, we learn about the weather, the cat's preference for being outside, the condition of the mat and finally we are told about something else the cat is doing; it's reading the newspaper.

We are also told that the mat requires cleaning. This additional information could have been added in a separate sentence, like this:

> Although it preferred to be out in the garden first thing, while it was raining outside the cat sat on the mat and read the newspaper. The mat needed cleaning.

The ideas do not follow smoothly here and our attention has to be drawn back to the mat in a second sentence which makes the mat seems far more important than it actually is.

> Although it preferred to be out in the garden first thing, while it was raining outside the cat sat on the mat, which needed cleaning, and read the newspaper.

In this final version, the information about the mat is tucked in neatly so that we know that something more important is still to come; what could be more important than the cat reading the paper? In this way the information that the mat needed cleaning is related in passing, without the distraction of a second sentence.

ACTIVITY 4

The answer to **(a)** is on the Exam Café CD.

(a) In pairs, identify the five bits of information given in the final version of this sentence.

(b) See how many versions of this sentence you can write, including all the information in each sentence. You may alter or replace words if necessary.

(c) Choose the version you prefer. Compare it to other students' preferred versions.

EXERCISE 2

(a) Write or select a sentence of no more than six words and expand it step by step in the same way that the sentence about the cat was expanded. At each stage, read what you have written very carefully so that it still makes sense.

One of the longest sentences in a novel is found in *Ulysses* by James Joyce. It has 4391 words, but there are now claims that Jonathan Coe's *The Rotters' Club*, published in 2001, contains a sentence with 13 955 words.

(b) Now, write a list of items to be included in a new long sentence and pass them to someone else to write out as a series of expanded sentences.

(c) Experiment with a simple sentence to see how long a sentence you can produce. Be prepared to read it aloud to the class or a group.

Summary

You have looked at reading involved stories and difficult explanations, with elements and meanings that are sometimes only hinted at. Reading and writing these kinds of passages can take a great deal of effort and time. You have explored the dramatic difference between the speed at which we read and write. This clearly showed the need for us to plan and write carefully in order for a reader to understand our work. You have practised checking your work, and that of others, to improve its effectiveness. Finally, you have looked at combining and separating ideas in longer sentences so that the information in them is presented as clearly as possible.

Chapter 4

Checking and correcting your English

Getting started

In this chapter you are encouraged to check and correct your own use of English, spoken and written. In particular there is an important section on punctuation to help you do this as independently as possible. Soon you will no longer have a teacher to check and correct your English for you and you will have to be responsible for the effectiveness of what you say and what you write. As part of this work, you will practise cooperative writing and consider ways of re-working written material to improve it.

Listening for full stops

Full stops are the most basic of controls on the flow of information. They signal a mental 'pause' before the next set of information comes through and this makes it easier to absorb information. Full stops are where we should start.

ACTIVITY 1

(a) The article that follows, from *The Times of India*, is about the kidnapping of a train crew in India. Close this book and listen carefully as your teacher reads the article aloud. Each time your teacher reaches the end of a sentence you should either clap your hands, raise a hand in the air or make some other agreed signal.

(b) When your teacher has finished reading the passage, then read through it yourself.

Times of India   27th October 2009

Terrorists Seize Train

KOLKATA: The government on Tuesday stated that the driver of the New Delhi-Bhubaneswar Rajdhani Express and his assistant, kidnapped by Maoists between Jhargram and Sarna stations of the South Eastern Railway this afternoon, have been released.

Home minister P Chidambaram today said the train and passengers on board were safe. "The train is safe. All passengers are safe and the good news is the train is safe," he told reporters. "State police have reached the spot and the area has been secured. There is no sign of any other adversary there," Chidambaram said. He also refuted reports that there was an exchange of fire between security forces and suspected Maoists. "There was firing and a civilian driver was injured but there was no injury to police personnel, "Chidambaram said.

He said the Centre has rushed a relief train to Orissa with doctors and relief supplies. The home minister said the train will bring back the passengers on the Rajdhani Express. Chidambaram said railway minister Mamta Banerjee was monitoring the situation from her office. A pro-Maoist group, the People's Committee against Police Atrocities, had claimed responsibility for the attack stating that the train drivers had defied them. TV reports had also suggested that PCPA had set the conditions for releasing the Rajdhani drivers. The pro-Maoist group sought the release of their leader Chhatradhar Mahato from the police custody, in a swap deal. The ministry has sought a report on the incident from the state government as well as the railway ministry, sources said.

The newspaper article has 275 words which are divided up and grouped into 15 sentences. Each sentence contains a very clear and manageable amount of information with a full stop at the end. The passage is a series of brief statements of fact. Clear breaks are important for informative writing so that the facts stand out clearly. We are going to practise presenting facts clearly in the exercise that follows.

 **EXERCISE 1**

Choose an event, real or imagined, and prepare a press release of 200 to 300 words long. Remember to provide a background or context to your event. You might do this by mentioning or explaining previous events that led to this event or give some information that will make your reader understand why your event is significant. Consequences of the event might also be relevant. You will need to give different points of view on the event and concerns about it from different people. Note that in the article about the terrorists seizing the train, there were accounts from India's Home Minister and the People's Committee against Police Atrocities.

> Don't forget to write key words first, as we practised in **Chapter 3**.

Punctuation – road signs for readers

Punctuation is much more than full stops. It also indicates how ideas are combined, by dividing words into clauses and phrases in order to clarify their meaning. Another of the many other functions of punctuation is to show when someone is speaking. We can see how important the role of punctuation is in the passage below.

> the party had started well but then the boat struck something there was a loud crash and a jolt and a number of people on the deck fell down the boat is sinking a man said its time to get off what shall i do said the woman who had boasted about the cost of her outfit swim said the man i cant said the woman another boat from the shore approached them help called the man theres someone here who cant swim

ACTIVITY 2

(a) Try to read the unpunctuated passage above quietly to yourself.

(b) Now try to read it aloud, in groups or in pairs.

(c) Discuss, was reading the passage aloud easier or more difficult? Try and explain why.

Remember how we measured the time difference between reading silently and reading aloud in **Chapter 3**.

We naturally use our hearing to hear what is said and our sight to see what is written so we should use these senses to help check our own English writing. When we read aloud, we can hear whether our punctuation and our grammar (the right words in the right order) are correct. When we read, it is our sight that we use to check our spelling.

EXERCISE 2

When you have finished you can compare your version with the original which is on the next page and in the Exam Café CD.

(a) Decide where the sentences end in the unpunctuated passage. Then copy it out, adding all the punctuation that you think is necessary.

(b) Now you are going to expand this passage, by adding a further sentence after each of the original sentences. You could add descriptive detail, further action or additional dialogue. The original is 83 words long so aim for about 150 words in your extended version.

Could you devise an easier way of indicating the end of sentences, a need to pause when reading, items in a list, the joining of two closely related sentences (a semi-colon), and a change of voice for reported speech? Try reading this version of the passage.

> (capital letter) the party had started well but then the boat struck something (full stop) (capital letter) there was a loud crash and a jolt and a number of people fell to the deck (full stop) (new line) (open speech marks) (capital letter) the boat is sinking (comma) (close speech marks) a man said (full stop) (open speech marks) (capital letter) it (apostrophe) s time to get off (full stop) (close speech marks) (new line) (open speech marks) (capital letter) what shall I do (question mark) (close speech marks) said the woman who had boasted about the cost of her outfit (full stop) (new line) (open speech marks) (capital letter) swim (exclamation mark) (close speech marks) said the man (full stop) (new line) (open speech marks) (capital letter) i can (apostrophe) t (comma) (close speech marks) said the woman (full stop) (new line) (capital letter) another boat from the shore approached them (full stop) (new line) (open speech marks) (capital letter) help (exclamation mark) (close speech marks) called the man (full stop) (capital letter) there (apostrophe) s someone here who can (apostrophe) t swim (full stop) (close speech marks)

There are 94 words of punctuation instructions here, but only 83 of text. It's rather like writing a computer program. Perhaps, one day, one of you will write a program that can insert punctuation automatically. In the meantime we will have to continue with the job of inserting our own punctuation marks.

By now, reading your work aloud, and listening to others reading your work aloud, should have become important ways for you to check your work. Remember, our ears provide the best means for checking punctuation and grammar and that is why it is best to read work aloud. If you are in a place where you cannot read aloud, try to imagine the sound of the material being read aloud.

Spelling also requires care and checking, although in different ways. It is our visual memory that recognises the way we spell words. Children learning to spell are often encouraged to look at words, and then cover them up before trying to spell them correctly from memory. Spelling is often arbitrary, for example, *sow seeds* but *sew buttons*, and phonetically illogical, for example, *light*. This spelling is simply a historical reminder that the word came from Germany 1500 years ago; its German cousin is spelt and pronounced *licht* (with the *ch* pronounced like the *ch* in *loch*). We just have to accept these spelling conventions, unspoken agreements, recorded in dictionaries.

Printing a passage you've written on a computer and seeing it on paper is a good way of seeing it in a fresh way and finding spelling mistakes and other errors. It is even better to read it again the next day.

Embarrassment about having our work read aloud is natural because we are concerned that we may have made mistakes and we do not like being embarrassed. Checking your work, however, is so important that you must learn to get over this if you are to make progress. Remember, there is nothing wrong with making mistakes; people who never make mistakes seldom learn much.

Joining sentences

Some ideas are better presented together, rather than separately, so joining sentences can improve the effectiveness of your writing. Consider the passages that follow.

> I dreamt once that ice cream tasted of fresh tomatoes. This had a devastating effect on me. For months afterwards I was unable to eat the stuff. Eventually I had to force myself to buy an ice cream to break the dream. Then I returned enthusiastically to Rossi's ice cream parlour. Rossi's had been my favourite maker of ice cream for years.

We can improve things:

> I dreamt once that ice cream tasted of fresh tomatoes which had a devastating effect on me. For months afterwards I was unable to eat the stuff so, eventually, I had to force myself to buy an ice cream to break the dream. Then I returned enthusiastically to Rossi's ice cream parlour because Rossi's had been my favourite for years and I no longer dreaded eating ice cream.

The answers are in the Exam Café CD.

ACTIVITY 3

Discuss, what has been done in the second version of the passage to improve it? In groups or pairs, discuss the changes and how they have been brought about.

Cooperative writing

Cooperative writing is brought about by people writing together, rather than individually. Think of scientists jointly working on a research paper which will convey their new findings. Consider a husband and wife team writing a school text book together, both using the best of their skills and knowledge and responding to one another's ideas as they proceed. Sometimes a writer and a publisher will work cooperatively and the manuscript goes to and fro as they try to perfect it. Practising cooperative writing is a good way to learn to improve your writing and it will help you develop confidence in handling ideas in the written form. It can also inspire you with new ideas for the story.

ACTIVITY 4

In this activity you are going to work in groups of about six to combine checking others' work with adding your own material to what they have already written. You will each need a sheet of paper to write on.

(a) Together, decide what sort of writing you are going to do. Will it be a report, a story, a newspaper or magazine article or an extract from a diary?

(b) Write your initials clearly in the margin at the top of the sheet. Write the first sentence, in pen. When everyone in the group has written their sentence, pass the sheet on to someone else.

(c) Read through the sheet that you now have in front of you. Put your initials clearly in the margin at the end of the piece you have read. Decide what you are going to do with this piece. Will you continue with the first writer's ideas and develop them, or will you try and move the piece in a new direction? Leave at least one line clear and then write the next sentence. When everyone in the group is ready, pass the sheet on again.

(d) Continue for six turns. On your sixth turn you should try to write a final sentence to complete the item in front of you. Return the sheet to the person whose initials appear at the top of the page.

This exercise can be adapted in several ways. You could each write half a page at each turn or you could try to make it tricky for the next writer to continue the passage. Alternatively, the initial brief could be more closely specified, for example, it could be set in a particular place or at a particular time. No doubt you will be able to think up many more variations of this game.

Think of the role of the editor or sub-editor. They take work that has been written by someone else and check it for meaning and try to make it easier to read and understand. They also check for any errors. The passage has got to be perfect as they, not the author, will ultimately have to take responsibility for any misspellings, typos, bad grammar and incorrect punctuation.

A note about grammar and spelling checkers when using a computer: be careful not to become reliant on these. They should only be used as a first indication that something may require your attention. Some grammar checkers cannot cope with complex sentence construction and will find fault with perfect sentences. You must be able to check your grammar independently. With a spelling checker, check whether you are using American or British spelling.

 **EXERCISE 3**

In this exercise, you are going to play the role of editor. You are going to transform a first draft of a piece of work into something more polished. You will need your original sheet from Activity 4.

(a) Read through the whole piece, at least twice, and decide what it seems to be about. Write this down at the end of the piece, in one sentence.

(b) Use a pencil to correct and amend what has been written. Try to find ways of making the ideas in the passage as clear as possible and link them together with additional words of your own if necessary.

(c) When you are clear about what needs to be done and the best way to do it, write out your version of the passage. Read it out aloud, remembering that someone else might be asked to read it out in class.

When this piece has been marked, file it away safely.

If there is any possibility that you will be taking the written coursework option for the IGCSE then you should take great care of any substantial written work once it has been responded to by your teacher. Further efforts on your part to edit, revise and correct the piece will be needed before you submit the work as coursework. In **Section Five** you will find additional guidance and suggestions about coursework.

Summary

Checking your work can sometimes seem to get in the way of finishing a task, but the importance of this, not least in examinations, should be more apparent now. The best way to check your passage for grammar and punctuation is to listen to it, so read it aloud (if possible). The best way to check the spelling is to look at the words carefully.

The work on punctuation and joining sentences, and the cooperative writing and editing you did, will help you become more aware of what is needed to write effectively. It should also improve your confidence when it comes to handling words.

Chapter 5

Understanding and responding to passages

Getting started

Identifying and organising information is an important part of understanding a passage. Doing this enables us to arrange our thoughts and ideas about the passage and then in turn communicate those ideas clearly and effectively. This chapter is going to develop both your ability to understand passages, and to respond to them. This may require you to select, explain, summarise or compare some of the information contained in passages. You will also have opportunities to write in response to some of the ideas you encounter.

Reading for understanding

We can show our understanding of a written passage both in discussion with others and by writing in response to questions. You will do both of these in response to this interesting passage which conveys both information and description. It comes from *Expatica*, a magazine for expatriates living in Switzerland.

My first Fête Nationale Suisse

American expat Carolyn Moncel wasn't sure what to expect from Switzerland's National Day, and explored Lausanne this 1 August to find out.

There's a famous Crosby, Stills & Nash song that has the lyrics, "…And if you can't be with the one you love, love the one you're with." Substitute the word "one" with the word "country" and my sentiments regarding celebrating Independence Day as an expatriate would be accurate. It's true. I haven't celebrated Independence Day on American soil in seven years. I still celebrate the Fourth of July no matter where I am, even allowing my children to miss school so we can barbecue and enjoy the day together. But I've learned to adapt to local celebrations in both France (Fête Nationale or Bastille Day on 14 July) and now this year in Switzerland (Fête Nationale Suisse on 1 August).

Honestly, I wasn't sure what to expect. Would it be like Bastille Day with large military parades, jets flying overhead, memorials at the Tomb of the Unknown Soldier, outdoor parties and fireworks, or would it be closer to the American Fourth of July with flags flying, hot dogs grilling, marching bands, parades and fireworks? It turns out that Fête Nationale Suisse is a bit of both with a little something new thrown in. For one, it turns out that there is no unified celebration as there are 26 Swiss cantons, each one free to celebrate the day any way they think their citizens would enjoy.

I ventured out early Saturday morning to see if there would be any celebrations in Lausanne but oddly enough the streets were empty. Later in the afternoon, I viewed a lot of celebrations across Switzerland on TSR1, a French-language television channel, which included a couple of historical re-enactments. When the sun set here in Lausanne, I headed down toward Ouchy where the entire city's residents seemed to be. Along the way, I could see Swiss flags flying proudly from balconies. Yes, there was a military band playing the Swiss National Anthem after all, along with greetings from the Mayor of Lausanne. Like in America, some people knew the national anthem by heart, while others needed the words supplied to them on paper as a reference.

When dusk turned into night, the fireworks began and I realised, had I been in Chicago in July, my celebration would have been a lot like this one; a comforting thought. There would have been lots of food by the lakefront (Lake Michigan this time), and of course fireworks at sunset.

Since I am living abroad, I do miss out on national holidays back in the United States. While I enjoy celebrations here in Switzerland, I sometimes feel as if I'm betraying my home country. It's like the lyrics to another famous song by Mary MacGregor, "Torn between two lovers, feelin' like a fool." This time, substitute the word "lovers" with "countries" and you get the idea.

But I've learned some important lessons. First, if you spend too much time focused on the glories of your home country, not only will you miss out on the attributes that make your host country equally special, you'll also miss an opportunity to reach common ground. For example, I now know that America doesn't have a monopoly on national pride, freedom or democracy.

Second, if we are indeed comparing "countries" to "lovers", then it's the only time when you can love more than one at the same time without feeling the least bit guilty. I can celebrate three Independence Days per year – one for the United States (my home country), one for France (my adopted country), and now Switzerland (my host country).

Observing host country celebrations like Nationale Suisse doesn't take anything away from me. Instead it offers a new global perspective and enriches my life experiences.

ACTIVITY 1

(a) Discuss in class, in groups or in pairs the theme of the article – what idea or interest or situation led Carolyn Moncel to write this piece? List the ideas that she explores as she pursues this theme.

(b) Discuss, what is the tone or mood of the article? Is it humorous, serious, reflective, informative, didactic, light-hearted or persuasive? Find evidence to support your claims.

Even when you are writing brief answers to questions such as these, remember to set out your responses in complete sentences using your own words. This will help you to clarify your ideas and ensure that they are communicated clearly.

EXERCISE 1

(a) In written answers, explore the article further.

(1) Explain the reference to the Crosby, Stills and Nash song. What contrast is suggested in Moncel's reference to another song by Mary MacGregor?

(2) What is distinct about national day celebrations in Switzerland?

(3) What has the writer learnt from celebrating other countries' national days?

The answers are in the Exam Café CD.

(b) Write a short article of about 300 words, for people who are coming to live in your country, about a national day you celebrate. Point out what you enjoy about it and what your fellow countrymen think is important about it.

Or

Write a more reflective piece (also about 300 words) about learning something new about yourself or your own country when travelling or meeting people for the first time.

Understanding by extracting and organising information

This article is also full of interesting information but is rather different in tone. It is about devastating floods in Brazil, and comes from the *Buenos Aires Herald*.

Buenos Aires Herald, *Oct 29th 2009*

PEOPLE ISOLATED AND AID STUCK

Brazilian floods claim 39 dead

As of Friday, 39 people were killed in the flooding, sparked by unusually heavy rains that have been falling for two months on 10 of Brazil's 26 states. Three times the size of Alaska, the affected area stretches from the normally wet rainforest to coastal states known for lengthy droughts.

Meteorologists blame an Atlantic Ocean weather system that typically moves on by April – and they forecast weeks more of the same.

Maria do Remedio Santos, whose fields of rice and manioc lay ruined underwater, said it was time to join those fleeing for safety. Heavy rains had begun seeping into her mud-brick, thatched-roof home, where nine relatives and neighbors were camped out. Outside, the dirt road was a muddy river.

"For now we're all sleeping in the living room, but we're going to have to leave," she said. "There's no other way out."

Some shelters were already packed with people, pets and livestock, and had little food or medical supplies. Even fleeing presented its own perils: In the same newly formed rivers that flood victims waded through or plied with canoes swam anacondas, rattlesnakes and legless, rodent-eating "worm lizards," whose bite is excruciating.

"So far no one has been bitten here. The main thing you tell the kids is to stay out of the water," Palmeiro da Costa said from a canoe in the town of Sao Miguel de Rosario.

Alligators swam through the city of Santarem, civil defense official Walkiria Coelho said. Scorpions congregated on the same high ground as people escaping the rising water. No injuries were reported.

Authorities worried about thousands of people isolated for days with little food or clean water, rushing aid to towns and cities. In some places, aid was stuck because there were no local workers to distribute it, said Maj. Wellington Soares Araujo, head of civil defense logistics in the hardest-hit state of Maranhao.

Rivers were still rising in Maranhao. The surging torrents wrecked bridges and made it too dangerous for relief workers to take boats onto some waterways – and mudslides were stranding trucks, preventing them from delivering food and aid to places cut off from civilization.

"They are stuck and waiting until we can clear the roads, which for some highways could be in a week if alternative routes aren't found," said Abner Ferreira, civil defense spokesman for Maranhao.

The army evacuated thousands of people from two Maranhao towns where tiled roofs barely poked above swirling waters. Residents packed into gyms and schools and huddled in tents.

In one particularly hard hit region, more than 1,000 homeless from areas near the city of Bacabel took refuge in a complex used for an annual farm and livestock fair, setting up camp in filthy stables.

"People unfortunately took shelter in places that were not sanitary. We are doing the best we can to find sanitary shelters so that people can live in adequate places," Ferreira said.

In the city of Itapecuru Mirim, residents stood on the back of flatbed trucks fleeing town. Tractors hauled trailers full of people trying to make it to higher ground.

Isolated cases of looting were reported in communities cut off by high water.

The mighty Rio Negro river that feeds the Amazon was just three feet (one meter) below a record set in 1953 near the jungle city of Manaus, and experts said the record could be broken by June. In the jungle city of Altamira, more rain fell in three hours than normally falls in two months, Mayor Odileida Sampaio told the state-run Brasil news agency.

"We don't know yet, but this could end up being the worst flooding ever in the region," said Joaquim Godim, a specialist with Brazil's National Water Agency. "It certainly is among the worst ever."

Near Altamira, Ocilene Ferreira da Silva barely had time to put her two young daughters into a canoe after a small dam collapsed.

"My neighbor came in screaming that the water was rising really fast, and then all of a sudden the water came rushing into my house," said Silva, 23. "It swept away all the dogs, cats and even parrots. It took everything."

Even as rains pounded the north, parts of southern Brazil are suffering through a two-month drought that has dried up the famed Iguazu falls, one of South America's leading tourist attractions, to less than a third of normal volume.

Some environmentalists said the Amazon wouldn't be hurt by the floods because the rainforest and its inhabitants have endured them for centuries.

But Paulo Barreto, a researcher at the Amazon Institute of People and the Environment, said the flooding comes just four years after a major drought. He blamed climate change and said such events put stress on the environment "that could affect the survival of plant and animal species."

ACTIVITY 2

Discuss these questions in groups or as a class.

(a) Consider an alternative headline for this article. Explain how you made your choice.

(b) Identify the sources used in the writing of this article.

(c) What do you find most troubling about the floods themselves, and the after effects?

(d) How does the writer convey an impression of the effects of the floods?

(e) If you were able to interview just one of the people mentioned in the article for television news, who would it be? Who would you choose for a discussion programme on television? Explain your choices.

EXERCISE 2

(a) Summarise what we learn from the article in the *Buenos Aires Herald* about the predictable and less predictable consequences of these floods in about 100 words.

(b) Summarise the different views reported of the causes of the floods in no more than 80 words.

Before writing your answers, you must read through the passage looking for references to consequences of the floods and the different views about the causes. Each time you find an appropriate reference, ask yourself whether it tells you anything new. If it does, use two or three words to note down the essence of what you have learnt. If the reference does not reveal additional information, move on.

Essentially you need to report, as briefly as you can, the points that are made. This must be done without repeating yourself and without including any additional information, evidence or descriptive detail that does not answer the question directly. To keep it brief, report what is said but do not quote people's exact words.

When you have listed the points needed for each summary, ensure that they are sensibly ordered then use them as a writing plan and incorporate them into complete sentences. Start with an introduction of two sentences and finish with a conclusion of about the same length.

> Remember that here you have only to summarise the two aspects of the article referred to in Exercise 2 (a) and (b); do not try to summarise the whole passage.
>
> The answers are in the Exam Café CD.

Appreciating and understanding longer passages

In the previous two passages you practised reading and then seeking specific information for specific purposes. You also looked at how to support your findings with a clear argument and evidence. In the next two passages you are going to practise demonstrating your understanding, and also appreciation, of longer and more complex passages. Consider the passage below.

> As we read material we must ensure that we have understood it, or at least work out the questions we need to ask in order to understand it.

No fun for kids, urban sprawls take toll on children's health

By Laura Stone, *Canwest News Service*

OTTAWA — Kids these days: they rarely walk anywhere. They don't ride bikes, they don't play outside — not like they used to, anyway. But can we blame them?

Not according to two new studies released by the Vanier Institute of the Family, a charitable Ottawa-based organization.

"The way that cities have evolved has been rather wrong-headed," said Katherine Scott, director of programs at the institute. "Lots of it has to do with urban sprawl."

The studies, released Tuesday, chronicle a generation of Canadian youngsters reared primarily in spread-out communities outside the

urban centre, where they can expect to be driven anywhere they want to go, even if it's just to a friend's house a few blocks away. The data is based both on literature and empirical research, conducted over the past year, said Scott.

"We have built cities that actively discourage walking and biking among children, certainly when we compare the experiences of today's children and those of their parents," writes Juan Torres, an urban planner and professor at the University of Montreal, in his study titled Children & Cities: Planning to Grow Together.

Aside from being environmentally problematic, urban sprawl has also taken its toll on the bodies and minds of children, said Torres.

"The biggest problem presented in the report is the fact that cities are being planned especially for cars and for adults," he said. "This is an important issue because alternative mobility is part of the things that children need in order to develop properly. Not only in terms of obesity and this problem of public health — that, of course, is deeply related with physical activity and the fact that children don't walk as much as before — but oftentimes of personal development."

Children gain a sense of independence and can better understand the concept of common space when they can navigate themselves outside, he said.

A second report, Caution! Kids at Play?, written by psychology student Belinda Boekhoven from Carleton University in Ottawa, finds that a decline in unstructured playtime and outdoor space in cities, also related to urbanization, can affect a child's self-motivation and self-reliance.

While organized activities are good, children need unstructured outdoor time — made difficult by an increasing car-reliant culture — for proper development, said Scott.

Scott said cities should start consulting with kids about what they want from their neighbourhoods — improved public transit, closer schools, more accessible communities — "so people aren't forced to travel long distances to access food and basic necessities."

Programs such as UNICEF's Child Friendly Cities, which consult with youth about planning and business initiatives, are offered in Ottawa, Calgary and Saskatoon.

ACTIVITY 3

(a) Consider the following questions about the article above. Discuss them in pairs or groups if it helps.

(1) What sources of information does the writer use?

(2) What has changed for the current generation of young people?

(3) 'The way that cities have evolved has been rather wrong-headed.' What is suggested by this sentence?

(4) What do you understand by the expressions, 'urban sprawl' and 'unstructured playtime'?

(5) What two concerns are expressed about children's development?

(6) Explain what seems to have changed in the way that urban children move from one part of an area to another.

(7) The article begins with the words, 'Kids these days: they rarely walk anywhere. They don't ride bikes, they don't play outside – not like they used to, anyway.' What effect is the writer trying to achieve here?

(8) Professor Torres says that urban sprawl has also taken its toll on the bodies and minds of children. What does this suggest about his views?

The answers are in the Exam Café CD.

(b) Remember the game *Just a Minute* which we played in Activity 4 of **Chapter 1**? You are going to give a speech of one minute again, but this time you will be given time to prepare – and you won't be interrupted! Plan, write and deliver a speech to a group or the class about one aspect of this article that you believe is important. You will have to identify this one aspect very clearly, then explain and back up your view. Remember to plan by making a brief list of about 5 to 10 words or a few key points which will remind you what it is that you want to say. Keep it short because you can probably only say about 100 words in a minute.

If you are entered for the optional Speaking and Listening section of the examination, look at pp 193–194 of **Section Five**.

EXERCISE 3

Summarise in two short paragraphs:

a) the harm to children that is mentioned in the article

b) the steps that could be taken to improve matters.

Only select material that directly answers what you have been asked for.

The answers are in the Exam Café CD.

When answering questions like these, read the question several times to make sure that you have fully grasped what it concerns and what it requires of you. Plan carefully. Establish a routine with which you are confident. This will be especially helpful if you find examinations stressful. List the points you want to make, the ideas you wish to convey and the impressions you want your reader to receive. Make sure that they are in the best possible order. Put the strongest argument, the most striking piece of description or the most surprising turn of events where it will be most effective.

Comparing passages

Comparing information from two sources provides important practice to improve and develop the way that you select and consider ideas. It is also a good way to develop an understanding of the ways in which different writers present their ideas. We will compare the previous passage about the impact of urban sprawl on children with the passage that follows which is adapted from *The Jungle Book* by Rudyard Kipling. In this passage, Mother and Father Wolf hear Shere Khan the tiger hunting nearby in the jungle.

Father Wolf listened, and below in the valley that ran down to a little river, he heard the dry, angry, snarly, singsong whine of a tiger who has caught nothing and does not care if all the Jungle knows it.

"The fool!" said Father Wolf. "To begin a night's work with that noise! Does he think that our buck are like his fat Waingunga bullocks?"

"H'sh! It is neither bullock nor buck he hunts tonight," said Mother Wolf. "It is man." The whine had changed to a sort of humming purr that seemed to come from every quarter of the compass. It was the noise that bewilders woodcutters and gipsies sleeping in the open, and makes them run sometimes into the very mouth of the tiger.

The purr grew louder, and ended in the full-throated "Aaarh!" of the tiger's charge.

Then there was a howl – an untigerish howl – from Shere Khan. "He has missed," said Mother Wolf. "What is it?"

The bushes rustled a little in the thicket, and Father Wolf dropped with his haunches under him, ready for his leap. Then, if you had been watching, you would have seen the most wonderful thing in the world – the wolf checked in mid-spring. He made his bound before he saw what it was he was jumping at, and then he tried to stop himself. The result was that he shot up straight into the air for four or five feet, landing almost where he left the ground.

"Man," he snapped. "A man's cub. Look!"

Directly in front of him, holding on by a low branch, stood a naked brown baby who could just walk – as soft and as dimpled a little atom as ever come to a wolf's cave at night. He looked up into Father Wolf's face, and laughed.

"Is that a man's cub?" said Mother Wolf. "I have never seen one. Bring it here."

Then the moonlight was blocked out of the mouth of the cave, for Shere Khan's great square head and shoulders were thrust into the entrance. Tabaqui, behind him, was squeaking: "My lord, my lord, it went in here."

"Shere Khan does us great honour," said Father Wolf, but his eyes were very angry. "What does Shere Khan need?"

"My quarry. A man's cub went this way," said Shere Khan. "Its parents have run off. Give it to me."

⚙ EXERCISE 4

(a) In a passage of about 300 words compare the situation of children in Canadian cities, described in the article 'No fun for kids, urban sprawls take toll on children's health', with the situation of Mowgli, the little boy who is being protected by wolves, in India.

(b) Follow the steps taken by Rudyard Kipling to build up tension in the passage from *The Jungle Book*. Explain by reference to words used in the passage how this is achieved and describe how these words have their effect. You should aim to write 100 to 150 words.

⊙ The answers are in the Exam Café CD.

Directed writing and composing letters

Often, the writing that you have to do is on behalf of someone else or in accordance with particular instructions. It might be for a very particular purpose where the focus is not on being creative but on getting the most important points across. When you do this kind of writing, you need to be certain in your own mind about:

- why you are writing

- the most important point that you need to make

- the impression that you want to leave with the reader

- the response you are hoping for from the reader

- the tone that you should write in (whether formal or informal). Informal notes, letters, emails and mobile phone text messages to your friends can be expressed in casual or note form with incomplete sentences, rather like a casual conversation. Formal letters and writing, however, require material expressed in a complete and correct form. For example, an informal message such as: 'No luck here. Going to nxt plce. See you' would become something like 'I have had no luck here. I am going on to the next place. I will meet you on Friday.'

In the letter-writing exercise that follows, you will practise writing a formal letter.

 **EXERCISE 5**

Yousuf Smith has not been doing well at school. He complains that the teachers are strict and that he does not understand the work, especially science. The teachers accuse him of being lazy and poorly behaved. His parents are looking for a new school and have obtained leaflets about Allways Academy and Wellbourne Grange. They have sent these to Yousuf's Aunt Marcia and have asked for her views.

Imagine you are Yousuf's aunt. Read the leaflets and write your letter to Yousuf's parents (Amna and Bob Smith), making clear why you believe one school is more suitable than the other. Explain your reasons carefully.

Write about $1\frac{1}{2}$ – 2 sides, allowing for the size of your handwriting.

Begin your letter 'Dear Amna and Bob'

> From *Cambridge International Examinations IGCSE English – First Language Specimen Paper 0500/03 Q1 May/June 2005*

Here are some hints on how to write good letters.

The first line must make it clear to whom you are writing: 'Dear Sir' or 'Dear Ms Smith'.

The opening paragraph should indicate what the letter is about. One should be able to perceive quickly whether it is a reply to someone else's letter, a request for information, a complaint, or a letter of congratulation, etc.

In the final paragraph you should sum up what you have said and indicate, if necessary, what you expect to happen next: 'I will call you next week' or, 'If I do not hear from you within two weeks I will consider this to be the end of the matter.' Remember that these will be your last words, for the time being at least, to the person to whom you are sending the letter.

If you have addressed the letter to someone by name, you should finish with the words: 'Yours sincerely', if not, with 'Yours faithfully'.

Allways Academy

Welcome to this premier school which maintains the high standards set by its founder, Martha Allways, when she opened it in 1950. It was Mrs Allways (who recently celebrated her ninetieth birthday and who still takes an active interest in the running of the Academy) who gave us the motto, *Strive for Excellence*.

That is what we do. Our 1000 boy and girl students and 55 staff are under no illusion as to what they are here for. Our Principal, Mr John Allways, demands a disciplined approach with plenty of homework, and a rigorous programme of regular reporting to parents. Science and mathematics are our key priorities, and the uniform rules are strict. Poor behaviour is not tolerated since the understanding of rules is considered paramount. Hence our examination results are excellent and former students occupy high positions in the professions.

The Academy has achieved success in a wide variety of team sports which we consider essential in encouraging discipline and strong character. Students become tougher and more ready to face the world through competition. Each day starts with a physical education (PE) class because a healthy body promotes a healthy mind.

The Academy stands in spacious grounds several kilometres away from the nearest town. There are therefore no distractions from work. Our buildings are imposing and date from 1975. We know you will be impressed.

Wellbourne Grange

Dear Parents,

When you were at school, how often did you dream of charming buildings blending with a wooded environment where you could wander at your heart's content and discover the exciting world of nature?

Or spend hours developing your special talents in the art room, or getting involved with the dance group, or playing on a beautiful Yamaha grand piano?

Well... you will find that the dream has turned into a reality when you visit Wellbourne Grange ... the school of your dreams! Here we do not herd children into large groups. Our twenty skilled teachers work with small groups in interactive teaching situations. Our students are free to choose their own curriculum: they are not forced to learn subjects that are foreign to them. They can also choose what to wear, as we believe everyone should express their individuality. This individuality is best achieved in a small school of 300 students.

John, the Principal, believes in success through self-discipline and positive relationships between students and teachers who are on first-name terms with each other. In this happy atmosphere, abnormal patterns of behaviour can be contained because there is respect for everybody.

We do not believe in team games, since competition is a poor way of building up self-respect and concern for others. Instead we pursue skills in individual sporting activities.

Our motto is Success through happiness and motivation, seen in our examination results which are beginning steadily to improve.

Effective composition

When writing a composition you need to choose your topic well as the more you know about the topic, the better. If it is a topic about which you feel strongly, even better. Anybody who marks examination papers will tell you that you will write better when you know your topic well, when you feel strongly about your topic and when you enjoy writing about your topic. If necessary, do some acting and take on the persona of someone who cares passionately about the topic you have chosen. So, once you have chosen a topic about which to write, engage determinedly in writing it. However, don't neglect the planning stage. Think carefully about your ideas and opinions, and jot them down, before you start writing your composition.

EXERCISE 6

You have now to choose, plan and write a composition of 350 to 400 words on ONE of the six topics that follow.

> Look carefully at the way these topics are paired and give some thought to just what it is that you are choosing to write.

Argumentative/discursive writing

'Big sporting events like the football World Cup and the Olympic Games are a complete waste of time.' To what extent do you agree with this view?

or

Explain why two or three places known to you should be protected for the benefit of future generations.

Descriptive writing

In the passage 'The Fancy Dress Competition', you will describe in detail the atmosphere of the competition (including the moment when the winner is announced) and the costumes of two of the people taking part.

or

Describe a busy scene in a shop or market place.

Narrative writing

You are going to write the beginning of a mystery story set in a large, old building that your main character has been invited to stay in. Focus on his or her arrival at the house. There is no one there to welcome him or her. Once inside the house, the atmosphere is peculiar, and then something unusual happens...

or

You overhear someone talking about you. Make this event an important part of a story called 'A true friend'.

When you think you have finished, read through your work slowly. If you are not able to read it aloud, imagine the sound of your voice reading it aloud. Hold a pen or pencil in your hand as you do so in order to mark or correct mistakes as you go.

Examiners would rather see clear alterations than careless work that has obviously not been checked. Use a single, diagonal line to strike out items you want to delete and write in additional words very clearly above or below the line.

Do not feel that you have to write the maximum length allowed – examiners will be far more impressed with work that is thoughtfully composed and clearly expressed than long rambling passages that seem to have no direction.

Summary

In this chapter we have consolidated and practised your ability to understand and respond to passages. Whether you are writing long or short passages, explaining contrasts and comparisons between passages, summarising material or ideas, writing letters or simply preparing notes about something you have read, you will be better prepared now to understand a wider range of written material, and to write on a wider range of topics.

These basic skills will help as you look more closely in the next sections at the material that needs to be covered for the examination.

Chapter 6

The threads of the story

Getting started

In **Section Two** we are going to look at the most natural form of writing – storytelling and the choosing and arranging of our words to develop a plot and storyline. We will also consider other people's views of things and other people as the subject of storytelling.

As far as we know, humans have been telling each other stories since time immemorial. The essence of a story is a narrative thread. This narrative is rather like the threads started if you blogged an online diary of your life. When you do this, you set loose a story which will run as long as there are people interested enough to listen or to read it, and you have the energy to keep writing.

Stories fulfil a number of purposes. They occupy us, entertain us, show or reveal important truths and teach us important lessons. Sometimes it is easier to follow a story, than to apply ourselves to a simple statement or a sequence of facts.

Examining the narrative

In this chapter we are starting to look at storytelling and what it is that turns a sequence of events into a narrative that we want to follow. Firstly, let's examine a very simple, straightforward narrative.

On a foggy night

On a very dark and foggy evening, two boys were given a lift home by a teacher; the journey home by bus would have taken them several hours. They left the school and headed towards Colchester, a large town some miles away, north-east of London.

Approaching a roundabout the car came to a halt in the slow lane. The traffic was bumper to bumper and, in the fog, it was possible to see only the car immediately in front. To their right, the driver of another car leaned over to his passenger window, wound it down and called out to ask whether they were going towards Colchester. The teacher turned to speak to the man but, before he could answer, one of the boys in the back opened his window and called back, telling the other driver that they were headed towards Birmingham.

Birmingham was in fact over a hundred miles away, back in the direction that they had come from. The other driver gasped, horrified. The teacher started to explain that the boy was joking when suddenly the traffic cleared in front of them and, before he could reassure the other driver, he disappeared into the fog again.

ACTIVITY 1

Work in groups or pairs.

(a) List very briefly the essential events of the story above. A simple numbered list would be ideal.

(b) Look at other, non-essential events. What effect do they have on the narrative?

(c) Besides the events of the story, there are other things that are explained. Identify them and explain their importance.

(d) List other information that could be added that would help make the story more interesting. You might want to emphasise the comic aspects, or the embarrassment of the teacher at the boy's behaviour, or the frustration and anger on the part of the other motorist. What might readers of this story want to learn next?

(e) Who might want to tell this story? To what sort of audience would you expect them to tell it?

Developing the narrative

The storyline is the bare bones of a story. To develop it further, you need to add some flesh to the bones. To do this, think about who the story is for, who the narrator in the story will be and for what purpose it will be told.

The narrator is the person who tells the story. The narrator can be a character in the story or they can be outside the story (a third person narrator). Some longer stories and books have more than one narrator.

EXERCISE 1

In this exercise you are going to develop the story 'On a foggy night' further, for a particular purpose on behalf of a particular narrator. You could add events that take place before or after the passage, possibly revealing the consequences of the events for any of the characters involved. You could also tell us more about the characters involved or enhance the descriptive details.

Decide whether you are going to tell the story from the point of view of one of the drivers, one of the two boys or someone who hears about the incident later. Decide on your audience. It might be friends on the playground, the school governors (perhaps the driver of the other car made a complaint) or some colleagues.

Your choices will determine the register that you adopt. You need to use the appropriate tone and level of formality or informality to match the narrator and the audience. The events could be seen as amusing – or serious, taking advantage of the other motorist's vulnerability.

The story here is about 200 words in length. Try to double it.

Sharing your story

Sharing is the key aspect of a story. A story is not a story until it has seen the light of day or someone has said to a friend, 'Have you heard about…?' Until someone tells the story, until it has reached more ears and eyes, it is merely an idea. Good storytellers bring their ideas to life by setting them up and launching them into a life that may endure for years, even thousands of years.

Whether your writing is based on fact or is entirely fictitious, it is important to try it out on an audience. Many good novelists either read the novels that they are working on aloud to friends or family members, or give it them to read. Without feedback you cannot tell whether your novel is interesting to your audience, flows nicely or just makes sense to someone who is new to it. For this reason you should not be shy of sharing your story with others. That's how your novel, and you, develop and grow.

ACTIVITY 2

Take it in turns for each student to read their new version of the story (written in Exercise 1) to the class. Discuss and list the developments that you find most effective in the different stories that have been written.

A story with a purpose

Many stories are written to share important information. Others convey an understanding of a character's thoughts or feelings. Others reveal a moral lesson or truth. The moral of a story will usually endure; we are more likely to take to heart lessons that others have learnt when presented in a story, than to accept instructions or advice directly. Being told what we are to do, or should do, is not always comfortable. It is much easier to learn from others' mistakes, especially when a story tells the consequences of those mistakes.

Many traditional tales in different cultures work like this. Here is a good example of a story where the sort of situation experienced by the main character is not one which we would want to undergo. From it, however, we can learn to appreciate important truths which apply to our lives.

A Fable from Ancient Kush
The Lion's Whisker

Once upon a time, a long time ago, there lived a young husband and wife in a small village in Africa. For some time now, the husband had not been happy with his marriage. He began to come home late from working in the fields. His wife thought he was the most wonderful man. But she was unhappy, too. His behavior was making her miserable.

Finally, she went to the oldest man in her village, the village elder. The elder was sad to hear her marriage was not a happy one. He had married them only two years before. At the time, he was sure that the marriage would be a good one.

"Of course I will end your marriage if that is what you want," he told the young wife, after listening patiently for a while. "You will be free to marry again. But is that really what you want?"

"I want my husband to be loving," she said. "I want to be loving. We are both miserable."

"I think I can help you," the elder said slowly. "I can prepare a secret potion that will change your husband into a loving man."

"Prepare this magic potion at once!" the young wife cried out excitedly.

"I could make it," he said sadly. "But I am missing an important ingredient. I am too old to get this ingredient for you. You must bring it to me."

"What do you need?" the young wife asked eagerly. "I'll bring it today."

"I need a single whisker taken from a living lion to make the potion work."

Her eyes widened in alarm. She bit her bottom lip. She straightened her shoulders. "I'll get it for you," she nodded.

The next morning, the young wife carried a huge piece of raw meat down to the river where lions sometimes came to drink. She hid behind a tree and waited. After waiting many hours, a lion ambled down to the river to have a drink. He sniffed at the raw meat. In three bites, the meat was gone. He raised his mighty head. He knew she was there. The young wife held her breath. The mighty lion moved slowly back into the forest and disappeared.

The next day, the young wife came again. This time, the lion appeared quite quickly. This continued for many days. Days became weeks. Each day, the woman crept from her hiding place behind the tree, moving closer and closer to the lion.

At the end of four weeks, she moved quietly next to the lion and sat silently while he ate. Her hand shaking, she reached out slowly and pulled a whisker from his chin. Holding her prize firmly in one hand, she sat frozen until the lion had disappeared back into the forest.

She ran to the elder, waving her whisker. "I have it," she shouted. "I have it!"

The elder was in awe when he heard her story. "You do not need magic to change your husband back into the loving man he once was. You are brave enough to pull a whisker from the chin of a living lion. It took cleverness and bravery to do what you have done. Can you not use that same patience and courage and wit with your husband?"

"But the potion," the young wife said eagerly. "Would not that work as well?"

"Perhaps," the elder told her. "But it would not last. Trust me, my child. Show your husband each day that you love him. Share his problems. Make him feel welcome. Make him feel wanted and needed. Give him time to change and see what happens."

The young wife went home and followed the elder's advice. Slowly, her husband began to return from the fields with the other men of the village. He began to look glad to see her. Within a year, their life was a happy one.

ACTIVITY 3

Discuss the story in class and consider the following questions.

(a) List four things that this story tells us about daily life in ancient Kush/Nubia.

(b) What is it that drives the story? What is recounted at the start?

(c) For what purpose is the author writing this story? Write a complete sentence that states the moral of this story.

(d) Why do you think that this story has endured for a long time?

(e) Can you imagine a version of this story in which the main character was male? Explain.

Children are more apt to remember stories than commands or facts. Writing for them can be lots of fun. When you write for young children, you could base your story on something that you remember from your childhood or on something that you make up.

Children's story books have lots of pictures to keep them interested and to help them remember the details of the story. When you write for children, remember to give memorable detail with words, descriptions and direct speech. These will help your story come alive.

Use humour, even if your theme is a serious one such as being wary of strangers. Remember that young children laugh very readily, especially if the joke is on an adult or figure of authority.

You are going to plan and write a short story for young children. The theme of your story, that is the idea which drives it, could be the need to warn young children about something or to encourage them to try something out. You want them to remember something important. You might, for example, belong to a successful organisation for young people and want children to consider joining when they are old enough. Once your story has been marked, again, be prepared to read it in class or to allow someone else to read it.

Stories inspired by real life

Enduring stories may be fact or fiction. As far as we know, real rabbits do not shout insults at foxes, but generations of children have enjoyed the stories of Brer Rabbit and Brer Fox. Fact can equally hold the power of a great story. Generations of adults have recounted the true story of the football matches played between British and German troops on the first Christmas Day of the First World War.

Some of the best stories are stories that are based on fact or real-life but then embellished by an author's imagination. You will find some of the best material and inspiration for story-writing if you keep your eyes open to the world around you. You might find the idea for a best-selling novel in your local newspaper or by listening to snippets of gossip at school or at home (without joining in)!

Novelists and film-makers have produced vast numbers of popular stories dealing with law-breaking and the people involved. Think of all the popular television programmes that you know or have heard of that involve criminals, unsolved crimes, police officers, private detectives, lawyers and judges.

The court report that follows comes from the heart of a justice system, an appeal court where judges are asked to examine the decisions of lower courts. This 'story' takes the form of extracts from a judgement in Ireland's Court of Criminal Appeal. In it a man wants the court to overturn his conviction which was based on phone calls between him and another man convicted of the same offences.

> What is the difference between 'stories' and 'accounts'? Strictly speaking, a story that is based entirely on fact is an account. An example is a historical record of a past event. We give an account of something that actually happened and, potentially, support the account with evidence. Fiction on the other hand, depends on a person's imagination.

People are fascinated by stories about crime and criminals. ▼

COURT REPORT

This is an application for leave to appeal against conviction. The applicant was convicted of membership of an unlawful organisation, that is, one styling itself the Irish Republican Army, otherwise Oglaigh na hEireann, otherwise the IRA, by the Special Criminal Court and was sentenced.

It is relevant to note two matters. The first is that the prosecution in this case followed on shortly after the trial of another man. This other man was arrested at Garryhundon, County Carlow, following an incident and a crash on a certain date, and was found in an outhouse at about 6.40 am on the following day, having left behind a firearm – a sawn off shotgun – and ammunition for which he was charged and pleaded guilty. He was also charged with membership of an illegal organisation, to which he pleaded not guilty, but was convicted and sentenced. The second is that this applicant (the man seeking to have his conviction overturned) was arrested on two charges: (a) possession of information in relation to the unlawful possession of a firearm at Garryhundon, County Carlow, on the first of these two dates, and (b) membership of an unlawful organisation on the following day.

Having regard to the findings set out above (17 pages containing 10 000 words), the court is not satisfied that it has been established that the applicant was guilty of the charge against him. This court will set aside the conviction of the applicant and direct a new trial.

Strictly speaking this court report is not a story, but part of a judgement written by a judge who is reporting the court's decision, giving an account of the decision he made along with two other judges.

We learn nothing about the characters involved, or the circumstances surrounding the incidents reported. We learn nothing about the atmosphere in the courtroom, or outside where the press or family and friends of the accused, or their victims, may be gathering.

All we learn is that the court has decided that the man's conviction was unsound and that he must face a retrial. How is it then that so much news, interest and entertainment is generated by the law?

ACTIVITY 4

(a) After you have read the court report, you will need a sheet of paper divided into two vertical sections. Working in groups or pairs, list in the left column anything that could be added to this court report that would turn it into a proper story that interests, entertains or causes us to think.

(b) Now read the following article from the *New Zealand Herald* about another criminal case. What information or ideas can you find in this newspaper report to add to your list of components that would improve a story? Add them to the right-hand column of the sheet of paper.

It was road rage, no mistake, says horrified witness

By *Rachel Tiffen*

5:30 AM Friday Sep 10, 2010

A horrified witness has spoken of how an enraged driver put his foot down and "just went for it" in a road-rage incident that left a man with two smashed legs.

In the first full account of Wednesday morning's hit-and-run in inner Auckland, the witness described the moments before an Asian man was knocked down and dragged several metres along Mt Eden Rd.

The victim - who is likely to need a series of operations - was last night stable in Auckland City Hospital.

"If you ask me, [the driver] cannot say 'it was a mistake' or 'my foot slipped off the accelerator'. He just went for it and [the victim] actually went under the wheels ... No after-thought, not slowly, nothing ... He just went, at speed," said the witness, who did not want to be named.

He said he was at work when he heard a lot of shouting about 9.40am.

He went outside and saw a middle-aged man with "salt and pepper" hair get out of a dark-coloured Saab, which was parked in the carpark next to Galbraith's Alehouse on Mt Eden Rd.

The Asian driver of a dark Mercedes had stopped in the middle of the street.

"I don't know why," the witness said. "Maybe he didn't give way to the guy coming out of the carpark or something silly like that."

He said the Saab driver pulled the Mercedes driver's door open and was shouting at the man inside.

"Then he slammed the door shut on him and walked back to his car."

The Mercedes driver then moved his vehicle from the middle of the road and parked. He strode over to the Saab, smacked the bonnet and began moving around to the driver's door.

The witness watched in horror as the Saab driver appeared to slam his foot down on the accelerator to drive straight into him.

"There was no way that man can say 'I didn't mean to'," he said.

The Asian man was dragged under the car for two or three metres and was left lying on the road screaming, his left leg at an unnatural angle.

The Saab driver, who had a middle-aged, dark-haired female with him, sped off.

"I could hear the [Mercedes] guy yelling and he was in pain, so I ran over to him and I assisted him as much as I could until the ambulance came," the witness said.

The injured man spoke limited English but the witness tried to keep him talking, to take his mind off the pain.

"I was holding his leg up and I could see his leg was twisted a bit and he couldn't put it down so I put it up to avoid the blood rushing to the spot."

Shortly after, paramedics arrived and took the victim away.

The witness later spoke to the injured man's partner, who had returned to get his car. "She said he was in hospital and was undergoing surgery, one of a long series of surgeries, I think," he said. "She said he had three breaks in his legs, one at the knee, two in the other leg, a ruptured blood vessel. All sorts of things."

Resident Jamie Ruscoe, who saw the aftermath of the crash, said police told him that the Saab driver had phoned to confess the hit-and-run.

"He refused to come back to the scene to talk to them, but he told them who he was and where he lived."

Police spokeswoman Noreen Hegarty confirmed staff had spoken to the driver but said no charges had been laid. Police had also spoken to the injured man briefly in hospital, and were talking to witnesses as part of an "ongoing inquiry".

Canterbury University criminologist Greg Newbold said road rage often came down to big-city stress.

"Auckland is a place with a huge traffic problem and people get stressed out and if you get someone stressed out at the wrong time, they can do something totally out of character.

"It's typical of big cities. It's not so typical of small towns, but it does happen everywhere."

Dr Newbold said "you don't know what sort of morning that bloke had" and Auckland was a "pretty aggressive sort of a city" compared to the likes of Christchurch.

http://www.nzherald.co.nz/crime/news/article.cfm?c_id=30&objectid=10672366

Look again at the components that you listed in columns in Activity 4. Use these ideas, and any others you can think of, to develop your story, the idea behind it, the characters involved, a sense of drama, a sense of justice, or whatever is important for you. Remember to plan by putting down key words before you start writing.

EXERCISE 3

(a) Using the sentence that follows as a beginning, write a story of any kind and with any purpose that you choose. Aim to write between 350 and 400 words.

They watched from some distance away.

(b) Once your story has been marked, be prepared to read it in class or to allow someone else to read it.

Summary

In this chapter we have considered what a basic narrative is, and how a narrative can be developed into a more interesting and detailed story. We have considered the people for whom we write, our audience, and the reasons for telling a story. We then thought about the reasons for reading our work to an audience, and practised it. Using crime reports, we considered how we can form stories from events, facts and ideas inspired by real-life.

Chapter 7

Narrative and the writer's purpose

Getting started

In this chapter we are going to look closely at the way authors use material and ideas to create the subjects and the themes of their stories. We will also consider further their reasons for telling stories – an author's intentions, motives and purposes. Sometimes the question of *why* they are writing is more important than *what* they are writing.

The narrator as a character

John Mortimer practised as a barrister, that is a lawyer who specialises in advocacy, representing clients in the higher courts in London. He was also a writer and invented a character, Harold Rumpole, an older London barrister who loved the courtroom and was prepared to defend any and all clients. As a class, read this passage from the short story 'Rumpole and the Man of God'. As you read, think about what Mortimer, the writer, had in mind in these opening paragraphs to the story.

Rumpole and the Man of God
By *John Mortimer*

As I take up my pen during a brief and unfortunate lull in Crime (taking their cue from the car-workers, the villains of this city appear to have downed tools causing a regrettable series of lay-offs, redundancies and slow-time workings down the Old Bailey), I wonder which of my most recent Trials to chronicle. Sitting in Chambers on a quiet Sunday morning (I never write these memories at home for fear that She Who Must Be Obeyed, my wife Hilda, should glance over my shoulder and take exception to the manner in which I have felt it right, in the strict interest of truth and accuracy, to describe domestic life à coté de chez Rumpole); seated, as I say, in my Chambers I thought of going to the archives and consulting the mementoes of some of my more notorious victories. However when I opened the cupboard it was bare, and I remembered that it was during my defence of a South London clergyman on a shoplifting rap that I had felt bound to expunge all traces of my past, and destroy my souvenirs. It is the curse, as well as

> This extract is from a first person narrative.

the fascination of the law, that lawyers get to know more than is good for them about their fellow human beings, and this truth was driven home to me during the time that I was engaged in the affair that I have called "Rumpole and the Man of God".

When I was called to the Bar, too long ago now for me to remember with any degree of comfort, I may have had high-flown ideas of a general practice of a more or less lush variety, divorcing duchesses, defending stars of stage and screen from imputations of unchastity, getting shipping companies off scrapes. But I soon found that it's crime which not only pays moderately well, but which is also by far the most fun. Give me a murder on a spring morning with a decent run and a tolerably sympathetic jury, and Rumpole's happiness is complete. Like most decent advocates, I have no great taste for the law; but I flatter myself I can cross-examine a copper on his notebook, or charm the

Uxbridge magistrates off their Bench, or have the old lady sitting number four in the jury-box sighing with pity for an embezzler with two wives and six starving children. I am also, and I say it with absolutely no desire to boast, about the best man in the Temple on the subject of bloodstains. There is really nothing you can tell Rumpole about blood, particularly when it's out of the body and onto the clothing in the forensic laboratory.

We often ask what something is about. Here we can easily distinguish between the subject and the major theme. The subject is Rumpole's intention to tell us about his professional appearances in the courts as a barrister, and the major theme is his interest in himself.

The answer to **(c)** is in the Exam Café CD.

ACTIVITY 1

(a) Discuss in class what the writer means by these words.
  (1) 'I wonder which of my most recent Trials to chronicle.' What is he announcing here?
  (2) 'I thought of going to the archives and consulting the mementoes of some of my more notorious victories.'
  (3) 'I may have had high-flown ideas of a general practice of a more or less lush (glamorous and well paid) variety.'

(b) Like the sentences in questions 1 to 3 above, many of the sentences in this extract begin with the word 'I'. What does this suggest about the character of Rumpole?

(c) Explain in your own words 'in Chambers', 'rap', 'a decent run', 'imputations' and 'embezzler'.

(d) Look now at the effect of the way the first paragraph is written. Between the first few words 'As I take up my pen' and the last words, 'that I have called, "Rumpole and the Man of God"', we learn a good deal. What is the effect of all this information? Does it serve to entertain or amuse us or does it prevent us from concentrating on the story?

EXERCISE 1

Write your answers.

(a) Explain what Rumpole complains of in the first sentence. What do you think of this?

(b) What did Rumpole learn about the practice of law once he got started?

(c) What evidence does Rumpole produce that would support his claim to be a good barrister?

(d) Do you think you would learn much about the law if you could read the rest of this story? What might you learn from Mr Rumpole?

(e) What do you think were John Mortimer's intentions in writing this story?

A writer's motives

Now we will look at another short story, 'The Case for the Defence', written by Graham Greene. Written in 1939 before the abolition of the death penalty in the UK, this story seems to be simply another story to do with the law. But remember to consider the writer's intentions and motives as you read.

The Case for the Defence
by *Graham Greene*

It was the strangest murder trial I ever attended. They named it the Peckham murder in the headlines, though Northwood Street, where the old woman was found battered to death was not strictly speaking in Peckham. This was not one of those cases of circumstantial evidence in which you felt the juryman's anxiety – because mistakes have been made – like domes of silence muting the court. No, this murdered was all but found with the body; no one present when the Crown counsel outlined his case believed that the man in the dock stood any chance at all.

He was a stout man with bulging bloodshot eyes. All his muscles seemed to be in his thighs. Yes, an ugly customer, one you wouldn't forget in a hurry – and that was an important point because the Crown proposed to call four witnesses who hadn't forgotten him, who had seen him hurrying away from the little red villa in Northwood Street. The clock had just struck one o'clock in the morning.

Mrs Salmon in 15 Northwood Street had been unable to sleep; she heard a door click shut and thought it was her own gate. So she went to the window and saw Adams (that was his name) on the steps of Mrs Parker's house. He had just come out and he was wearing gloves. He had a hammer in his hand and she saw him drop it into the laurel bushes by the front gate. But before he moved away, he had looked up – at her window. The fatal instinct that tells a man when he is watched exposed him in the light of a street-lamp to her gaze – his eye suffused with horrifying and brutal fear, like an animal's when you raise a whip. I talked afterwards to Mrs Salmon, who naturally after the astonishing verdict went in fear for herself. As I imagine did all the witnesses – Henry MacDougall, who had been driving home from Benfleet late and nearly ran Adams down at the corner of Northwood Street. Adams was walking in the middle of the road looking dazed. And old Mr Wheeler, who lived next door to Mrs Parker, at No 12, and was wakened by a noise – like a chair falling – through the thin-as-paper villa wall, and got up and looked out of the window, just as Mrs Salmon had done, saw Adam's back and, as he turned, those bulging eyes. In Laurel Avenue he had been seen by yet another witness – his luck was badly out; he might as well have committed the crime in broad daylight.

"I understand," counsel said, "that the defence proposes to plead mistaken identity. Adam's wife will tell you that he was with her at two in the morning of February 14, but after you have heard the witnesses for the Crown and examined carefully the features of the prisoner, I do not think you will be prepared to admit the possibility of a mistake."

It was all over, you would have said, but the hanging.

After the formal evidence had been given by the policeman who had found the body and the surgeon who examined it, Mrs Salmon was called. She was the ideal witness, with her slight Scotch accent and her expression of honesty, care and kindness.

The counsel for the Crown brought the story gently out. She spoke very firmly. There was no malice in her, and no sense of importance at standing there in the Central Criminal Court with a judge in scarlet hanging on her words and the reporters writing them down. Yes, she said, and then she had gone downstairs and rung up the police station.

"And do you see the man here in court?"

She looked straight at the big man in the dock, who stared at her with his Pekingese eyes without emotion.

"Yes," she said, "there he is."

"You are quite certain?"

She said simply, "I couldn't be mistaken, sir."

It was all as easy as that.

"Thank you, Mrs Salmon."

Counsel for the defence rose to cross-examine. If you had reported as many murder trials as I have, you would have known beforehand what line he would take. And I was right, up to a point.

"Now, Mrs Salmon, you must remember that a man's life may depend on your evidence."

"I do remember it, sir."

"Is your eyesight good?"

"I have never had to wear spectacles, sir."

"You are a woman of fifty-five?"

"Fifty-six, sir."

"And the man you saw was on the other side of the road?"

"Yes, sir."

"And it was two o'clock in the morning. You must have remarkable eyes, Mrs Salmon."

"No, sir. There was moonlight, and when the man looked up, he had the lamplight on his face."

"And you have no doubt whatever that the man you saw is the prisoner?"

I couldn't make out what he was at. He couldn't have expected any answer than the one he got.

"None whatever, sir. It isn't a face one forgets." 70

Counsel took a look around the court for a moment. Then he said, "Do you mind, Mrs Salmon, examining again the people in court? No, not the prisoner. Stand up please, Mr Adams," and there at the back of the court with thick stout body and muscular legs and a pair of bulging eyes, was the exact image of the man in the dock. He was even dressed the same – tight blue suit and striped tie.

"Now think very carefully, Mrs Salmon. Can you still swear that the man you saw drop the hammer in Mrs Parker's garden was the prisoner – and not this man, who is his twin brother?"

Of course she couldn't. She looked from one to the other and didn't say a word.

There the big brute sat in the dock with his legs crossed, and there he stood too at 80 the back of the court and they both stared at Mrs Salmon. She shook her head.

What we saw then was the end of the case. There wasn't a witness prepared to swear that it was the prisoner he'd seen. And the brother? He had his alibi, too; he was with his wife.

And so the man was acquitted for lack of evidence. But whether – if he did the murder and not his brother – he was punished or not I don't know. That extraordinary day had an extraordinary end. I followed Mrs Salmon out of court and we got wedged in the crowd who were waiting, of course, for the twins. The police tried to drive the crowd away, but all they could do was keep the road-way clear of traffic. I learned later that they tried to get the twins to leave by a back way, but they wouldn't. One of 90 them – no one knew which – said, "I've been acquitted, haven't I?" and they walked bang out of the front entrance. Then it happened. I don't know how, though I was only six feet away. The crowd moved and somehow one of the twins got pushed on to the road right in front of a bus.

He gave a little squeal like a rabbit and that was all; he was dead, his skull smashed just as Mrs Parker's had been. Divine vengeance? I wish I knew. There was the other Adams getting onto his feet from beside the body and looking straight over at Mrs Salmon. He was crying, but whether he was the murderer or the innocent man nobody will ever be able to tell. But if you were Mrs Salmon, could you sleep at night?

EXERCISE 2

Provide written answers to these questions.

(a) Explain what you understand by 'circumstantial evidence'.

(line 4)

(b) What was it about Adam's appearance that Greene describes in the early part of the story? Why is this important?

(c) Why does Greene say that Adams' 'luck was badly out'?

(line 28)

(d) How does Greene establish Mrs Salmon as a reliable witness? Why is this important?

(e) What is Greene trying to do to the pace of his story in lines 82 to 84? How does he achieve this?

The answers are in the Exam Café CD.

This passage is much more involved than the previous three passages which also deal with crime and the courts. One of the ways in which it is more complex is that the legal thread runs through it, from the commission of the crime to the judgement. But then you have to ask, is it the judgement of the court that matters? Or is it the judgement of someone's conscience, or of God or a deity of some sort? (Graham Greene was a Christian, a Roman Catholic.) Or did fate determine that the twins got what they deserved? Perhaps it is us, the readers, who have to make a judgement.

As you work together on Activity 2 below, especially on (b), consider the way the story is structured. What is happening to the story between line 34, 'It was all over, you would have said, but the hanging…' and line 68, 'I couldn't make out what he was at…'?

Why do you think, in his story, Greene has counsel for the defence question Mrs Salmon about her eyesight? Also, why does the writer, Greene, emphasise his own experience as a crime reporter, 'If you had reported as many murder trials as I have…'?

Remember when you are summarising this story that you need to find an essential thread or main theme that runs through it. This needs to be the thread that other ideas are built on; do you think that Greene wrote his story with events in mind, or a character or an idea?

Do you think that Greene himself might have experienced something like this court trial in his life?

Do you think Greene might have met someone who looked menacing – with a muscular body and bulging eyes?

Do you think that Greene might have been pondering the question of evil?

ACTIVITY 2

(a) Working in pairs or small groups, name the guilty parties, that is, all the people in Greene's short story who may carry a share of guilt.

(b) Write in one paragraph your own response to the story, that is, your reaction to what you have just read.

(c) In groups or pairs, discuss and write a summary of the story. Take particular care to identify the turning points in the story, that is, the points at which this story changes unexpectedly.

The answers are in the Exam Café CD.

EXERCISE 3

(a) Write a factual report of about 200 to 300 words on the trial for a newspaper or a television news report.

(b) Choose ONE of the topics that follow for a composition of 400 to 500 words.

- On your travels you find yourself outside the courtroom in a small town. Set the scene for your reader or your television audience.
- A friend of yours is on trial for murder. You are determined to support your friend and you attend every day of the trial. What happens on the last day?
- You are the sole witness of a violent crime committed by someone you know. What do you do?

When you have written your story, write asterisks in the margin to indicate where the turning points are.

Summary

You have read two very different 'legal' stories, in both of which the writers had underlying reasons for writing their stories.

The first one, 'Rumpole and The Man of God' by John Mortimer, is based on a character who is telling the story. The character and his views (often quite comical) on his story are just as important as the story itself. In the second story, 'The Case for the Defence', the writer Grahame Greene aims to get us thinking about different philosophical questions around crime, justice and judgement. Consideration of these two stories reveals to us how great the differences can be between a basic narrative or story and the ideas and motives that drive a writer.

There are several collections of John Mortimer's *Rumpole* stories and Graham Greene's short stories. You might want to get your hands on a set.

Chapter 8

Techniques that writers use

Getting started

It can be difficult, while you are actually setting out your ideas in writing, to consider the effect that your choice and use of words will have. If we are aware of the ways that writing can be made more effective by choosing the right words, then it will become easier to write well. In this chapter you will look closely at ways in which people tell stories and find the confidence to look critically at the ways in which you select and organise words when you write.

Choosing words

This is the opening scene of *Great Expectations* by Charles Dickens. With a bit of luck your teacher will tell you to shut the book, and your eyes, while this passage is read to you. Listening with your eyes shut can help you to concentrate and to imagine and more clearly visualise the scene in which a story is set.

My father's name being Pirrip, and my Christian name Philip, my infant tongue could make of both names nothing more explicit than Pip. So, I called myself Pip, and came to be called Pip.

I give Pirrip as my father's family name, on the authority of his tombstone and my sister – Mrs Joe Gargery, who married the blacksmith. As I never saw my father or my mother, and never saw any likeness of either of them (for their days were long before the days of photographs), my first fancies regarding what they were like, were unreasonably derived from their tombstones. The shape of the letters on my father's gave me an odd idea that he was a square, stout, dark man, with curly black hair. From the character and turn of the inscription, "Also Georgiana Wife of the Above," I drew a childish conclusion that my mother was freckled and sickly. To five little stone lozenges, each about a foot and a half long, which were arranged in a neat row beside their grace, and were sacred to the memory of five little brothers of mine – who gave up trying to get a living exceedingly early in that universal struggle – I am indebted for a belief I religiously entertained that they had all been born on their backs with their hands in their trousers-pockets, and had never taken them out in this state of existence.

Ours was the marsh county, down by the river, within, as the river wound, twenty miles of the sea. My first most vivid and broad impression of the identity of things, seems to me to have been gained on a memorable raw afternoon towards evening. At such time I found out for certain, that this bleak place overgrown with nettles was the churchyard; and that Philip Pirrip, late of this parish, and also Georgiana, wife of the above, were dead and buried; and that Alexander, Bartholomew, Abraham, Tobias and Roger, infant children of the aforesaid, were also dead and buried; and that the dark flat wilderness beyond the churchyard, intersected with dykes and mounds and gates, with scattered cattle feeding on it, was the marshes; and that the low leaden line beyond was the river; and that the distant savage lair from which the wind was rushing, was the sea; and that the small bundle of shivers growing afraid of it all and beginning to cry, was Pip.

"Hold your noise!" cried a terrible voice, as a man started up from among the graves at the side of the church porch. "Keep still, you little devil or I'll cut your throat!"

A fearful man, all in coarse gray, with a great iron on his leg. A man with no hat, and broken shoes, and with an old rag tied round his head. A man who had been soaked in water, and smothered in mud, and lamed by stones, and cut by flints, and stung by nettles, and torn by briars; who limped, and shivered, and glared and frowned; and whose teeth chattered in his head as he seized me by the chin.

> If you had your eyes closed while you listened, you might have jumped at the sound of the convict's first words, 'Hold your noise!'

Charles Dickens wrote in the Victorian times. He was sensationally popular and most of his novels were published in weekly instalments – many people would buy the newspaper just to read the next bit of the saga. His works highlighted many of the problems in his society such as poverty, orphanhood, crime and the corruption of the criminal justice system. He experienced many of these problems himself as his own father was thrown into prison as a result of debt problems when Charles was twelve years old and so he had to work to support his family from a young age. Because of this, Dickens was able to understand the fears and suffering of many of the common folk and portray their emotions and situations very clearly in his novels, making for really powerful writing.

Some of these questions have as much to do with how a writer achieves effects with words as with what is actually happening.

The answers are in the Exam Café CD.

Writers arrange words just as artists arrange things that we see and musicians arrange things that we hear. We will look more closely at this again in **Section Four**.

ACTIVITY 1

(a) Working in pairs, discuss these questions.

    (1) What do you understand by the words, '…who gave up trying to get a living exceedingly early in that universal struggle'?

    (2) From their tombstones, what impression does Pip have of his brothers? How does he describe them?

    (3) In the third paragraph what does Pip come to realise? What effect does this have on Pip?

    (4) What is suggested by the boy speaking of himself as 'Pip', rather than 'Philip Pirrip'?

    (5) What is the implication of the leg iron worn by the man?

(b) Summarise, in one written sentence, what is happening in the first three paragraphs of *Great Expectations*.

When reading *Great Expectations* we need to interest ourselves in the ways in which *Dickens'* choice of words, and the way that he uses them, makes the scenes that he describes very powerful. His words also convey the atmosphere of the scene – the pain and later the fear. In some ways, the images that he creates with words are even more vivid than the actual events that he is telling us about. We'll look more closely at his techniques for doing this below.

The sounds that writers use

When you write, there are times when you need to be aware of the sounds that the words that you are using make. Authors can use the power of sound to great effect.

The sounds of words are made up of vowels and consonants. Vowels (the letters *a, e, i, o* and *u*) represent the basis of speech sounds, while the other 21 letters, the consonants (the word consonant means 'with the sound'), indicate how we shape or modify the sounds with our mouths. Note that *y* also functions as a vowel in words such as *try*.

Three vowels are said to be strong: c*a*t, c*o*t, c*u*t; the two others, weak: w*e*t, w*i*t. The word w*ea*k also has a weak vowel sound – ignore the spelling and listen to the <u>sound</u> of the word.

ACTIVITY 2

Discuss in small groups or as a class.

(a) In the first paragraph of *Great Expectations* which three words are used most? What does the writer seem to be doing here?

(b) Look at these pairs of names and contrast the impressions given by each name in each pair:

Tom and Tiddles
Robert and Robbie
Milly and Maud
Paul and Saul

What impression of Pip do you gain from his name?

(c) Philip Pirrip is Pip's full name. The three names all have a small, weak vowel sound, like cl*i*ck or k*i*tten. Compare these with words with heavy, strong sounds such as *clout* or *commando*.

(d) Consider what we are told about the man who terrifies Pip. What do you think are the key words in the last paragraph?

(e) Can you spot any other ways in which Dickens organises his words in this paragraph to build up the sense of Pip's horror?

> By using the name 'Pip', which is chosen from a vast range of English names, Dickens suggests things about the character.

> Notice how Dickens breaks the formal rules of grammar in the last paragraph; there are no properly constructed sentences. Look also at the length of the sentences /groups of words in the third paragraph and the way they seem to grow, until they become overpowering.

Writers are not continuously aware of every word they use. However, good writers work to become aware of the possible impact of every word that they use. When they are consciously looking for the best word, their own experience of reading will help remind them of the particular effects certain words can have. That is one reason why you need to be a good reader in order to be a good writer.

It is important that you try out your own ideas in your writing in order to get a feel of the kinds of words that you would choose for particular purposes. The next exercise will allow you to do this. The more effective the words you choose, the more impact they will have.

EXERCISE 1

Write a paragraph of about 50 words for each of the following ideas:

(a) a common event, but seen in slow motion

(b) a creature of some sort, domestic or wild

(c) instructions for using a simple piece of equipment, real or imaginary

(d) the outline of a strongly held view or opinion.

Before you submit this work for marking or assessment, read it aloud in groups or pairs and amend it as necessary.

Placing words in a sentence

Read these three sentences from the beginning of Pip's story. Note the positioning of the underlined words

---

'My father's name being Pirrip, and my Christian name Philip, my infant tongue could make of both names nothing more explicit than <u>Pip</u>.'

'The shape of the letters on my father's gave me an odd idea that he was a <u>square, stout, dark man</u>, with curly black hair.

"<u>Hold your noise!</u>" cried a terrible voice, as a man started up from among the graves at the side of the church porch.'

In the first sentence, Pip explains his name, which is formed of a single, weak sound and seems insignificant. By placing it at the end of the sentence, however, he manages to give it significance; placed elsewhere it might be lost amongst stronger words. In the second sentence, Pip's main description of his father, who he thinks of as a sturdy man, is in the middle of the sentence as if placing it there makes him seem even more sturdy and secure. In the third sentence, the drama is conveyed by the first words which come as a surprising and terrifying command. The careful and selective placing of words in this way is a good technique for making the words that you use more effective.

> The thematic significance of this develops through the novel.

EXERCISE 2

Write a dramatic piece of about 200 words in which you vary the position of important words as Dickens does in the example above. You might describe someone entering a room suddenly, or waking up in the middle of the night, or hearing a strange noise.

Varying the length of sentences

Read this extract from an article published in *The Sunday Independent*, a South African newspaper. It was written by Eddie Daniels, who was imprisoned with Nelson Mandela, and was published on 19 July 2009 to celebrate Mandela's 91st birthday.

As you read, remember that the impact of sentences can be greatly increased by their length. Using longer and shorter sentences is an important technique that writers use. Things happen. Tension rises. Shock is sudden. Events can be set out, starkly, dramatically, in short sentences, and short sharp phrases. Descriptive passages or explanations, on the other hand, can be made more effective in longer sentences which allow the writer to build up a momentum with words.

A man at home with all people

After isolation for about a week I was allowed to join my fellow prisoners in what was then known as the "isolation section". At the end of my first day of hammering large slabs of slate into gravel I was making my way to the common bathroom when my progress was barred by a big man. I looked up and recognised Nelson Mandela. I said "Good afternoon, Mr Mandela". He offered me his hand and said: "The name is Nelson. Welcome."

That was the beginning of an enduring friendship in which I was, by far, the main beneficiary. In prison we had created an illegal committee which was made up of representatives of all the political organisations in our section. In spite of my being the only member of my organisations, the Liberal Party of South Africa and my illegal organisation, the African Resistance Movement (ARM), I had the same voting rights as the delegate representing the African National Congress (ANC).

At times disagreements occurred. Mandela, in a humble manner, went to the leaders of the other political organisations in our section to try to persuade them to return to the committee. He pointed out that it was very important to show a united front to our common enemy.

Once a week Mandela and I would spend the day together at the quarry, just chatting about our respective lives, the Struggle and our future hopes for our country.

One day, on returning from the quarry, Mandela inquired: "Where is Danny? I did not see him at the quarry today." He was told that I was ill and lying on the floor in my cell. He came into my cell, sat down on the floor next to me and comforted me (at that time we in our section were barred from attending the prison hospital).

He was then locked up in his cell and I in mine. The next morning Mandela came into my cell carrying his bucket under his arm

(we did not have water-borne sewerage in our cells). He put his bucket on the floor and again sat down next to me and comforted me. He then got up, picked up his bucket under his one arm then picked up my bucket under his other arm. He carried my bucket to the common toilet, emptied the contents, cleaned it and brought it back to me.

To put the story into context, Mandela, as an international figure, leader of the most powerful organisation fighting the apartheid government and the most important political prisoner in South Africa, could easily have requested any member of the ANC in our section to look after me. And who was I? I was a non-entity, I was practically illiterate (Grade 8), I was the only member of my organisation on Robben Island. I had no political influence or muscle, but yet he came to look after me. He came down to my level in more ways than one.

Why was Mandela so generous and compassionate to me? It is because he is so magnanimous. He can walk in the company of the elite and in the company of the downtrodden, and will be equally at home in both environments.

Work in groups or pairs.

(a) Discuss Eddie Daniels' feelings about Mandela. Find evidence to support your views.

(b) Examine the length of the sentences in the first, seventh and eighth paragraphs. What does Daniels emphasise in his short sentences? How does this affect the rest of each paragraph?

(c) Write a paragraph of about 80 words on any topic you like, using a series of sentences that grow longer and longer. The first sentence should have a maximum of four words. Read and discuss your paragraphs in turn.

(d) Write a paragraph of about 80 words on any topic you like, using a series of sentences that start off long but then shrink to a final sentence of only one word. Remember, this last one-word sentence should be a verb. Read and discuss your paragraphs in turn.

Remember the impact that sentence length has.

EXERCISE 3

Look around the place that you find yourself in at present. Write a dramatic story that begins in this place. To help establish and build tension and excitement, try to use some of the techniques that writers use that were discussed in this chapter. Think carefully about your choice of words and their sounds, and where you place them in a sentence. You should also vary the length of your sentences. Aim to write 400 to 500 words. It might help you to start your story with these words:

The door opened.

Summary

The work in this chapter is aimed at helping you to use and handle the English language effectively. Especially in storytelling, writers choose and organise words and sounds to have the effects that they need. They also need to place those words in the right place in a sentence, and ensure that the sentences are of the right length. Short, sharp sentences more easily convey a sense of drama and action while long ones are better for building visual images or developing ideas.

Whatever we want to say, it can be said, and written, well. To achieve this we have to listen to ourselves. We must also check our writing by seeing what effect it has on other people – just as we should watch people to whom we are speaking, to see the effect of what we are saying.

Chapter 9

Getting an audience to respond

Getting started

There's often a story behind a story. When you read something, consider what the writer wants to achieve with the passage or article. How can we tell what this is?

Writers write for an audience, for particular readers, and in some cases they are hoping that, after reading their work, the audience will think, feel and maybe even do something about what they have read.

Finding an audience

Here is a piece of writing which does one job while appearing to do another. Think about the impact the writer is hoping to have on his audience. He may have more than one goal.

The first resort

The Guardian
Saturday 14th March 2009

Turkey's original seaside retreat escaped the ravages of mass tourism. But now the Black Sea gem is under threat – from black gold.   by Benji Lanyado

The cliché assures travellers that getting there is half the fun. But some journeys force you to reconsider that ratio. We've taken the long route to Amasra – a six-hour overnight bus from Istanbul – and arrive at a bus station in the hill town of Bartin to find it entirely shrouded in fog. If this is half the fun, it doesn't bode well for the rest of the holiday. And we're not even there yet. Our final destination, on the other side of the mountain range, is Amasra, allegedly the finest town on Turkey's 2,000km Black Sea coast. It had better be. Things start looking

Quintessential seaside town ... Amasra.

up as we start looking down. The sun begins to rise as the road arcs over the tip of the mountain, swiftly dispersing the fog to reveal vast ripples of escarpment stretching along the coast and coated in dense forest. This is the Turkish vista that few tourists see – the lush, fertile richness of the north. And Amasra is the jewel in its crown.

From our window seat we can see two coves divided by a long, thin promontory jutting out into the water, with two small islands a stone's throw from its tip. The larger of the two is ringed with white, craggy rock and the remains of fortifications, funnelling towards a small Roman bridge connecting to the mainland. Red-topped houses are giddily arranged over the camber of the peninsula and the habitable rim of the island, with only the minarets of the Fatih mosque rising above Amasra's low skyline.

Well before the Aegean and Mediterranean coasts were developed for tourists, Amasra was Turkey's first holiday resort. As the closest sea port to Ankara, it became a summertime haven for the capital's creative elite in the 1940s.

But when Turkish tourism began to attract an international crowd in the 70s and 80s, Amasra turned to coal, focusing its efforts on blasting the local hillsides for their reserves. It was the coal that saved Amasra from large-scale development.

At our hotel on the western of the two coves we lounge on sofas in the breakfast room overlooking the seafront as the town wakes up. A few fishermen loiter around their boats as a couple of old men swim out into the bay in slow-motion front crawl. Soon others follow, many of them women in head-to-toe waterproof burkas. A father reads the paper on the promenade as his son is dispatched to the bakery, and next to him, a policeman eats his breakfast.

Over the past few years, Turks have started to return to Amasra, but there are still barely any foreigners here. It feels like all quintessential seaside towns, only prettier – the sort of place where regular patrons take their normal lives, habits and routines, and simply transplant them to the seaside.

We head for the flattened peak of Boztepe island, one of the two lumpy outcrops just beyond the tip of the peninsula. We cross the water on a crumbling Byzantine bridge and walk to the peak via the remains of Genoese towers and a handful of Ottoman-era wooden houses. There are no tourist signposts or tours for these things; Amasra wears its history on its sleeve.

Towards the peak, a small wooden cafe dishes out tea to grannies sitting on benches admiring the view and posing for photographs. Where the hill levels out on to rocky grassland with views over the entire town we bust a couple of canoodling teenagers. There's something slushily romantic about Amasra, the perfect spot for a cheesy holiday romance.

We can see down to the main beach on the eastern side of the peninsula, and pick out tiny fishing boats chugging back to shore, their catches about to be scattered across the town's restaurants. On one of the town's two bays the stump of a Roman lighthouse has been colonised by local lads as the perfect spot for daredevil leaps into the water. Behind us, the smaller, barren island that sulks further out to sea has also been colonised – by a gang of 100 black-and-white rabbits, just visible through our binoculars.

By night, the central square and the short thoroughfare linking the two sides of the peninsula are buzzing. We mimic the locals and wander slowly, arm in arm. By eight o'clock, the whole town smells of grilled fish and meat.

The edges of the peninsula are lined with restaurants, and each night we dine on the fresh catch. Fried haddock and Black Sea whitebait are prolific, eaten with oily fingers and a squeeze of lemon. Everything is accompanied by the 36-ingredient Amasra Salad – a pile of waffle-cut vegetables that includes carrots, beetroot and tomatoes.

Uncle Mustafa's (Cukuk Liman Cadessi 8), on the western side of the peninsula, is surely one of the country's best located restaurants, with a handful of tables scattered along a candlelit shingle beach, and a lucky few seated on the small jetty reaching out above the water.

As in all Turkish towns, images of Mustafa Kamal Atatürk, the Father of the Republic, abound in restaurants and shop windows. But here another face is almost as prominent. The long-haired, smouldering visage of Baris Akarsu can be seen every 10 paces or so. Few things better symbolise Amasra's charm than their adoration of this local hero, winner of the first Turkish Pop

Idol in 2004. Beloved for his habit of hugging everyone he met, he died in a car crash in 2007.

Unfortunately, Baris's death may not be the last tragedy to beset the town. The government plans to restart the coal blasting on Amasra's western fringes, an event that many locals believe will smother the city in fumes. A small but determined campaign is underway to stop the development, but if it fails, Amasra has a limited shelf-life as a holiday destination.

The difficult journey will immunise the town from any packaged bombardment for a long time, assuming the government doesn't deliver the coup de grace itself. But for now, Amasra is what many places claim to be, but few really are: a true escape. Let's hope it stays that way.

Striking details in this passage force you to pay attention. There are out of the ordinary words or combinations of words that seize your attention. They could be nouns such as 'retreat' and adjectives such as 'mass' in the introductory sentence, or adverbs such as 'yet' in the first paragraph. Each of these words puts into effect what the writer is trying to achieve.

Sometimes it is rather more than one or two words that catch the eye such as 'a long, thin promontory jutting out into the water' in the third paragraph. This is something that we can imagine and is suggested by the photograph. Here the promontory is represented by the image that we can form in our minds with the help of the words chosen.

Sometimes a simple verb can get our attention, suggesting the particular nature of some action, 'bust' for example in the eighth paragraph. In the same passage, the word 'canoodling' is used. This is dated slang for kissing, cuddling or 'snogging'. The latter is, of course, an example of more recent slang.

The author has more than one purpose in this passage. He wants to tell people about this travel destination, but he has a more important message to share about the fact that it is in danger of being ruined by coal blasting. If the article was just about the concerns he has about the blasting, it might not be read that widely. But he reaches a wider audience as he appears to have directed his passage at travellers and people interested in reading about other parts of the world.

ACTIVITY 1

Work in pairs.

(a) Identify and list the main events in this story of the town of Amasra.

(b) Choose any three paragraphs from the 2nd to the 15th paragraphs of this article. Mark up all the words or groups of words in them that you find striking.

(c) Look at these words and phrases in the first and last paragraphs. Using a thesaurus, find effective alternatives for them.

  (1) 'cliché', 'half the fun', 'entirely shrouded in fog', 'bode well', 'allegedly the finest town on Turkey's 2,000km Black Sea coast'

  (2) 'immunise', 'packaged bombardment', 'coup de grace', 'a true escape'

(d) Each of you should give this story a new title and then write a summary of the story in one paragraph. Read it to your partner so that they can comment on what you have written.

(e) Discuss what else we are told about Amasra. What impression of the town are we given in the second half of the piece?

(f) What do you think are the writer's aims in writing this story? What impact might he want to have on his audience? Does he hope that they might believe something, and maybe even do something about it?

EXERCISE 1

Write a story in which you use a threat or warning of some sort to encourage your reader or readers to do something. Where you can, choose words that will make them feel that they must take some kind of action. Aim to write between 350 and 450 words.

Writing with a direct purpose

The piece that follows goes much further in looking closely at the words used to tell a story behind a story. It also goes a long way to show how visual material can complement words or challenge words, and the powerful effect that words and pictures can have together.

The advertisement that follows shows how the marketing and writing skills that are so often deployed to turn us and our money towards the advertiser's ends can also be used to direct our thoughts, feelings and actions towards people who are far less fortunate than we are. In it, the writer makes her purpose immediately clear and then goes on to explain something that has caught her attention. The article features the photograph of the three refugees which further adds to its impact.

to advertise: to draw attention or describe favourably (from the French, *avertir,* which means to inform or warn; linked to *divert* which means to turn away)

refugees are so lucky

They have no idea how much it costs to renovate a house these days.
Brazilian hardwood. Stainless steel appliances.
Kitchen backsplash at $12.55 per square foot.
Their home furnishings tend to be a little more basic. Tarps. Rope. Cardboard.
Anything that can help protect from the harshness of the elements.
And give them a fighting chance at survival.

The text of the print ad reads:

refugees are so lucky… They have no idea how much it costs to renovate a house these days. Brazilian hardwood. Stainless steel appliances. Kitchen backsplash at $12.55 per square foot. Their home furnishings tend to be a little more basic. Tarps. Rope. Cardboard. Anything that can help protect from the harshness of the elements. And give them a fighting chance at survival.

What we take for granted 21 million people wish they could have back. Please give to the UN Refugee Agency. Visit unhcr.ca.

Karen Hegmann is a respected marketing and communication professional with a specialty in brand storytelling and advertising. This is what she wrote about the advertisement:

> "It's not often that a print ad captures my attention and imagination, but a recent campaign designed by BBDO Toronto in conjunction with the United Nations High Commissioner for Refugees (UNHCR) did just that. The ad was in a recent edition of *Canadian Living Magazine*, and featured a photo of three refugees standing in a sandstorm, with nothing but a few parcels and the clothes on their backs. The tagline literally stopped me in my tracks, and I wondered what story the advertiser was trying to tell. The copy was at total odds with the desperate mood of the photo, and I found myself drawn into the story and compelled to learn more…
>
> "Talk about a powerful message. The campaign is going global and includes a series of TV and print ads designed to raise awareness about the plight of more than 20 million refugees.
>
> "What was interesting about the ad is that it drew me into the refugee experience by contrasting their lifestyle against our own. In contrast to the chaotic world of a refugee, our problems seem so insignificant…"

One of the designers of the advertisement Patrick Scissons, Creative Director of BBDO Toronto, said:

> "We've all seen the news reports and images of refugees around the world, but the challenge in telling their stories is that their experiences are so far removed from our daily lives. Now imagine coming home after a long day at work to find that all your personal possessions and the home you know have been taken from you. This is an experience we can all relate to and we used this as our starting point for the campaign so people could begin to understand what refugees around the world go through on a daily basis."

Think about how this passage relates our experience of life to that of refugees. Note how they've used something that we might worry about to get us thinking about what refugees have to worry about.

(a) In pairs or groups discuss the refugee advertisement and the comments about it. Identify anything you consider surprising or striking about the advert and the comments.

Make sure that you find out the meaning of any words or expressions that you don't understand.

(b) Discuss these questions:

(1) What was it about the advertisement that first caught Karen Hegmann's interest?

(2) How does she sum up her response to the advertisement?

(3) At whom is the advertisement aimed?

(4) What is the most important way in which it seizes the attention of its audience?

(5) How do the words used in the advertisement combine with the picture to affect us?

EXERCISE 2

(a) Working on your own, answer the five questions in Activity 2 (b) with a single sentence each.

(b) Respond in writing, in whatever way you choose, to the last sentence of Patrick Scissons' comment. What he says concerns the spread of tolerance, compassion and understanding. Aim to write about 300 words.

Writing for a specific audience

Different types of audiences need different types of writing. This is especially true when we compare the kinds of writing that young children and adults can appreciate and understand. Writing in the way that is right for our audience will help us to attract and retain their interest in what we have to say.

Many children's stories are written with a purpose in mind. Writers use funny or interesting stories to get children's attention while they teach them a moral or life lesson, for example, to encourage them to act more thoughtfully, more wisely, or with greater sympathy. In the story of the three Billy-goats gruff, the first goat persuades a troll to let him cross a bridge by telling the hungry troll that he should wait for his brother. The second goat does the same. The third brother is so much bigger that he butts the troll off the bridge. This story is a warning against greed.

As a writer you want to get your message across so you need to write in a way that suits your audience.

Children love a story that can make them laugh. ▼

Do you remember books like this one in the picture on the right – very few words on the page and a picture with exaggerated colours and shapes?

 **ACTIVITY 3**

(a) In groups, list the characteristics of these children's storybook pages which mark them out as stories for very young children.

(b) As a class, list stories that you remember from your childhood. Include stories that you have encountered on television or film, as well as written stories.

(c) Do any of these stories that you remember have a purpose other than to entertain a small child?

EXERCISE 3

Complete both these writing exercises.

(a) Plan and write a grown-up version of one of the stories that you remembered in Activity 3. Before you start your story, set out in one sentence a reason for telling the story to someone your own age.

(b) Plan and write a child's version of a grown-up story about someone who is well-known. Begin with the words 'Once upon a time…' or 'There was a little prime minister called…' or a similar phrase.

An adult version of *Three Billy Goats Gruff* might begin like this:
'It's not always wise to wait for a bigger and better opportunity to come along. It might be that the chance you've been waiting for ends up being too big for you to handle'.

'Once upon a time, the President…' does not sound like the start of a history text book but it might be good fun to write in this way.

Summary

In this chapter we have considered our choice of words and the purposes for which we use them when we write.

The exercise with the thesaurus gave us an idea of the wide choice of words that we have. There are over 200 000 words in the English language with many of them only having slight differences in meaning from other words. In the article about Amasra, we hear that it has escaped 'mass' and 'large-scale' tourism. We could also use the term 'modern tourism' here. Then the word 'lucky' is not one which we normally associate with the word 'refugee', yet combined in this advertisement the words have a striking effect, for to be a refugee is to be seen as terribly unfortunate. An effective choice of words can enable a writer to convey his or her message powerfully.

Sometimes a writer has more than one message to convey in his piece of writing and sometimes the writing has one direct purpose. Writers need to consider their audiences – their age, interests, concerns and what is relevant to them – in order to get them to listen and to have the impact on them that they, the writers, are hoping for.

Chapter 10

Seeing from others' perspective

Getting started

Learning to think from someone else's perspective will make you a better writer (and a better person!). In this chapter we are going to work on thinking from the viewpoint of others in some activities and writing exercises.

Firstly, you are going to make uncertainty less worrying for someone a few years younger than you. If you've experienced something yourself, it is easier to imagine how others feel.

After that you will consider how being aware of what other people are thinking – what they know (and what they don't know) – can be used to create some great writing. Sometimes writers keep one or more characters in their book, and the reader, in the dark as to what is happening or is going to happen. Then when both the character, and you, finally realise what is going on, you as the reader can really identify with the character in the book and feel how that character felt.

Thinking about how others feel

For many of us, changing from primary to secondary school is one of the first big challenges of our young lives. In the activity below you need to think about how young people feel entering secondary school for the first time.

ACTIVITY 1

(a) In groups, describe to one another the most difficult aspects for each of you of moving into senior school.

(b) Each of you should make your own list of these difficulties, in order of seriousness.

(c) Discuss what could have been done to make the change of school less worrying. Make a brief note of the group's recommendations.

EXERCISE 1

Set out, in a series of paragraphs that will form part of a booklet, advice for younger children who are going to join your school next year. If you have ideas for pictures or diagrams that would help your readers, write brief instructions <enclosed in angle brackets> for the designer of the booklet.

Understanding other people

Mystery and detective stories often rely on the author being very aware of what their readers know and don't know, can guess and can't guess – what they are thinking and, even better, what they are feeling. In that way good writers build up suspense and keep you, the reader, turning the pages. Then, when you least expect it, they bring in a brilliant eureka moment and you shout out in surprise, 'Oh, he's the guilty one!'

How do good writers do this? They achieve this by being very aware of their audience and the impact of their words.

Some writers have a knack of putting you in a situation where you feel that you don't know what is going on or understand what is happening. It can seem puzzling, or even annoying, but there are good reasons for writers doing this, such as in the two extracts from novels that follow. These writers are trying to help you to imagine, understand and sympathise with the uncertainties facing their characters.

In the first extract Hooper's father is about to marry Kingshaw's mother. Kingshaw and his mother will be moving into the Hoopers' family home. It's a big change for them but the adults find little time for their sons, both of whom are about ten years old.

Extract from

I'm the King of the Castle
by Susan Hill

"What did it do?" Hooper puckered up his face. "Was it a naughty crow, then, did it frighten Mummy's baby-boy?"

Kingshaw whipped round. Hooper paused. The recollection of Kingshaw's fist on his cheekbone was vivid. He shrugged.

"Why did you go off, anyway? Where did you think you'd get to?"

"Mind your own business. I don't have to tell you anything."

"Shall I tell you something, Kingshaw?" Hooper came up close to him suddenly, pressing him back against the wall and breathing into his face, "You're getting a very rude little boy, aren't you, you're very cocky all of a sudden. Just watch it, that's all."

Kingshaw bit him hard on the wrist. Hooper let go, backed a step or two, but went on staring at him.

"I'll tell you something, baby-baby, you daren't go into the copse."

Remember these points.

- Things that are familiar to you will need explaining to new students.
- Simple explanations, such as why one year group at a time is summoned for lunch, can make it easier for 'newbies' to understand unfamiliar activities and places.
- Your readers need to know what to do when things seem to go wrong and who to go to for help.
- Be encouraging – help the newcomers feel welcome and confident.
- Use humour where possible.

Kingshaw did not reply.

"You went and looked and stopped, because you were a scaredy, it's dark in there."

"I changed my mind, that's all."

Hooper straddled a chair beside the bed. "All right," he said, in a menacing, amiable voice, "O.K., go in there, I dare you. And I'll watch. Or into the big wood, even. Yes, you daren't go up into the big wood. If you do it'll be O.K."

"What will?"

"Things."

"I'm not afraid of you, Hooper."

"Liar."

"I can go into the wood any time I want."

"Liar."

"I don't care if you believe me or not."

"Oh yes you do. Liar, liar, liar."

Silence. Kingshaw bent down and began to fiddle with his sandal strap. He had never been faced with such relentless persecution as this.

"I dare you to go into the copse."

"Oh, stuff it."

Hooper stuck his hands up on either side of his head, and waggled his fingers about. He found Kingshaw frustrating. He was at a loss to know how to get past this stone-walling, the dull, steady stare. All he could do was bait and bait, seeing how far he could go, trying to think of new things. He despised Kingshaw, but he was curious about him. He had watched him change, even in the week since they came here. He was closer, more suspicious. Hooper wanted to know what was going on inside his head. He sat on the chair again, and watched.

![ACTIVITY 2]

ACTIVITY 2

Write a single sentence response to each question about the above extract.

(a) Read the paragraph that begins with Hooper saying, "Shall I tell you something, Kingshaw?" What do you notice about the way he addresses Kingshaw? Why do you think Hooper is doing this?

(b) Describe what you think Kingshaw is trying to do.

(c) How would you describe the atmosphere between the two boys?

Sometimes it is important to understand how someone else is feeling, for example an unhappy child.

▼

It can be very challenging to know or understand what other people are thinking. In some situations we don't spend much time wondering what others are thinking, for example, our fellow passengers when we travel by public transport. Sometimes, however, it is important to try to understand what someone else is thinking and feeling, for example, a victim of some sort, someone who is seriously ill or a child who is lost or frightened.

Sometimes we need to understand someone who is a threat or risk to us or to other people who we care about. Like a police detective who is piecing together information to figure out a criminal's mind or determine his next step, we have to use our imagination to try to understand what is going on in the mind of another person. One way of doing this is to see things from the other person's point of view.

Extract from

Boy A

by Jonathan Trigell

Jack's feet feel fresh in the box-fresh, bright white trainers that Terry gave him to wear. They cushion and bounce him, lift him up. Terry says that his son wears them, that they're the height of fashion. Jack's seen the new lads coming in with them for a while now, but he's still pleased with them. They've set the seal on his day. New and radiant and airy. That's how it feels; there's so much space around him. He could run in any direction in his new Nikes and nothing would stop him. He knows he could outrun Terry easily. Terry's old enough to be his dad. He looks at him: the soft smoke curls in his grey sideburns, gentle eyes, brown like his Ford Sierra. Jack used to wish he was his dad, used to think that none of it would have happened if he had been. He could never outrun Terry, because he'd stop when called. Jack could never let Terry down.

"How you feeling, son?" Terry asks. "What do you think of the wide world?"

"I dunno." He always feels childish around Terry. A chance to let down barriers and bravado. "It's big."

He realizes "wide world" is not just an expression. Streets are broad, houses high, horizons unimaginably vast, even corner shops are commodious. Big dens of pop and videos, fags and beer. The trees are greener close up, the walls are redder, the windows more see-through. He wants to tell Terry all of this, and more. He wants to tell him how great wheely bins are, how every house should have a name like the one back there did, how telephone wires drape like bunting. He wants to shake Terry's hand with thanks and hug him with excitement and have Terry hold him tight to quell the fear.

But he only says: "It's big."

They pass a skip painted dazzling sunflower-yellow. Jack remembers skips as full of [rubbish] and bricks, but this one's empty except for a cocoa armchair. He wonders if only Stonelee skips were full of [rubbish]; but the flies wafting above the chair must believe it's on its way.

It was Terry who suggested that they walk the last few terraced streets to Jack's new home. Their driver is waiting outside, in a biro-blue Camry with a stick-on taxi-sign. The letters of its number-plate spell "PAX". Jack thinks this is a good omen, like they used to say when they were kids. Before "the incident," as his assigned psychologist called it. Pax meant you make up, that the past was forgotten, a truce and an amnesty declared, begin afresh.

The Camry is the third car that Jack and Terry have been in today, weaving a false trail, even though apparently unfollowed. The press know that he's being released; even the liberal papers called for a working committee. *The Sun* said "Tell The Public Where He's Going And Let Them Sort Him Out." Terry says they're just being sensationalist, that most people believe he's served his time. Terry reminds him that they haven't got a photograph taken since puberty. That he's a special case, not going onto the offenders' register, untraceable. Even Jack didn't know where he was going until an hour ago.

When you have finished writing this piece it will still need to be checked for:

- mechanical accuracy, spelling and punctuation
- ease of reading. If you are not able to read your work out aloud, you should read it slowly, trying to _imagine_ how it would sound. Make the movements with your mouth as if you were reading aloud.
- enjoyment of reading. Did you use clear images and sentences that are straightforward? Have you bothered to separate ideas or combine them in sentences to make the flow of your material easier?
- the way that you have placed each of your main ideas; at the beginning, the end or in the middle of the sentence?
- clarity of ideas. Would someone else immediately grasp what you are trying to say?

This is an important part of writing that we will return to in **Section Four**.

ACTIVITY 3

Work in pairs.

(a) Decide what is happening in this passage.

(b) Discuss these words taken from the passage:
  (1) 'the new lads coming in with them'
  (2) 'there's so much space around him'
  (3) 'because he'd stop when called'
  (4) 'But he only says: "It's big."'
  (5) 'Jack's new home'
  (6) '"the incident," as his assigned psychologist called it'
  (7) 'apparently unfollowed'.

Do you want to change your answer to **(a)** now?

(c) Identify the point in the story at which a piece of significant information is revealed.

(d) Why do you think the story is written in this way?

EXERCISE 2

Plan and write a story in which uncertainty plays an important part, both for characters in the story and the reader. Try to find ways of reducing the uncertainty, perhaps by allowing characters in the story to make discoveries and find out key information. Aim to write 350 to 500 words. If it helps, begin your story with the words:

The door closed behind them/him/her.

Summary

Sometimes we have to tell things exactly as they are, for example, if we are witnesses giving a statement to the police or if we are asked for information or directions from someone. Sometimes, however, we need to understand better the situation of the person or audience we are addressing. We need to appreciate their feelings in order to be able to communicate with them. For example, if we want to reassure them, we will do so more effectively if we are aware of what is upsetting them, and have thought about how that might make them feel.

Really good writers usually have a good understanding of people and are very sensitive to the impact of their written words on their audience. They use words carefully and control the flow of information to control their reader's emotions, whether it is to build up suspense, despair, fear, hope or joy.

If we want to help someone to understand another person then we have to appeal to their imagination. If you want your reader to really understand and sympathise with the character you have created in your writing then you have to help your reader get 'inside' your character and to be able to imagine, and even feel, how they feel.

Chapter 11

Characters

Getting started

Can you 'think outside the box'? Many people use this expression to describe a person who is able to think in new or unusual ways, especially when faced with a problem to resolve. Good writers often need to see things from unusual angles or perspectives, and they need to create characters who can do so too.

This chapter looks at how writers create and present characters in their stories. In the first half of the chapter there are two very interesting passages in which the two writers present us with changed worlds in which ordinary people make extraordinary efforts to survive. What techniques do the writers use in their presentation of the characters so that we as readers can relate to and understand them? Later we learn about two very determined real-life people with interesting tales to tell.

Developing characters using extraordinary situations

Look at the next two pieces of writing as examples of writing about powerful ideas, ideas which some readers might find difficult to accept initially. Consider their similarities and differences and how the authors present their unusual ideas and situations in ways that we the readers can understand, 'get into' and even relate to.

John Wyndham is a well-known English science fiction writer. In *The Day of the Triffids*, which was published in the early 1950s, he imagines a world in a post-apocalyptic future. In it, people face unbelievable chaos and threats to their lives following catastrophes in the natural world. In this extract, Wyndham describes a triffid.

The Day of the Triffids has been ▶ adapted for radio, film and television.

Nowadays when everyone knows only too well what a triffid looks like it is difficult to recall how odd and somehow *foreign* the first ones appeared to us. Nobody, as far as I know, felt any misgiving or alarm about them then. I imagine that most people thought of them – when they thought of them at all – in much the same way that my father did.

I have a picture in my memory of him examining ours and puzzling over it at a time when it must have been about a year old. In almost every detail it was a half-sized replica of a fully-grown triffid – only it didn't have a name yet, and no one had seen one fully grown. My father leant over, peering at it through his horn-rimmed glasses, fingering its stalk, and blowing gently through his gingery moustache as was his habit when thoughtful. He inspected the straight stem, and the woody bole from which it sprang. He gave a curious, if not very penetrative attention to the three small, bare sticks which grew straight up beside the stem. He smoothed the short sprays of leathery green leaves between his finger and thumb as if their texture might tell him something. Then he peered into the curious, funnel-like formation at the top of the stem, still puffing reflectively but inconclusively through his moustache. I remember the first time he lifted me up to look inside that conical cup and see the tightly-wrapped whorl within. It looked not unlike the new, close-rolled frond of a fern, emerging a couple of inches from a sticky mess in the base of the cup. I did not touch it, but I knew the stuff must be sticky because there were flies and other small insects struggling in it.

More than once my father ruminated that it was pretty queer, and observed that one of these days he really must try to find out what it was. I don't think he ever made the effort, nor, at that stage, was he likely to have learned much if he had tried.

The thing would have been about four feet high then. There must have been plenty of them about, growing up quietly and inoffensively, with nobody taking any particular notice of them – at least, it seemed so, for if the biological or botanical experts were excited over them no news of their interest percolated to the general public. And so the one in our garden continued its growth peacefully, as did thousands like it in neglected spots all over the world.

It was some little time later that the first one picked up its roots, and walked.

 **ACTIVITY 1**

In groups, discuss the following questions:

(a) What is the main idea in each of the five paragraphs? Identify them and write each of them down.

(b) Why is the introduction of the writer's father important? What effect does his presence have on the tone of the second paragraph and why is this important?

(c) What is the effect of the last two words of the extract? Explain the importance of this.

The extract that follows is from *The Handmaid's Tale* by the Canadian author Margaret Atwood. She described this book, which was published in 1986, as speculative fiction – as opposed to science fiction. According to her, the difference between the two is that the events in speculative fiction could really happen.

In this story it is not the natural world that is turned upside down but the social order, the arrangements and understandings by which people try to organise their lives together in civic society. In the book, human reproduction, for example, is totally controlled by an all-powerful state.

I got a better apartment after that, where I lived for the two years it took Luke to pry himself loose. I paid for it myself, with my new job. It was in a library, not the big one with Death and Victory, a smaller one.

I worked transferring books to computer discs, to cut down on storage space and replacement costs they said. Discers, we called ourselves. We called the library a discotheque, which was a joke of ours. After the books were transferred they were supposed to go to the shredder, but sometimes I took them home with me. I liked the feel of them and the look. Luke said I had the mind of an antiquarian. He liked that, he liked old things about himself.

It's strange, now, to think about having a job. *Job*. It's a funny word. It's a job for a man. Do a jobbie, they'd say to children, when they were being toilet-trained. Or of dogs: he did a job on the carpet. You were supposed to hit them with rolled-up newspapers, my mother said. I can remember when there were newspapers, though I never had a dog, only cats.

The Book of Job.

All those women having jobs: hard to imagine, now, but thousands of them had jobs, millions. It was considered the normal thing. Now it's like remembering the paper money, when they still had that. My mother kept some of it, pasted into her scrapbook along with the early photos. It was obsolete by then, you couldn't buy anything with it. Pieces of paper, thickish, greasy to the touch, green-coloured, with pictures on each side, some old man in a wig, and on the other side a pyramid with an eye above it. It said *In God we trust*. My mother said people used to have signs beside their cash registers, for a joke: *In God We Trust, All Others Pay Cash*. That would be blasphemy now.

To answer these questions, you will find it helpful to think about these words from the first passage:

'I remember the first time he lifted me up to look inside that conical cup and see the tightly-wrapped whorl within. It looked not unlike the new, close-rolled frond of a fern, emerging a couple of inches from a sticky mess in the base of the cup.'

Also look at these words from the second passage:

'All those women having jobs: hard to imagine, now.'

ACTIVITY 2

(a) Discuss these questions in groups.
 (1) Who was Job? For what is he remembered?
 (2) Books and paper money – what reminders do you find in your life, in your home and among friends and family of the way things were for earlier generations?
 (3) Can you think of things that are familiar to you that you might have to explain to your grandchildren one day?

(b) Still in groups, compare the ways in which the two writers try to help their readers understand unfamiliar futures.
 (1) How do they suggest that things have changed for the worst?
 (2) How do they use familiar things and ideas?
 (3) What impressions or clues to the background of the two writers do we gain; what sort of work might they have done, what sort of interests and hobbies might they have pursued, and what sort of things do you think might have mattered to them?

Nazi book burning in Germany in the 1930s. ▶

For some people the idea of destroying books is worrying because it is a reminder that destroying books has been a way of destroying or controlling knowledge. In medieval Europe books that were condemned, usually for ideas that challenged the authorities and the established church, were burned by the public hangman. Even translations of the Bible into any language, other than Latin, were burned. Religious books approved by the Roman Catholic Church are still printed with the words '*Nihil obstat*' (Latin for 'May nothing obstruct this book') and '*Imprimatur*' (which means 'This may be printed') on the reverse of the title page.

In the Soviet Union books that undermined communism could be outlawed and people found to possess them were punished, as could happen under fascism.

For someone such as a librarian, concerned with books and writing, and the business of ideas and communicating them, the destruction of books would be a very serious matter. Saving books from destruction, which is what the character in *The Handmaid's Tale* is doing, may entail terrible risks for her.

 **EXERCISE 1**

(a) Imagine a scenario in which a group of people are in a position of great uncertainty about what is going on around them. You might start with a natural disaster such as a flood, or a man-made situation, such as a riot or political coup. Decide and note down what it is that concerns the people facing this disaster.

(b) Use your notes to develop your scenario into a prose narrative, a script, a series of diary entries, verse or lyrics for a song. Write between 200 and 300 words.

Extraordinary characters

You have already met and learned about determined people, for example, Nelson Mandela. Here are two more, one an American pilot and the other a Dutch sailor.

Biography - Amelia Earhart
(1897–1939)

In an era when the adventures of aviation pioneers were as much in the news as today's pop idols and the whiz-kids of the world of IT, Amelia Earhart (pronounced <u>Air</u>hart) became the first woman to fly across the Atlantic, to fly between Hawaii and California and between Africa and India. Between the 1920s and the1930s, the western world was adjusting itself to the idea that women might sometimes prefer to wear trousers, and sea journeys, the only practical way for people to travel across the oceans of the world, required several days between Europe and America, and a matter of weeks if you were bound for Australia or New Zealand from most parts of the world.

In the early days of aviation most people rarely saw aeroplanes; they were a novelty. In both the US and the UK pilots who had flown in combat during the First World War tried to keep flying and a number of them set up flying circuses which travelled around the country, putting on displays of flying, sometimes with dancers strapped to the wings to perform while in the air, and to give short flights. It was a risky but exciting business and it only took a ten-minute flight at such a display to change Amelia Earhart's life.

Early in life, Amelia had shown a determined and independent streak that would enable her to overcome early set-backs. Her parents' marriage was unstable – her father struggled with alcoholism and was an unreliable provider. At times, with her younger sister, Amelia was left in the charge of her grandmother and enjoyed an adventurous and independent childhood but frequent moves made it difficult for her to settle into friendships or make something of her academic and sporting potential.

She left home determined never to be dependent on anyone else. Once she had tasted the thrill of flying – remember this was the era of open cockpits, goggles and a deal of warm clothing, she took any work she could to pay for flying lessons. In fact Amelia gave herself up completely to flying, reading all she could lay her hands on concerning the subject and spending a good deal of time at airfields.

Amelia Earhart's first flight across the Atlantic, in 1928, resulted in her becoming famous, as the first woman to fly the Atlantic, as a passenger. The flight lasted twenty-two hours, about four times longer than required now by commercial airlines, long enough nowadays to reach the far side of the world. By the time she died she had become the first woman to fly solo across the Atlantic, in 1932. Then, in 1937, she set off to circumnavigate the globe along the equator only to be lost in an accident which has never been explained.

Besides the recognition that followed her achievements as a pilot, as something of a role model for ambitious young women and establishing her own clothing brand – garments which she made on her own sewing machine – official, formal recognition also followed. President Hoover presented Amelia with the Gold Medal from the National Geographic Society. From the U.S. Congress there came the Distinguished Flying Cross and, from the French government, the Cross of the Knight of the Legion of Honour.

_____

In the news …

A single-handed sailor, a girl of 13, put into care for planning to sail the world, alone

In the autumn of 2009 a Dutch court ruled that a thirteen-year-old girl should be placed, temporarily, under state supervision. The decision effectively put a halt to her plans to become the youngest person to circumnavigate the globe single-handed.

Laura Dekker was born on her parents' boat in New Zealand and spent her first four years at sea. She began sailing when she was six and four years later began to plan a voyage around the world. In an interview she said that she would simply delay her trip; she was confident that her boat was good enough and that she had the ability to undertake the project.

Laura explained that the longest time she would be alone at sea would be three weeks since she would often call into port and she dismissed worries about her education saying that she will continue her studies via distance learning.

Dutch child-welfare authorities had other ideas and considered it irresponsible to allow Laura to set off.

Laura's father was instructed to share custody with the state – Laura's parents are now separated. The ruling, a very frustrating one for Laura, came just one day after British 17-year-old, Mike Perham, completed a single-handed voyage around the planet, a trip that lasted nine months.

Earlier in the year Laura reached England after a single-handed trip across the North Sea. Despite instructions from the British authorities that her father should return with her, she returned on her own. Her adventure has fuelled debate on

parents' responsibilities for their children's involvement in risky adventures.

The case was scheduled to be reviewed in October, by which time Laura will have reached fourteen, the age at which Mike Perham crossed the Atlantic single-handed.

✸ ACTIVITY 3

(a) In pairs, compare what you have learned about Amelia and Laura, about their circumstances and their characters. Draw up two columns and make a note of the similarities.

(b) In groups or as a class, identify and discuss the questions raised in this article about Laura, about the age at which young people should be allowed or encouraged to take responsibility for themselves.

(c) Laura's father ignored instructions from the British police that he should sail back to Holland with Laura, a voyage of some 400 km (250 miles). What is your view of this? How should adults treat young people who are extremely intelligent, able and adept?

(d) What do you think might have happened to Amelia? What might she have achieved had she survived? What do you think will happen to Laura? Will she set sail in time to become the youngest person to circumnavigate the globe?

Determined characters facing difficult situations can provide dramatic writing material.

 **EXERCISE 2**

(a) Choose ONE of these topics for a composition of about 400 words.

- Plan and write a story in which you, or your character, strive to get round obstructions placed in your way by well-intentioned adults.

- Plan and write a story in which great determination is required to show others that you, or your main character, is able to achieve something that others thought was impossible.

(b) Choose ONE of the following topics for a composition of about 400 words and give it an eye-catching title.

- Continue Laura's story or the story of a young person in similar circumstances.

- Imagine that Amelia Earhart or some other 'achiever' was able or decided to communicate with us now. What do you think she or he would say now about their achievement?

- The diary of a dangerous expedition to a remote place is found. The diary might have turned up on a mountainside, in the wreck of a submarine, in an abandoned space station or outside your back door. Piece together the story of the expedition in a continuous narrative, revealing not only events but the characters of the people involved.

> Stepping away from the care and demands of people, such as teachers and parents, who have responsibility for us and care for us is not always easy, but it is an important part of growing up. In adult life too, people sometimes believe that they should strike out on their own, and 'do their own thing', even if that also means taking risks.

Stories about the great and the good

Martin Luther King thought outside the box; he used civil disobedience and non-violent protest to help end racial segregation in the United States.

People say that things are impossible because:
- they know that they cannot happen
- they believe that they should not happen
- they don't want them to happen
- they don't want you to realise that they could happen.

Can you think of examples of this? If you can, you've got good ideas that can be developed into interesting stories.

▲ Martin Luther King

(a) Plan and write a story in which an important dream comes true. Decide how much of the story will be true and how much fiction, but you do not need to tell your reader. Just make it the best story you can. Write between 300 and 500 words.

(b) Write a letter about the story that you wrote in (a) to a publisher, film director or television producer. Introduce yourself and explain why you are writing, tell them why you think the story deserves a wider audience and indicate the response you are hoping for. Begin and finish the letter formally.

Summary

You have encountered four stories, two fictional narratives and two articles centred on people. Good stories rely on having good strong characters. In this chapter we have looked at two important techniques that authors use when working with characters. You have ordinary people stretched to do extraordinary things, and then you have very extraordinary, strong-willed or determined people living their lives. Think hard about your characters, and the situations that they face, when you write.

As readers we often have to imagine things and events that might seem impossible or unacceptable because that is what characters in fiction often have to do. Writers help us to understand these situations by creating characters whom we can relate to. Then things become possible, in a range of stories from science fiction to romance. Characters, created by writers, can lead us to accept what we would previously have rejected.

However, strange things also happen in real life – remember that real people in real life often face situations that seem unimaginable before they happen.

Chapter 12

Developing characters

Getting started

People are fascinated by people. In this chapter we'll continue to look at developing character – whether in non-fiction or fiction. We will consider some of the aspects of narrative that occur in the accounts of people's lives and how these can be used to develop character.

We also look at the business of taking over a character in a story, be it a real or fictitious person, and deciding what we are going to say about the character and how we are going to say it – essentially how we shape and develop the characters that we write about.

Describing a person

Think about the ways in which lifestyle magazines, all over the world, try to attract your attention and convince you that they are the thing that you should be reading – the most exciting and interesting publication on the shelf. It's not quite advertising, but then what is it that entices you to take a peek inside? Marketing people might describe it as promotion, marketing, engaging the reader or reaching the target audience.

The most important way in which magazines attract attention is with other people – their stories, photos, advice, scandals, heartaches and victories. This is especially true with women's magazines. The covers of most magazines have a face on them.

ACTIVITY 1

Everyone should bring a lifestyle magazine into class. Put them on a table and look at the covers. Note down the pictures and text on the covers of these magazines which provide clues to what audience the magazine is appealing to and what articles might be inside the magazine. What is the main focus of most of the magazines?

Below is some advice for writing a good advert for a 'lonely hearts column' from a New Zealand lifestyle website, www.nzs.com.

Are you searching for the love of your life, looking for a date for the weekend, or just trying to find a like-minded companion? Today, there are countless dating sites featuring New Zealand personal ads and dating profiles. But that hasn't made the art of matchmaking any easier. With so many punters out there, you'll only get noticed if you write an effective, interesting and unique ad to hook your potential love interest from the first word.

- **Spend some time writing your personal ad:** think of it as an investment in your future and the key to meeting your special someone. Spend time thinking about what you want to include, then write two or three drafts, each with a slightly different emphasis. As a guide, write 40% about yourself, 40% about what you're looking for in someone else and 20% on what kind of relationship you're seeking. Remember, this snippet about you will be a first impression, so make it a good one.

- **Market yourself well:** think about your points of difference and the things that make you who you are. Try to see your ad as others will see it: What kind of person do you want to attract? What kind of person do others want to meet? Try to make your ad have personality and punch!

- **Include a photo of yourself:** sure, you'll be putting your mug out there on the Web for everyone to see, but a face will add character, personality and impact to your ad. Personal ads with photographs get a much greater number of replies, compared with those using text only.

- **Have a good opener:** your opening line should be the synopsis of your ad, so make it a true representation of 'you' and create a line with some pizzazz. Instead of 'Single girl seeks male in Auckland', try 'Single girl searching for fun guy with personality and style'. Your username should be enticing too. Kate395 has no personality, so go for something that tells the reader about you: KarateKate, KuddlyKate or KookieKatie.

- **Impress with stunning syntax:** write in full sentences and check that your spelling and grammar are correct. For a great ad, avoid too many exclamation marks, avoid writing in all capital letters and steer clear of 'txt speak' like 'u r my #1'.

- **Be yourself:** if you lie in your personal ad, you're fooling your potential love interest and yourself. Be true to your personality in your ad: if you're honest about your likes, dislikes and relationship expectations, you're far more likely to find a good match. And if you're one of those people who lie about being married or in a relationship – get a grip on reality!

- **Have realistic expectations:** for those who want a serious, committed relationship, be aware that you're never going to change someone with the username Lookin4hotchicks. Be aware of what those who read your ad will see. Put key requirements in your ad – if you want a casual date, long term relationship or a summer fling, then make sure your ad reflects what you're seeking.

- **Remember there's more to you than meets the eye:** many personal ads include a physical description – hair colour, eye colour, physical build and so on – but there's more to you than that. Include personality clues in your ad, such as your interests, favourite music and movies, pets and interesting titbits about you. Don't give them your life story, but make sure your ad is more than just the physical facts.

- **Be positive:** rather than listing all the things you don't want in a partner, list the things which appeal to you or are requirements. This will help reduce the number of 'dead end' replies you receive. If you're a workaholic, paint yourself as a career driven individual; if you're scared that your children will frighten off potential suitors, state in your ad that you love spending time with your family.

- **Don't get too personal:** always avoid including your last name, phone number or street address. Most people who meet people on dating sites are harmless, but some are not.

Good luck finding your Mr or Miss Right! There are many couples who have met over the Internet and have gone on to lead happy lives together. These people come from all walks of life and from every part of the world, but one thing is for sure – they all had interesting, eye-catching personal ads!

This advice is about presenting yourself. It suggests ways of giving an account of yourself, telling your story and marketing yourself. It also contains good advice about written communication and useful warnings about using the internet.

There is no need to remind you that dating sites are sometimes used by people whose intentions are questionable. This should be borne in mind by anyone using such sites.

 ACTIVITY 2

(a) In just ten minutes, and on your own, write down brief responses to the following questions.

(1) Why do you think the internet article above starts with a question?

(2) What is the writer trying to do in the first paragraph with the words, 'With so many punters out there'?

(3) What do you understand by 'personality and punch' in paragraph three?

(4) Can you think of circumstances when 'KuddlyKate' would not want her nick-name used?

(5) In the final paragraph we read, 'There are many couples who have met over the Internet and have gone on to lead happy lives together.' What do you think is the purpose of this sentence? Would it convince you of anything?

(6) Which paragraph is the most honest or straightforward?

(7) For you, what would be the most important advice given here? Explain why.

(b) Now work in pairs or small groups.

(1) Discuss your responses. Change your responses in the light of this discussion, if appropriate.

(2) List the ways you are encouraged in this piece to consider the people who might read your ads.

How do we know that what is being said is true? As we have already seen, courts often spend a great deal of time trying to establish whether someone's story is true – just think of Graham Greene's twins in *The Case for the Defence*.

 EXERCISE 1

Plan and write a review of this item for people of your own age. Make clear what the writer is trying to say. Comment on the way the item is written and indicate what you think of the idea of dating online. Aim to write about 400 words.

Bringing a character to life

One of the earliest novels in English, *Pamela,* was written in 1740. Before then fiction had been written in verse and as drama, for performance rather than private reading; before the eighteenth century, many people in England could not read and write. However, with a growing number of people who could read, other ways were sought to present fiction. Samuel Richardson, the author of *Pamela,* was also a printer and he gathered together ways of telling stories and from them his novel grew. Pamela, a lady's maid, is terrified when her employer dies and she is left with the employer's son. The plot is simple. He wants to seduce her or make her his mistress; she will settle for nothing less than an honourable marriage. The result is a 'soap', a dramatic story with new instalments made available daily or weekly, that was wildly successful over two centuries ago.

Some of the techniques that Richardson used were letter writing and diary entries. Here are some brief extracts from his work:

This is an extract from a letter to her parents.

> Dear Father and Mother,
>
> I have great trouble, and some comfort, to acquaint you with. The trouble is that my good lady died of the illness I mentioned to you....
>
> And so comes the comfort, that I shall not be obliged to return back to be a clog upon my dear parents! For my master said, "I will take good care of you all, my good maidens. And for you, Pamela," (and he took me by the hand; yes, he took my hand in front of them all), "for my dear mother's sake, I will be a friend to you."
>
> ...and gave me with his own hand four golden guineas, which were in my employer's pocket when she died; and said, if I was a good girl, and faithful and diligent, he would be a friend to me. And so I send you these four guineas for your comfort.

Four golden guineas was an enormous sum of money, equivalent to quite a few thousands of pounds.

This is an extract from a letter of reply from her parents.

> *Dear Pamela,*
>
> *Your letter was a great trouble, and some comfort, to me and your good mother...*
>
> *But our chief trouble is, and a very great one, for fear you should be brought to any thing dishonest or wicked, by being set so above yourself. Every body talks how you have come on, and what a genteel girl you are; some say you are very pretty. But what avails all this if you are to be ruined or undone.*

Later, Pamela writes a diary entry in which she quotes from an anonymous letter which warns her of a wicked plan.

> *"...The squire is absolutely determined to ruin you; and because he despairs of any other way, he will pretend great love and kindness to you, and that he will marry you. You may expect a parson, for this purpose, in a few days; but he is a disgraced lawyer, hired to impersonate a clergyman."*

As Pamela's story unfolds, Richardson inserts the device of the anonymous letter to add to his character's difficulties. He does not have to produce factual evidence as we would in a courtroom, for example. In fiction, events can be added to suit, to increase the tension, to cause laughter, to reveal things about a character or to hint at what might happen later.

ACTIVITY 3

Work in pairs.

(a) List the events relayed in these extracts.

(b) List Pamela's concerns.

(c) Pamela's parents' first concern is her ambition, that she may be hoping to marry her wealthy employer. What is their second concern?

(d) What is suggested about the character of Pamela from the words she puts in brackets in the first letter?

The answers are in the Exam Café CD.

EXERCISE 2

(a) Draw up the description of a character. It could be someone you know or a fictional character. List basic information first, such as name, age and the place where the person lives. Then try to add in details about the person's character, interests, ways of behaving, values, beliefs and ways of seeing things.

(b) Use your character to start a story. Before you start, write in one sentence one of the things that your character will do or experience. You may write the story in whatever form you like, as a prose narrative, script or poem. Make sure that you introduce your character and his or her situation or circumstances. At the end of the story try to establish that there will be at least a pause in the action. You may want to point out conclusions drawn by the character or what may happen in the future. Aim to write between 400 and 500 words.

(c) Read the story written by one of your classmates. Read the whole story or sections of it to the group or class, and explain what it is about the character that they have created that you find interesting or enjoyable.

Developing characters further

Some of the greatest stories around started with one character or set of characters, which the author has then developed and taken further. Sometimes a character stays very much the same, but sometimes a character changes and grows or matures over time. Some of your favourite movies are like this. Think of the movies *Free Willy 1*, *Free Willy 2* and *Free Willy 3*. In *Free Willy 1*, the star of the show, Jesse, starts out as an angry runaway boy who is fostered into a family where he learns to listen and love again through his experience with an orca (a killer whale). In *Free Willy 3*, Jesse emerges as a serious grown-up hero, taking on the whalers. In other films, the characters stay the same. An example is *Toy Story 1*, *Toy Story 2* and *Toy Story 3*. The heroes of that show, Buzz Lightyear and Woody, don't change much – they just have new adventures.

EXERCISE 3

Imagine that a publisher or television producer has asked your advice to help an author develop ideas for a follow-up book or film, or a second series of a TV show that he or she has written. The plan is that you give ideas to develop the story further using the same characters that already exist in the book or film.

(a) Select a story that you know and enjoyed – from a book, film or TV series such as a soap. If you prefer, you could ask your teacher or school librarian to help you find a short story.

Decide in what direction the author must take the story.

- Will the character(s) change or stay the same?
- If the character(s) change, how will they develop?
- If the character(s) stay the same, how will you ensure that their new adventures reflect their existing personalities?
- Consider the plot (the things that will happen in the new story).
- How will the themes, such as friendship or telling the truth, which run through the original story continue into the new one that you are suggesting?

Allow one paragraph for each of these points.

Summary

In this chapter we looked at some helpful advice about describing ourselves from a website that was encouraging its readers to try out online dating. We can use this same advice when we think about how to describe ourselves or imaginary characters when we are writing stories.

We also looked at some of the techniques that the writer Samuel Richardson used to make his main character, a young woman named Pamela, come alive. He used letter writing and diary entries to make her seem very real, even though her actual existence has never been established.

We then thought about how some characters change as the story develops, while in other cases the characters stay the same. This is something to decide about when you start writing.

Chapter 13

Using humour

Getting started

Making people laugh is an important way of keeping people entertained. Writers often use humour to keep people interested in their work. To use humour we need to know why people laugh. In this chapter we will look at what makes something funny. We'll also look at satire to see how this is used to poke fun at people.

Making people laugh

Most of us will laugh at cartoons and amusing pictures, but can we explain why? Knowing what makes people laugh, and why, is important for a writer.

 *'Mom said if I just smiled no one would notice.'*

✦ ACTIVITY 1

Collect pictures of well-known people and bring them to school. In pairs or groups, write funny captions or speech balloons for them. Show the best examples to other groups and the class. Be ready to explain why you are amused by the words that have been put in these people's mouths.

Storytelling involves making things happen and giving other people something to say and do.

ACTIVITY 2

"Please turn it down - Daddy's trying to do your homework."

Work in pairs or small groups.

(a) Examine the picture in this cartoon then answer these questions. Make a brief note of your answers. For now, cover and ignore the caption (the words printed underneath the picture).

(1) What is familiar in this picture?

(2) Are the people in the picture doing the sort of thing we would expect them to do?

(3) Are there any objects in the picture that are surprising or unusual?

(b) Now consider the words of the caption.

(1) Do fathers or mothers ever help with homework?

(2) Do parents ever ask their children to consider the inconvenience they might be causing to grown-ups?

(3) Do parents ever ask their children to turn down the television?

(4) Is there anything unusual here?

(5) Is it just one part of the caption, or the two parts put together, that make it funny?

EXERCISE 1

On your own, use the answers to the questions in Activity 2 to help you write a paragraph explaining why you think we laugh at this cartoon. You will probably need to write four or five sentences, between 60 and 80 words.

Why people laugh

In the Middle Ages soldiers spent months, even years, travelling away from home to fight.

ACTIVITY 3

"Is there someone else, Gervaise, or do you really go to the Crusades every Thursday?"

Work in pairs or small groups. Examine this cartoon then answer these questions. Make a brief note of your answers.

(a) Are the people in the picture doing the sort of thing we would expect them to do? Are there any objects in the picture that are surprising or unusual in such a scene?

(b) What is suggested by the expression on the man's face? Is he bored by the same old question from a wife who does not understand the logistics of warfare?

(c) Does the woman really think that you can set off on a crusade every week or is she being sarcastic? What is really worrying her?

Irony is involved in both these cartoons. It is unintended humour caused by the mother's lack of concern that her son is doing nothing about his homework and the medieval wife's complete unawareness that men do not go to war as they might go off to work that make us laugh, despite their seriousness.

EXERCISE 2

(a) On your own, use your answers to the questions in Activity 3 to help you write a paragraph explaining why you think we laugh at this cartoon. You will probably need to write four or five sentences, between 60 and 80 words.

(b) Decide which of the two cartoons that you have considered you prefer and explain why. Otherwise, describe another cartoon that you particularly like and explain your preference for it.

ACTIVITY 4

A self-caricature of Dave Brown, (drawn by himself), cartoonist of *The Independent* of the UK

(a) Work on your own.

   (1) List the exaggerated features of this caricature of Dave Brown and note briefly what you think is suggested by each of these features.

   (2) Set out in one sentence what this cartoon suggests about the business of drawing cartoons. What do you think this self-caricature tells us about Dave Brown?

   (3) Do you think that this self-caricature is a good way for Dave Brown to communicate his ideas? Explain your opinion in two or three sentences.

   (4) Write a caption for this picture.

(b) Share and discuss your responses in pairs or small groups.

caricature: literally an 'over-loaded picture'. It is an exaggeration of a person's appearance to amuse or cause ridicule.

Using satire to make people laugh

Humour is also an important tool to keep people interested in a story. Lots of people listen to stories, and watch movies, to have 'a good laugh'. Writers, even journalists, use humour to get people reading their work.

We've spoken about how writers need to look at things in new ways, and help their readers do the same. Humour can be an important tool to do this. Poking fun at something or someone is also a good way of getting people to see the problems with a situation or person that you are concerned about.

In the extracts from the following articles, we'll see how humour is used to poke fun at celebrity culture. First is an extract from a 'spoof' diary entry that was published in a newspaper. It is one of a number of diary entries which were made up as if written by various well-known people, such as entertainment celebrities and politicians. This one was written as if by Elton John.

This series of extracts from newspaper articles are an example of a story that, in journalism-speak, 'runs'. When journalists say that a story 'runs', they mean that it develops and continues to interest people, and that they can continue to publish new articles on the story.

A spoof diary is a satirical (witty and maybe a little scornful) 'fake' diary by someone.

A peek at the diary of ... Elton John by Marina Hyde
The Guardian, Saturday 5 July 2008

What a few days it's been. First I sang Happy Birthday to my dear, dear friend Nelson Mandela – I like to think I'm one of the few people privileged enough to call him Madiba – at a party specially organised to provide white celebrities with a chance to be photographed cuddling him, wearing that patronisingly awestruck smile they all have.

The next night I welcomed the exact same crowd to my place for my annual White Tie & Tiaras ball. Lulu, Kelly Osbourne, Agyness Deyn, Richard Desmond, Liz Hurley, Bill Clinton – I met most of them 10 minutes ago, but we have something very special and magical in common: we're all members of the entertainment industry. You can't manufacture a connection like that.

The style in which this diary is written is called satire and it is the business of mocking, teasing, ridiculing or poking fun at someone or something. Sometimes its intention is simply to amuse; sometimes to reveal foolishness.

What follows is two accounts of the consequences of the spoof diary entries. The target of this joke, Elton John, did not see the funny side of things and took the publishers to court.

Elton John's libel claim against the Guardian thrown out
The Guardian, Friday 12 December 2008

John had been seeking an apology and damages after he was the subject of the "A Peek at the Diary Of …" column in The Guardian.

John claimed that it poked fun at his celebrity fundraising and suggested that his annual fundraising White Tie and Tiara Ball was used to meet celebrities and for self-promotion.

Guardian newspapers said in a statement: "We're sorry that Elton John lost his sense of humour over this article.

The judge – and, we suspect all readers – saw the article for what it was; a piece of mild satire. Newspapers have published satire since the 17th century in this country: the judgment is an important recognition of the right to poke the occasional bit of fun."

Elton John drops libel claim against Guardian over spoof diary
The Guardian, Thursday 26 March 2009

Sir Elton John has ended his libel claim against the Guardian newspaper over an article that poked fun at his celebrity fundraising.

John had accused Hyde (the writer of the diary) of defamation and using a "gratuitously offensive, nasty and snide tone" in the piece. In December a high court judge struck out his claim for libel, agreeing with the

Guardian that the article did not carry the factual meanings that John had claimed.

Mr Justice Tugendhat also refused John permission to appeal and ordered him to pay costs.

Finally, last week, the court of appeal rejected a written application seeking leave to appeal, giving the singer one week to launch a further challenge, which expired today.

ACTIVITY 5

In pairs, work methodically through the questions that follow. Note down your responses briefly, in writing.

(a) What is suggested about public interest in this story by the three dates?

(b) Why does the writer, Marina Hyde, use the following words and expressions in the diary: 'privileged', 'white celebrities' and 'patronisingly awestruck'?

(c) What is suggested about Elton John in this sentence: 'I met most of them 10 minutes ago, but we have something very special and magical in common: we're all members of the entertainment industry'?

(d) In the court case, as described in the second extract, what were the opposing views taken of the matter by Elton John and by *The Guardian*? Explain in one sentence.

(e) What is it in the last two sentences of the second extract that indicates how *The Guardian* may feel about all this? Explain your opinion in one sentence.

(f) In the third article we are told why Elton John found the spoof diary offensive. Do you think that it was offensive? Explain your viewpoint, in no more than two sentences.

EXERCISE 3

You are going to write about a character, real or fictitious, who annoys you or other people. Decide what it is about this person that is annoying. Make a note of this. You may choose to write about this person in one of the three ways listed below.

- Plan and write a story of about 400 words in which your main character (the annoying person) reveals what she or he is really like. Use humour in your story. Maybe something funny happens and your character reacts in a comical way.

- Write a design brief, a set of instructions, for an artist who is going to draw a caricature or cartoon of this person. You will need to indicate what you want in the picture, and why, explaining what it is about this person that you are trying to communicate. If you want a cartoon drawn, you may want to include other figures, a background and clues about the character of the main person. Write 200 to 300 words.

- Write a spoof diary in which the annoying character of this person is brought out. Think about what might interest them and how they would write or speak about it. Write 250 to 300 words.

Plotting a story for maximum humour

The story about Elton John, above, follows three steps: first there was the spoof diary, then there was a court case against the publisher of the diary and then there was the announcement that Elton John was dropping the case against the newspaper, *The Guardian*.

This story could have been 'assembled' with the three steps arranged and balanced in any one of six different orders, depending on the effect that the writer or editor wished to achieve. The order reported above reflects the natural order of events which gives the story a convincing sense of orderliness. However, if written after all these events, it could have started with the drama of Elton John's failed attempt to sue *The Guardian* or with a sense of relief, or disappointment, that the case had been dropped. If you want to use humour in a story, it is a good idea to think about which order of events would be most suitable for introducing some humour or providing a funny twist. For example, if someone is absolutely convinced that they are going to win a court case, but then lose it, that could be the starting point for some fun.

EXERCISE 4

(a) Write a report of the Elton John story in which you arrange the material in a different order. Use humour in your story. The three original reports contain a total of 359 words. Aim to write between 300 and 400 words.

(b) Choose ONE of the following options.

- Write up your version of a story that has 'run'. It could be fictitious or one with which you are familiar. Decide what are the important steps or developments in the story, decide the order in which you are going to present them and then expand your ideas into a complete story. Try not to write more than 300 words.

- Write a narrative or a report in which something is revealed of someone's character. You could choose to reveal something shameful, or something good. It can be creditable or fanciful, or just funny. Plan carefully and keep your writing sharply focussed on the essentials. Write between 350 and 500 words.

Remember these points about storytelling:

Write about
- something you know
- something you have found out about, or
- something that matters.

As part of your writing
- plan your ideas with a minimum of words
- expand these ideas with additional words and arrange them in order
- then write your passage clearly so that it is easy for your reader to follow what you are saying.

When you think you have finished
- check your work against your plan and the instructions you are following
- read the material aloud or imagine the sound of your voice as you read it silently.

Summary

You have to be very confident and competent to sum up a character so that other people can recognise quickly and easily what you are trying to show about them. Some artists can do this with a few deft strokes of a brush and some musicians need only a chord or a few carefully chosen notes.

It can be difficult to do this with words. If your words have impressed others, or caused genuine laughter, then you should feel pleased with yourself. Humour, including the use of satire, can be a very important tool to keep your audience interested in the events and the people that you write about.

You also have been reminded of the need to plot events to increase the impact of whatever it is that you want to say.

The power of observation

Getting started

In **Section Three: Descriptive**, we will look at ways of describing things and events, including other people's feelings. We'll practise close observation and describing what we see, using comparisons and building images (word pictures). We will also use description to enhance a sense of drama or to convey emotion.

From minute detail to overall impressions, we observe the scene around us. When we need to convey these impressions or observations to others, we first have to be really sure about what we see and observe carefully. Then we have to select just what we are going to refer to, just what we think is important. Looking and choosing – that's how we need to get started with descriptive writing.

Starting with the familiar

We will start our work describing something familiar so that it can be done with a degree of confidence.

ACTIVITY 1

For this activity you will need to be in small groups ready to make notes.

(a) Think of a place that you know well. Make a list of what you can see when you think about this place. Ask yourself what you would want to tell somebody else about it. One of you describes their place while the rest of the group listens and makes notes. It may help you to concentrate on what you are trying to tell the others about the place if you close your eyes while you talk.

(b) When you have completed your description, the rest of the group should each write a paragraph of continuous prose describing the place that you have spoken of. Each person in the group takes a turn.

When taking notes, if a member of the group refers to, for example, a red bus that is always waiting at a certain place, at a certain time then writing the word 'red' or 'bus' should be enough for you to recall whatever was said about a red bus.

It is important to mention difficulties as well as successes because, by talking about them with others, you may well find ways around them.

(c) Pass these written descriptions around for all of you to read. Make notes of any words or expressions that you find particularly helpful in imagining the places. What it is that makes some words and expressions particularly helpful? Which are the words that surprise you, and better help you to imagine the places?

Challenge

(d) Make a note of aspects of the places that you found difficult to describe and ask other members of the group how they tried to surmount this difficulty.

EXERCISE 1

Look at the two illustrations above. For each one, list the details that get your attention. Then write a description of each of the pictures. Aim to write about 150 words for each illustration.

Decide whether you are going to describe each point on your list with some realistic detail such as its colour, shape or size, or whether you are going to compare it to something else.

Decide whether it is detail in the jungle landscape that is important or the individual person. In the urban picture, is it the human figures or the buildings that form the most important aspect of the picture?

Words that you can see

Now you are going to match up words with things we can see or imagine. Read this description of Abbeystead, a village in the north of England, from the book *Beautiful Britain: The Lake District and Lancashire*.

A steep descent between neat beech hedges leads to Abbeystead in the sheltered valley of the Wyre. Built on the site of a long-vanished Cistercian abbey, the village has some farms which look like manor houses, a fine school, an ornate horse trough and a colourful tangle of cottages. Surrounded by heather moors, Abbeystead is noted for its fine grouse and its bees – many of the farms and cottages have honey for sale.

The two arms of the Wyre, Marshaw Wyre and Tarnbrook Wyre, meet at the village. Where they converge, the woods crowd right across the junction – a domain of green shade in summer and a crisp, golden world in autumn. No sooner have the two Wyres met, than their combined waters swell broadly across the valley, impeded by the dam of Abbeystead Reservoir half a mile below the village. It was constructed in the 19th century to provide water for textiles factories downstream at Dolphinholme and beyond. The still water reflects the woods that crowd upon its eastern shores. A path runs along the north bank of the reservoir, first among the trees, and then through the open county beside the river as it emerges from the dam. This is fine strolling country, crisscrossed by a network of easy paths. Many wildfowl can be seen gathering on the slowly silting shores, particularly in the winter.

About a mile beyond Abbeystead is Christ Church-over Wyresdale, known locally as the Shepherds' Church. This is because its porch faces rich green water meadows – ideal grazing for sheep. The inscription over the church door reads: "O ye shepherds hear the word of the Lord."

ACTIVITY 2

Work in pairs.

(a) Identify each aspect of the village which is described in this piece. Using one word for each of these features, make a simple list.

(b) Look at these words in the first paragraph:

'neat', 'beech', 'sheltered', 'fine', 'ornate', 'colourful tangle', and 'surrounded by heather moors'.

For each of these words or expressions find at least two alternatives that could have been used in the passage instead.

Look at these words in the description of Abbeystead, and the way they are used:

'leads', 'meet', 'converge', 'swell across', 'runs', and 'emerges'.

They are all verbs which are words that denote action or activity. What sort of action or activity does each of them represent here? Why is this important in this passage?

(c) What effect does the word 'beyond' have in the final paragraph?

(d) List other aspects of Abbeystead which are not described, but which might also draw your attention. What is it about them that is interesting or intriguing?

Notice how the verbs that indicate movement reveal how the reader is carried or led through the village.

As you describe the place you have chosen, try to lead your reader through the place as you describe and explain it. Rather than overwhelming them with everything at once, you might want to introduce things in the same order that you might notice them as you arrived and maybe walked through the place. This way your reader can imagine things happening and feel as though he or she is actually there.

EXERCISE 2

Plan and write a description of a place that you have visited. Aim to write between 250 and 400 words.

Using comparison

You've heard the words starting, 'It's like...'. Knowing that other people have seen, heard and generally experienced many of the things that we have experienced allows us to use comparison to help convey what we mean. Comparison enables us to link the familiar to the unfamiliar and reassures us that we already have something on which to base our encounters with things that seem very new or different.

The extract below is from the book *Traveller in Rome* by H V Morton. While writing about his time in Rome, H V Morton takes time to escape from the heat of the city to the countryside town of Tivoli, just as the Romans still do.

Tanagra is ancient Greek pottery.

An **aquatint** is a watercolour painting.

It is extraordinary how the air in summer alters after an hour's journey from Rome, and even at an altitude, like that of Tivoli, of only seven hundred feet (300 metres) above the sea. I walked on through the little town and came to the famous cascades where the river Anio takes a tremendous leap into the valley below. Then glancing up, I saw in the distance, high on the edge of a hill, the pretty little circular temple of the Sybil, wearing its low roof like a hat on a tanagra figure. I suppose of all the relics of antiquity this is the one most frequently reproduced in the English countryside by our forebears. Like the Colosseum, it is something one has always known. Yet it was a surprise to see it standing up there, looking so exactly like an old aquatint.

The entrance to the Villa d'Este was damp and decayed, and unlike what I had imagined it would be: but stepping on a terrace and looking down, I saw plumes of water shooting up above the heads of tall dark cypresses. I descended from this terrace into the sheerest fantasy. It was the extravaganza of falling water; of rising water; of water thundering up into snowy Alps under tremendous pressure; of water whispering and tinkling as it finds its way through moss and fern; of water lazily curving from the mouths of urns, and even, in some surely Freudian moment, from the breasts of sphinxes.

I came upon dark avenues flanked by colossal cypresses, nourished for centuries by the perpetual flood, where spouts of water arched from ancient masonry and gurgled away to a lower level, to be used again in some new fantasy. The old Arab extravagance of the water staircase, whose balustrades slide with rushing streams, which I seem to remember in the Gardens of the Generalife in Granada, added to the impression that I was wandering in the dream perhaps of a Bedouin or of someone from a parched land.

ACTIVITY 3

(a) Start by working on your own.

   (1) List the things Morton describes.

   (2) List the words he uses to suggest that he is moving, maybe walking along while describing Tivoli.

   (3) List the words that he uses to convey the sound of water. What other descriptive words can you find in the passage? What is it about these words that helps you to find them?

(b) Now work in pairs.

   (1) Identify the other locations with which Morton compares Tivoli. Why do you think he does this?

   (2) Identify the three similes in the first two paragraphs.

   (3) How does each of these similes help the reader to appreciate what Morton is trying to communicate?

   (4) In the third paragraph Morton refers to water a number of times. How does the use of contrast here help us to imagine and focus on the appearance and atmosphere of Tivoli?

   (5) Examine the final words of the extract, 'the impression that I was wandering in the dream perhaps of a Bedouin or of someone from a parched land.' How does the idea of a dream help the writer here? What does it enable him to suggest to the reader?

   (6) What do you think were Morton's purposes in writing this piece?

Challenge

A **simile** is an explicit comparison using *like* or *as*. An example is: *He snored like an old man.* Another example is: *The telegraph pole reached as high as the roof.* The comparison is between two clearly identified things.

A **metaphor** is an implicit comparison. *Candice flew around the ice rink.* Here Candice is compared to something that flies, possibly a bird. The comparison is not direct, it is suggested or hinted at.

To write effective descriptions, you need to practise being observant. Look around the room you are in. Count the number of things there are in the room, the people, the items of furniture, the bags, books and other items of equipment. Now count the light fittings, the switches on the walls, the windows and the window fittings.

Look again at the things in the room and consider their differences, for example, a large bag, a small one, one that is open and perhaps another that is sealed. You might have a smiling face and one that is sad, angry or bored. Look at the window fitting properly, is it one that the decorators simply slapped paint on without much care, or is it neatly and precisely done? The people who find things that interest them are likely to be the ones who care to look.

EXERCISE 3

Plan and write a description of an imaginary place in which you focus your reader's attention on an important, central feature. Build into this description comparisons with familiar things to help your reader visualise this feature. Aim to write about 400 words.

It may help you to start with a place or type of place that you are familiar with, that you yourself can visualise clearly, but then set it in a different time or shift it to another part of the world.

The central feature that you describe could be a human figure, a wild or domestic creature, or a man-made or a natural feature. It could also be something caused by the time of day or by the weather. Use phrases such as 'It sounds like...' or 'You remember....' to introduce comparisons.

Descriptions that convey a message

Descriptive passages can easily be used to serve other purposes, to enhance drama, for example or, as in this case of the article that follows, to help the reader understand or believe what the writer is trying to say.

In 1984 Nick Danziger, a British photo-journalist, set off to travel the Silk Road, a network of ancient trade routes which link China and the eastern Mediterranean. In order to do this he had to travel illegally, disguised as a nomadic muslim. It was the time of the Soviet occupation of Afghanistan. Here is a description of Danziger's arrival in Herat, an ancient city of that country. Notice how he uses description and close observation to get his message across.

In the picture above, there is much from which to select for closer examination. You could try to take in and describe the general scene of chaos, or you could focus on some detail that is central to the picture, or look even closer at a particular point of detail. Read this description of the scene by Danziger, published in his book *Danziger's Travels – Beyond Forbidden Frontiers.*

The western part of the city was devastated. It was far worse than any pictures I had seen of Dresden or London: it called the total wreck of Nagasaki to mind. The great city of Herat, which has stood for 2500 years and witnessed the passage of Alexander the Great, Genghis Khan and Tamerlane, is being reduced to rubble. I looked aghast at the destruction. Twisted timber beams jutted from collapsed walls like arms reaching out for help from a buried body. Embedded in walls were rockets, still unexploded, their fuses clearly visible in their tail-sections. Everywhere was the litter of modern warfare, and across it ranged the mujahedeen, scavenging for reuseable weaponry.

The bombing here had been more than intense. In some places there were craters three metres deep, which now contained pools of stagnant water. Herat had been so hard hit because the government troops and their Russian allies had decided to deprive them of any cover for attacks on army installations. But the mujahedeen lived on in the shells of the buildings, behind splintered doorways at the ends of blasted gardens. Their rooms were bare save for a few cushions on the floor, and the Kalashnikovs and ammunition pouches that hung on the walls from bits of wood driven into the mortar between the mud bricks. Many of their guns were decorated with gaily-coloured Islamic decals and invocations; others, for good luck and protection, had small chains attached to the gun-barrels, or a small triangular pouch with a Koranic script inside. These latter were also often worn around the neck or upper arm, like a garter.

ACTIVITY 4

(a) Discuss in class.
- (1) What else is described beside the devasted city? Make a note of this.
- (2) Select and list four brief details of description.
- (3) Select and list four images from the passage.

(b) Prepare your thoughts on these items, and then explain briefly to your group:
- (1) your first reaction to the destruction of Herat
- (2) compare it with any destruction that you have seen yourself
- (3) the effectiveness of one of the descriptive details and images that you have listed in **(a)**.

> **Images** are 'word pictures', pictures suggested by words. Examples are 'the total wreck of Nagasaki' or 'arms reaching out'. These are not difficult or complex words individually but used together, in this description of a city under attack, they help us to visualise more clearly something of what it must have looked like.

EXERCISE 4

(a) Look closely at the previous passage and explain in your own words the following quotations from the passage:
- (1) 'the total wreck'
- (2) 'reduced to rubble'
- (3) 'scavenging for reuseable weaponry'
- (4) 'to deprive them of any cover'
- (5) 'lived on in the shells of the buildings'.

> Try to imagine yourself in the situation of these young people living in and fighting for their city.

(b) Why do you think that Danziger described the guns in such detail in the second paragraph?

Challenge

(c) What clues does he give about his own sympathies for the two sides in this war?

(d) Write a summary of between 300 and 400 words of the main differences between Tivoli (page 102) and Herat as presented in the two passages.

> The answers are in the Exam Café CD.

(e) Plan and write a description of an act of destruction, good or bad, real or imagined – from slum clearance to vandalism. Your description could concern something about which you feel very strongly: the demolition of a play area perhaps or a memorial to someone who was popular in your area. Concentrate on closely observed detail to focus your readers' attention. Aim to write about 400 words.

Summary

From observing and selecting you have moved on to consider the way that description works and the way that the choice of words helps a writer to create a picture in the mind of the reader. When learning to write your own descriptions, you discovered that starting with something familiar can be helpful and that using comparison can build images in your readers' minds.

You are also beginning to consider the reasons why a writer wants to describe things – how he can use his powers of observation to describe details that will make an impact on the reader. For example, a description of the destruction of war can make readers think about how bad war is.

The last exercise required you to focus on the important or significant aspects of whatever it is that you want to describe.

Chapter 15

Descriptions and feelings

Getting started

Description is required for many types of writing. For example in **Chapter 14** we encountered writers who wanted to convey the history of a landscape by describing its historic features to encourage the reader to travel. Another writer described the wanton destruction of a beautiful and historic city which had horrified him.

In this chapter we will continue to look at the ways in which writers use descriptive writing to achieve their purposes. Descriptive writing can enhance a sense of drama and then our feelings of sympathy, concern and perhaps anger.

We'll also look at the importance of using our senses when we write and read and we will learn how writers are able to convey impressions and ideas by involving our senses.

Building dramatic tension

The *Lord of the Flies* by William Golding is set on a tropical island, just after the Second World War. A group of schoolboys, aged about twelve, have survived a plane crash and they are now trapped there without any adults. After a while, they realise that their only hope of rescue is to light a fire so that perhaps the sight of the smoke by day, or the flames by night, will attract a passing aircraft or ship.

In their eagerness the boys start a small fire which soon gets out of control and threatens the whole island, and them.

"You got your small fire all right."

Smoke was rising here and there among the creepers that festooned the dead or dying trees. As they watched, a flash of fire appeared at the root of one wisp and then the smoke thickened. Small flames stirred at the bole of a tree and crawled away through leaves and brushwood, dividing and increasing. One patch touched a tree trunk and scrambled up like a bright squirrel. The smoke increased, drifted, rolled outwards. The squirrel leapt on the wings of the wind and clung to another standing tree, eating downwards. Beneath the dark canopy of leaves and smoke the fire laid hold on the forest and began to gnaw. Acres of black and yellow smoke rolled steadily towards the sea. At the sight of the flames and the irresistible course of the fire, the boys broke into shrill, excited cheering. The flames, as though they were a kind of wild life, crept as a jaguar creeps on its belly towards a line of birch-like saplings that fledged an outcrop of the pink rock. They flapped at the first of the trees, and the branches grew a brief foliate of fire. The heart of flame leapt nimbly across the gap between the trees and then went swinging and flaring along the whole row of them. Beneath the capering boys a quarter of a mile square of forest was savage with smoke and flame. The separate noises of the fire merged into a drum-roll that seemed to shake the mountain.

ACTIVITY 1

(a) When you have read the passage, write one sentence in which you note how the growth of the fire is brought to our attention.

(b) In pairs or groups, discuss what you understand by these phrases from the passage:
  (1) 'creepers that festooned the dead or dying trees'
  (2) 'the bole of a tree'
  (3) 'the irresistible course of the fire'
  (4) 'swinging and flaring'
  (5) 'the capering boys'.

(c) The fire is compared to a squirrel. List the ways in which the movement of the fire is made to resemble the movements of a lively creature.

(d) What exactly are we told about the reactions of the boys to their fire?

(e) Compare the initial description of the fire with what is indicated in the last two sentences of the passage. Summarise in one or two sentences the transformation of the fire.

(f) Identify the place in the passage where you realise that the fire is out of control.

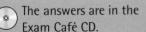 The answers are in the Exam Café CD.

EXERCISE 1

Develop ONE of the following situations in a short composition of 350 to 400 words, focussing on our feelings in the situation.

- You are alone in the dark. There is no light by which to see, and you have no torch, but you can move around. You hear a door shut. Outside there are noises made by people searching for something or someone. Describe your experiences during the next ten minutes.

- The sound of a nearby explosion has deprived you of your hearing. Two friends are rushing you to hospital. Naturally you are all extremely anxious; describe the journey.

- You are a prisoner, tied up and gagged in a hot, airless room. An armed guard dozes nearby. Describe the moment you are rescued.

- During a sports game (it could be rugby, soccer, hockey, cricket, baseball, American football or any team sport) you realise that you are seriously injured. Although there is little pain, you are told to lie very still and not to move your head at all. The medics encase you in a padded blanket and support and secure your head. Describe your experiences as you are eased onto a stretcher, loaded into an ambulance and taken to hospital.

ACTIVITY 2

(a) Discuss in groups, or as a class, reports that you have heard or seen of natural or human disasters. You will probably call to mind earthquakes, floods, bushfires, tsunamis, famine or the results of terrorism or warfare. Discuss how these disasters made you feel.

(b) Prepare to give a two minute talk to your class in which you describe how you felt when you heard about a particular disaster. Indicate what it was that particularly moved you. When you give your talk, you can refer to brief notes. Don't rush, and speak clearly.

When you are speaking formally like this you will do so far more effectively if you:

- in advance, think carefully about what you want to say
- note down, or write out fully, what you want to say
- practise what you are going to say and time yourself
- glance out, while you are speaking, at the members of your audience who are farthest away – then everyone will feel that you are speaking to them particularly and will pay closer attention
- if you need to, pause and force yourself to wait briefly to get your audience's attention, especially just before you mention something that is particularly important.

Description and opinions

About 150 years ago the failure of the potato crop in Ireland brought about starvation on a massive scale and contributed eventually to the political separation of much of Ireland from the United Kingdom. In this amended extract from *The London Illustrated News*, we can see how some journalists tried to describe to the rest of Britain the appalling situation that people in the Irish countryside were facing.

Each paragraph of this passage should be read aloud by a different member of the class.

SKETCHES IN THE WEST OF IRELAND, BY MR. JAMES MAHONY
THE ILLUSTRATED LONDON NEWS, 13 Feb 1847

"I started from Cork, saw little until we came to Clonakilty, where the coach stopped for breakfast; and here, for the first time, the horrors of the poverty became visible, in the vast number of famished poor, who flocked around the coach to beg alms: amongst them a woman carrying in her arms the corpse of a fine child, and making the most distressing appeal to the passengers for aid to enable her to purchase a coffin and bury her dear little baby.

OLD CHAPEL-LANE, SKIBBEREEN.

"In nearby Bridgetown I saw the dying, the living, and the dead, lying indiscriminately upon the same floor, without anything between them and the cold earth, save a few miserable rags upon them. Not a single house out of 500 could boast of being free from death and fever, though several could be pointed out with the dead lying close to the living for the space of three or four, even six days, without any effort being made to remove the bodies to a last resting place.

"We proceeded to High-street, or Old Chapel-lane (*See the Sketch*) and there found one house, without door or window, filled with destitute people lying on the bare floor; and one, fine, tall, stout country lad, who had entered some hours previously to find shelter from the piercing cold, lay here dead amongst others likely soon to follow him.

"We next proceeded to the Chapel-yard, to see the hut, of which Dr. Donovan gives the following graphic account in his diary:--

"*Six members of one family, named Barrett, who had been turned out of the cabin in which they lodged, had struggled to this burying-ground, and literally entombed themselves in a shelter. This shed is exactly seven feet long, by about six in breadth. By the side of the western wall is a long, newly-made grave; by either gable are two of shorter dimensions, which have been recently tenanted; and near the hole that serves as a doorway is the last resting-place of two or three children; in fact, this hut is surrounded by a rampart of human bones, which have accumulated to such a height that the threshold, which was originally on a level with the ground, is now two feet beneath it. In this horrible den, in the midst of a mass of human putrefaction, six individuals, males and females, labouring under the most malignant fever, were huddled together, as closely as were the dead in the graves around.*

"*On reaching this vault, I thrust my head through the hole of entrance, and had immediately to draw back, so intolerable was the foul stench; six fellow creatures were almost buried alive in this filthy tomb. When they heard my voice, one called out, 'Is that the Priest?' another, 'Is that the Doctor?'*

"Having returned to Skibbereen, we found that a man of the name of Leahey had died in the parish of Dromdaleague about a fortnight ago; his wife and two children remained in the house until the putrescent exhalations from the body drove them from their companionship with the dead; in a day or two after, some persons in passing the man's cabin, had their attention attracted by a loud snarling, and on entering, found the gnawed and mangled skeleton of Leahey contended for by hungry dogs."

BOY AND GIRL AT CAHERA.

A famished boy and girl turning up the ground at Cahera to seek for a potato to appease their hunger

To get yourself thinking, look at the first sentence of this passage. Ask yourself; why has the coach stopped in Clonakilty? What is the woman with the dead baby doing? Breakfast would have been familiar to the readers of this magazine; compare their situation with that of the people who are flocking around the coach.

EXERCISE 2

(a) List the five locations at which the descriptions of the passage are based. For each location, pick out the part of the description that you find most moving.

(b) Make sure that you understand the following expressions:
  (i) 'who flocked around the coach to beg alms'
  (ii) 'save a few miserable rags upon them'
  (iii) 'turned out of the cabin in which they lodged'
  (iv) 'a rampart of human bones, which have accumulated to such a height that the threshold, which was originally on a level with the ground, is now two feet beneath it'
  (v) 'putrescent exhalations from the body'
  (vi) 'contended for by hungry dogs'.

If you're unsure, discuss your uncertainties with a classmate near you.

(c) Consider what you find most moving about each of the two pictures that accompany this article. Note down these impressions in one sentence each and then write a brief description of about 100 words for each picture.

(d) Summarise in a paragraph of about 100 words the situation of the people described in this article.

Challenge

(e) Imagine that you are an aid worker who has been working in a part of the world that is going through extremely difficult times. Plan and write a report, real or imagined, in which the description of misfortune, tragedy or suffering is of paramount importance in order to motivate people to do something about the situation and prevent its recurrence. Aim to write between 400 and 500 words.

Description and the senses

Our awareness of what is happening around us is the result of our senses operating. These senses tell our brains about everything around us. Our senses are not only what we see, but what we hear, touch, smell and taste. Writers will appeal to our senses in order to communicate with us and to help us to appreciate what they are describing. The awareness that our senses can provide can be extended by our imaginations to imagine things that we have never in fact seen, heard, smelt nor tasted.

Here are some interesting facts about our senses. There is also a sixth sense, but not the intuition that some people are said to possess. This sixth sense is the kinaesthetic sense. It operates inside our bodies and tells us, for example, when we have a stomach ache or what position we are as we wake from sleep.

Language is normally communicated to us via our sense of sight or hearing. Braille, however, allows blind people a recordable language through the sense of touch. The patterns of raised dots on paper or card, used in Braille, read like the alphabet.

The sounds and smells of cooking are well-known triggers of hunger because they are associated with, or remind us of, what it is like to eat. Some appeals to our senses will arouse shared memories, such as the smell of urban traffic or the noise of someone approaching the back door of the house. Others may be more particular, the smell of a pipe that a grandfather smoked, or noises made by a smaller brother or sister. With these sensory memories we can also be reminded of the emotions that accompanied them. We remember the sight of a favourite ice cream being scraped into a cone and the excitement as we waited for it to be handed over to us.

Look at the picture above.

(a) Which of these people's senses are likely to be engaged here? What will they be hearing, tasting, smelling, seeing and touching?

(b) List the emotions that they are likely to be experiencing.

Challenge

(c) Can you explain any links between what is sensed with the senses, and what is felt emotionally?

Keeping in mind these links between our senses and our emotions, read the passage that follows which was written to accompany the picture above.

Later, as they came round a corner and mounted some steps, the girl tripped on a piece of stone that had fallen from one of the nearby buildings. It had been a tall, elegant building but now they saw how it squatted drunkenly, leaning perilously, about to tumble further out into the road. In other circumstances it would have made them laugh.

To keep herself upright she grabbed at her friend's arm and felt again the tremor of the quake which had travelled up the legs of her desk, through her body and forced her elbows to slide suddenly away from her. It was as if something inside her had recalled the tremor.

"Come on." She was standing upright now. "We can't stay here."

She let go of her arm and steadied herself on a chunk of broken masonry which felt rough and gritty against the palm of her hand.

Behind them another chunk of building slid across metal sheets then struck one of the plate glass windows. They hurried on, towards the park, the open ground, where the others should be waiting.

Round the next corner they stopped. They had stopped on this very spot so many times before, alone sometimes, sometimes with friends, and ordered a pizza, or a burger – Mr Cho's fried onions, the very very best. One of the delivery scooters was there, parked just off the pavement, with the handlebars twisted round so that they would have to wriggle to get past.

They could have shut their eyes and smelt that they were in the right place; it had been a joke that a blind student would have no difficulty finding Mr Cho's. The aroma of onions was almost a comfort with its familiarity, but the stall with its shelves, the cans of drink and the piles of buns waiting to be filled had all disappeared under a pile of rubble, a child's toy thrown to one side.

EXERCISE 3

(a) Find words in this passage which provide links to each of the five senses.

(b) What do you think is the purpose of the writer in writing this passage? Why do you think that some of the description is communicated through the memories of the people in the picture? Explain your view.

Draw comparisons between what is seen and what is remembered.

(c) Plan and write a description of the two people in the picture which was discussed in Activity 3. Use as many of the senses as you can to help your reader imagine what it must be like to be in their situation. You could make use of drama or dialogue to enhance your description. Aim to write 400 words.

Summary

In this chapter we looked at how describing feelings can help us to build dramatic tension when we write. It can also help us transmit our own feelings and opinions on an issue to our readers. To do this successfully, we should appeal to their senses. This will help them better imagine what we are trying to convey.

Describing feelings is at the heart of what we need to do when writing, whether we are describing a scene, telling a story, reporting a tragedy or trying to persuade people to take action.

Normally when we write, we rely on other people's understanding of abstract words or expressions we use. When we engage our reader's feelings we can address them more directly because our senses and emotions are shared more closely than our understanding of abstract words and concepts.

Chapter 16

Using the familiar and the unfamiliar

Getting started

Choosing a word, from a vocabulary of over 200 000, gives us many opportunities to find the right one, but also the potential to use the wrong word. Taking care with the words we use is important in descriptions, whether we are describing the appearance of something, the way it moves or functions or the way other people react to it.

First practise your descriptive writing by describing familiar things. Introducing things that your reader will recognise is a good way to get them interested. When you move onto things that are less familiar, you can actually harness your own feelings of fear, delight or surprise to create powerful descriptions.

Recognition and description

What is it that enables us to recognise something or someone familiar? Sometimes it needs only a glance, or the sound of their footfall, for us to be confident that we know who or what it is.

When you describe something, you may want to set out the colour, size and shape of it or of some of its features. Other things will be best described in other ways, for example, living creatures have particular ways of moving or might make distinctive sounds. Some people are recognisable by the sound of their voices, or the sort of things that they frequently say. Some people and creatures have habits that we can describe and are easily recognised. Some things are more easily recognised when we compare them to other things. We can point out what it is that makes them similar and what makes them different.

The description of some things can be enhanced by including a reference to the reactions of other observers or listeners to that thing. For example, a reference to a crowd's reaction to a popular band or poisonous snake can tell us more about the band or creature than the actual description of it. When a crowd gets to its feet, screams and gasps, or when a crowd follows, or flees from, something then that something is brought more closely to our attention. Use this technique to help you to describe things.

◀ Use other people's reactions to something to help describe that something.

ACTIVITY 1

(a) You are going to write a description of each item on this list to read to the class. For each item write a maximum of 20 words describing it, but without actually mentioning what it is.

(1) pet

(2) wild creature

(3) piece of machinery or equipment

(4) member of your family

(5) place where you like to meet with your friends

(6) local shop or supermarket

(7) friend's car or motorbike

(8) well-known politician, sportsman or woman, or entertainer

(9) material that you like to work with

(10) someone in school

(11) someone in your class

(12) someone in uniform

(b) Take it in turns to read one of your descriptions to a group or the class. Allow two to three minutes of discussion before the others decide what it is that you have described. If the thing or person is identified successfully, ask what the key words were that described the item most clearly. If the others are unable to identify the person or thing, reveal its identity and try to discover what your description is lacking. Work in pairs to improve the descriptions in light of the others' observations.

Choose two subjects from the list in Activity 1. Combine them in a more sustained piece of descriptive writing of about 200 words.

Using drama to enhance description

Just as we have seen description being used to enhance a dramatic passage, as in the extract from *Great Expectations* at the start of Chapter 8, so we can also find drama being used to enhance a descriptive passage. The dramatic events might be action related to the thing being described or it might be others' reactions to the thing.

The passage below is from *The Jungle Book* by Rudyard Kipling. Mowgli is a lost Indian boy, adopted by wolves. Now he has been kidnapped by a band of monkeys. Two of his friends, Baloo, a bear, and Bagheera, a panther, want Kaa the python to help rescue him from their clutches.

They found him stretched out on a warm ledge in the afternoon sun, admiring his beautiful new coat, for he had been in retirement for the last ten days, changing his skin, and now he was very splendid – darting his big blunt-nosed head along the ground, and twisting the thirty feet of his body into fantastic knots and curves, and licking his lips as he thought of his dinner to come.

"He has not eaten," said Baloo, with a grunt of relief, as soon as he saw the beautifully mottled brown-and-yellow jacket. "Be careful, Bagheera! He is always a little blind after he has changed his skin, and very quick to strike."

Kaa was not a poison-snake – in fact he rather despised the poison-snakes as cowards – but his strength lay in his hug, and when he had once lapped his huge coils round anybody there was no more to be said…

Now a snake, especially a wary old python like Kaa, very seldom shows that he is angry, but Baloo and Bagheera could see the big swallowing-muscles on either side of Kaa's throat ripple and bulge…

Generations of monkeys had been scared into good behaviour by the stories their elders told them of Kaa, the night thief, who could slip along the branches as quietly as moss grows, and steal away the strongest monkey that ever lived; of old Kaa, who could make himself look so like a dead branch or a rotten stump that the wisest were deceived, till the branch caught them. Kaa was everything that the monkeys feared in the jungle, for none of them knew the limits of his power, none of them could look him in the face, and none had ever come alive out of his hug.

The poem 'Snake' was written by D H Lawrence who is particularly remembered for his collection of poems entitled *Birds, Beasts and Flowers*. He explored the relationship between humankind and the natural world and used drama to reveal something of this relationship.

A snake came to my water-trough
On a hot, hot day and I in pyjamas for the heat,
To drink there.
In the deep, strange-scented shade of the great
dark carob tree
I came down the steps with my pitcher
And must wait, must stand and wait, for there
he was at the trough before me.

He reached down from a fissure in the earth-
wall in the gloom
And trailed his yellow-brown slackness soft-
bellied down, over the edge of the stone trough
And rested his throat upon the stone bottom,
And where the water had dripped from the tap,
in a small clearness,
He sipped with his straight mouth,
Softly drank through his straight gums, into his
slack long body,
Silently.

Someone was before me at my water-trough,
And I, like a second comer, waiting.

He lifted his head from his drinking, as cattle
do,
And looked at me vaguely, as drinking cattle do,
And flickered his two-forked tongue from his
lips, and mused a moment,
And stooped and drank a little more,
Being earth-brown, earth-golden from the
burning bowels of the earth
On the day of Sicilian July, with Etna smoking.

The voice of my education said to me
He must be killed,
For in Sicily the black, black snakes are
innocent, the gold are venomous.

And voices in me said, If you were a man
You would take a stick and break him now, and
finish him off.

But I must confess how I liked him,
How glad I was he had come like a guest in
quiet, to drink at my water-trough
And depart peaceful, pacified, and thankless,
Into the burning bowels of this earth?

Was it cowardice, that I dared not kill him?
Was it perversity, that I longed to talk to him?
Was it humility, to feel so honoured?
I felt so honoured.

And yet those voices:
If you were not afraid, you would kill him!

And truly I was afraid, I was most afraid,
But even so, honoured still more
That he should seek my hospitality
From out the dark door of the secret earth.

He drank enough
And lifted his head, dreamily, as one who has
drunken,

And flickered his tongue like a forked night on
the air, so black,
Seeming to lick his lips,
And looked around like a god, unseeing, into
the air,
And slowly turned his head,
And slowly, very slowly, as if thrice adream,
Proceeded to draw his slow length curving
round
And climb again the broken bank of my wall-
face.

Each of these passages is essentially a description of a snake in which the drama of the setting enhances the description. In the extract from *The Jungle Book*, Kaa is a useful ally in the rescue of Mowgli and the description of him strengthens the tension of the rescue attempt. In the poem, Lawrence is surprised and disturbed by his encounter with a snake and by his own reaction to it.

The answers are in the
Exam Café CD.

Ask yourself about the different views taken of snakes by each author.

ACTIVITY 2

(a) Briefly look at the passages on your own.

(1) For each passage, write a one-sentence summary of what is being communicated, that is, the events that are taking place (apart from the descriptions of the snakes).

(2) For each passage, sum up the impression and description given of each snake.

(b) Work in groups or as a class.

(1) Look at the similes and metaphors used to describe the snakes. How do they add to the impression given of each snake?

(2) What are the reactions of Baloo and Bagheera to Kaa the python?

(3) Examine Lawrence's reaction to the snake he encounters. Does he regard it as friend or foe?

EXERCISE 2

(a) Choose ONE of these assignments, then plan and write an essay of between 300 and 400 words.

- You have just escaped from somewhere (it could be school, care, prison, kidnappers, a court, your parents or a gang). You arrive at a friend's house, unexpected. How does he or she react? Describe your friend's reaction to your arrival and to whatever happens next. You may wish to use dialogue as well as a description of the physical details of your friend's appearance and actions.

- Two people have arranged to meet. As one approaches, the other person is able to watch unobserved. It becomes obvious to the observer that the first person, who is just arriving, is in some sort of danger. However, the observer cannot intervene as he or she is too far away. All he or she can do is call out, perhaps, and watch. Describe what happens. Include the observer's reaction to events as well as a strong description of the location, the second person and the threat.

Sometimes when we watch something bad happen and are powerless to do anything to stop it, it is like we see the whole event in slow motion with every detail vivid in our minds.

Challenge

(b) You have been called as a witness to a court of inquiry which is investigating an incident. You will need to imagine the event and the scene afterwards, then convey carefully and accurately a description that will inform rather than entertain your audience. Describe both the event and the scene. It could be one of the following incidents:

- a road accident
- the collapse of a building
- the escape of a dangerous animal
- over-crowding in local public transport.

Approaching the unfamiliar

In the pictures on the next page we can see some familiar objects, a tool shed, a wooden beehive, a pair of hands, a kitchen knife and a jar of honey. We also see large numbers of bees which, for many of us, are very unfamiliar. The thought of the close presence of bees is likely, initially at least, to make us feel frightened, anxious or disturbed. We'd probably expect them to react to us in the same way too, which doesn't help matters.

If you are trying to describe something familiar, you might want to think about how you felt and what interested you the first time you saw that thing. Think also about how you could describe things and events that are unfamiliar to you. Where do you start? It can be a good idea to 'harness' some of your strong feelings about new things, whether positive or negative, into your descriptions of those things. When we see something for the first time, it can be a very good idea to immediately jot down our feelings and reactions to what we see – what we notice and what stands out to us, and how that makes us feel. These feelings can heighten our sense of awareness which in turn increases our ability to describe something vividly.

ACTIVITY 3

Come and join us!

Study this picture of older people.

Your parents tell you that you are going to move in and share a home with these people. You would be the only person under sixty in the house.

In pairs, discuss and answer the following matters:

(1) Your reaction

(2) Whether you would try to escape

(3) Your feelings and experiences of older people

(4) Anything good you could anticipate in this move

(5) What you think you might be like in fifty years' time.

Report back to the class.

Branches cut away, a swarm awaits a beekeeper.

Bees and their sheets of wax comb in a garden shed which they have invaded.

A beekeeper inspecting a colony.

Releasing honey from the comb.

A hive, home to 50 000 bees.

Hive bees caring for larvae in the cells (some sealed and some open).

(a) For each picture write two sentences. In the first, state what it is about the picture that attracts your attention. In the second sentence, describe in some detail the most important thing that you can see.

The final product, something we all know.

(b) Explain in a brief paragraph what you think your reaction would be to encountering bees like these in real life.

(c) What impressions of bees and honey production do these pictures convey? What questions would you want to put to a beekeeper if you met one?

(d) Make a note of any sudden meetings with other unfamiliar things that you or your friends have experienced. Arrange a list of them with the most frightening at the top.

(e) In groups or as a class, discuss your answers to **(a)**, **(b)** and **(c)**.

EXERCISE 3

Try to remember (or imagine) how it felt when you first spent time with strangers, or discovered your hobby and what you loved about it, or experienced a tremendous shock. In your description, try to convey those feelings to your readers.

Plan and write a description of ONE of the following situations. Aim to write about 300 words.

- You are going to spend two days with a few complete strangers in a remote forest for a reality television programme. Write the script of a trailer for the programme revealing the start of the adventure, the place you'll be and the people who will join you. Then hint, briefly, at what is expected to be a big source of tension.

- Describe a hobby, sport or leisure activity that you enjoy (or would like to do) to people who have not taken part in that before.

- Describe a character you know who is about to open a garden shed like the one in the second picture in Activity 4. Choose a different surprise for them if you prefer to. Shape the description of the events so that it reveals something of this character. Don't forget to include in your description the opening of the door.

:::: EXERCISE 4

In this exercise you are going to write a passage using your reactions, and the reactions of some of your classmates, to a picture.

(a) Find a picture that interests you. If it is a really big picture, poster or graffiti on a wall that interests you, then try to photograph it and print it onto a sheet of paper.

(b) Write a clear but short statement in which you set out what it is about the picture that particularly interests you, then write a detailed description of the picture of between 100 and 200 words.

(c) Read your description aloud, if possible. Decide whether re-ordering the sentences in your description will make your passage better. Think of ways to vary the words and impressions you give. Rewrite it, if this will help.

(d) Show the picture, but not your writing, to two or three of your classmates and ask them what they think of the picture. Make a note of their reactions. Write descriptions (of about 50 words each) of each person's reaction to the picture.

(e) Connect the passages (in any way that you like) to make a complete article of about 400 words that reads well. Check your work and rewrite it, if necessary.

Remember you can describe the way things appear, sound, smell, taste or feel. You can also describe the way they move or behave. You can also describe your reactions – do you like to move away, get closer or simply to watch?

Other observers' reactions to the things you describe will help you. For example, how might your friends react if you told them that you had decided to become a ballet dancer, a Morris dancer, a nun or a Buddhist monk?

Summary

By looking carefully at things that seize our attention, we can learn to write good descriptions. By understanding why these things cannot be ignored, we can learn how to describe them in ways that hold a readers' attention and help them to appreciate the things that we appreciate.

Remember, clear and effective descriptions can help us communicate whatever it is that we are trying to convey – a story, a picture or an impression of something, an argument or a new idea.

Chapter 17

How description works

Getting started

We need to engage our imagination when we want to describe or explain something. We also need to engage our imagination in communicating with an audience; we must consider how much they know about what we are explaining and describing.

Sometimes descriptions need to be quite long in order to paint a full picture for our readers and at other times we just need a single word to draw a mental image. Words often have more power to take the reader through a landscape than even a map or a photograph does.

Explanations and demonstrations

Does this simple circuit diagram help you to imagine what this piece of equipment would look like in real life? Does it help you to understand how it functions?

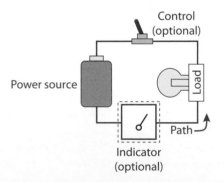

It's said that a picture is worth a thousand words, but sometimes things are actually better explained or demonstrated when described in words. A good example of this is in the extract that follows from *Down the Mine* by the author George Orwell.

George Orwell is well-known as the author of *Animal Farm*, a so-called fairy tale, in which he demonstrates the shortcomings and hypocrisy of communism, and of *1984*, a novel in which he shows how a futuristic, totalitarian state could misuse and pervert language in order to hold on to power. As a journalist he was always ready to champion people who were less fortunate and he concerned himself with presenting plain truths as plain truths. He always made a great effort to describe unfamiliar things in plain words so that as many people as possible could understand what he wanted to say. Simple words, carefully chosen and arranged, along with personal modesty, were the tools of his trade.

This extract from *Down the Mine* is a piece of journalism which makes clear his ability to encourage understanding by means of good description. It is in his typically self-effacing style.

When you have been down in two or three pits you begin to get some grasp of the processes that are going on underground. (I ought to say, by the way, that I know nothing whatever about the technical side of mining: I am merely describing what I have seen.) Coal lies in thin seams between enormous layers of rock, so that essentially the process of getting it out is like scooping the central layer from a Neapolitan ice-cream. In the old days the miners used to cut straight into the coal with pick and crowbar – a very slow job because coal, when lying in its virgin state, is almost as hard as rock. Nowadays the preliminary work is done by an electrically-driven coal-cutter, which in principle is an immensely tough and powerful band saw, running horizontally instead of vertically, with teeth a couple of inches long and half an inch or an inch thick. It can move backwards or forwards on its own power, and the men operating it can rotate it this way or that. Incidentally it makes one of the most awful noises I have ever heard, and sends forth clouds of dust which make it impossible to see more than two to three feet and almost impossible to breathe. The machine travels along the coal face cutting into the base of the coal to the depth to which it has been undermined. Where it is "difficult getting", however, it has also to be loosened with explosives. A man with an electric drill, rather like a small version of the drills used in street-mending, bores holes at intervals into the coal, inserts blasting powder, plugs it with clay, goes round the corner if there is one handy (he is supposed to retire to twenty-five yards/metres distance) and touches off the charge with an electric current. This is not intended to bring the coal out, only to loosen it. Occasionally, of course, the charge is too powerful, and then it not only brings the coal out but brings down the roof as well.

After the blasting has been done the "fillers" can tumble the coal out, break it up and shovel it on to the conveyor belt. It comes out first in monstrous boulders which may weigh anything up to twenty tons. The conveyor belt shoots it on to tubs, and the tubs are shoved into the main road and hitched on to an endlessly revolving steel cable which drags them to the cage. Then they are hoisted, and at the surface the coal is sorted by being run over screens, and if necessary is washed as well. As far as possible the "dirt" – shale, that is – is used for making the roads below. All that cannot be used is sent to the surface and dumped; hence the monstrous "dirt-heaps", like hideous grey mountains, which are the characteristic scenery of the coal areas. When the coal has been extracted to the depth to which the machine has cut, the coal face has advanced by five feet. Fresh props are put in to hold up the newly exposed roof, and during the next shift the conveyor belt is taken to pieces, moved five feet forward and reassembled. As far as possible the three operations of cutting, blasting and extraction are done in three separate shifts, the cutting in the afternoon, the blasting at night (there is a law, not always kept, that forbids its being done when other men are working nearby), and the "filling" in the morning shift, which lasts from six in the morning until half past one.

Even when you watch the process of coal-extraction you probably only watch it for a short time, and it is not until you begin making a few calculations that you realise what a stupendous task the "fillers" are performing. Normally each man has to clear a space four or five yards wide. The cutter has undermined the coal to a depth of five feet, so that if the seam of coal is three or four feet high, each man has to cut out, break up and load on to the belt something between seven and twelve cubic yards of coal. This is to say, taking a cubic yard as weighing twenty-seven hundredweight, that each man is shifting coal at a speed approaching two tons an hour. I have just enough experience of pick and shovel to be able to grasp what this means. When I am digging trenches in my garden, if I shift two tons of earth during the afternoon, I feel that I have earned my tea. But earth is tractable stuff compared with coal, and I don't have to work kneeling down, a thousand feet underground, in suffocating heat and swallowing coal dust with every breath I take; nor do I have to walk a mile bent double before I begin. The miner's job would be as much beyond me as it would be to perform on a flying trapeze or win the Grand National. I am not a manual labourer and please God I shall never be one, but there are some kinds of manual work that I could do if I had to. At a pitch I could be a tolerable road-sweeper or an inefficient gardener or even a tenth-rate farm hand. But by no conceivable amount of effort or training could I become a coal-miner; the work would kill me in a few weeks.

George Orwell wanted people to know how hard coal-miners had to work. ▶

There are a number of elements in this extract which make it a particularly effective piece of descriptive writing:

- George Orwell's modesty – he claims not to have technical knowledge of his subject and has a knack of presenting himself as someone to whom what he is telling the reader about is relatively new and unfamiliar
- his ability to make helpful comparisons, for example, the miner's drill compared to the drill we see at road works
- the ordering of his material so that we can follow the process from start to finish
- his admiration for the men who do this difficult and dangerous work and his modest assertion that he would not be up to the job.

When we are faced with unfamiliar things, we are much more alert and much more receptive to impressions. Orwell makes expert use of this fact.

The activity and exercise which follow will help you to appreciate better how Orwell achieves his purpose.

ACTIVITY 1

Discuss the following in pairs or small groups.

(a) What is the overall purpose of this passage?

(b) What three aspects of mining are described in the first two paragraphs?

(c) Two items of machinery are referred to in the first paragraph. What are they? With what more familiar items does Orwell compare them?

(d) What simile is used to describe the process of mining?

(e) List the verbs in the second paragraph which reveal the next stages in getting the coal out of the mine.

(f) What change occurs in the third paragraph? Which stage of the mining process is described here?

(g) What else does Orwell draw to our attention in the third paragraph? How does he set about this?

EXERCISE 1

Use the three of stages of mining – cutting, blasting and loading – discussed in Activity 1 (b) above for these written assignments.

(1) Describe these three stages in a paragraph of your own, using alternatives for verbs *cutting*, *blasting* and *loading*.

(2) You have been asked to prepare a series of pictures or diagrams to explain mining. Make a list of the pictures or diagrams that would be required. For each one, write one or two sentences of instructions for the artist.

(3) Describe an hour's activity in a place, such as a school classroom, that you know well. Write the description in such a way that a reader on another planet could understand the purpose of what is going on. Aim to write 400 words.

Description for effect

The first example of Orwell's writing, *Down the Mine*, was taken from a piece of non-fiction. The adapted extract which follows is from his novel *1984*. The extract below has been adapted and shortened for use in this student book in order to focus on descriptive sections that contribute to the drama. In the book, one of the tactics of the government is to weaken family ties as these strengthen individuals who might then oppose the state. Winston is the prisoner of O'Brien. O'Brien is using torture to try to make Winston betray a family member.

> A guard came in, carrying something made of wire, a box or basket of some kind. He set it down on the further table...
>
> It was an oblong wire cage with a handle on top for carrying it. Fixed to the front of it was something that looked like a fencing mask, with the concave side outwards... (Winston) could see that the cage was divided lengthways into two compartments and that there was some kind of creature in each. They were rats.
>
> O'Brien picked up the cage and brought it across to the nearer table...
>
> There was an outburst of squeals from the cage... The rats were fighting; they were trying to get at each other through the partition...
>
> O'Brien said, "You understand the construction of this cage. The mask will fit over your head, leaving no exit. When I press this lever, the door of the cage will slide up. These starving brutes will shoot out of it like bullets. Have you ever seen a rat leap through the air?"

What makes Orwell's description so powerful here is that he is using such a different approach to the item that he is describing.

Think of the context or setting – Winston was a prisoner.

Think of the physical qualities of the object – the cage was divided lengthways.

Consider the reaction of people to the object – O'Brien speaks of the trap in a very matter-of-fact way.

Then there is the uncertainty about the item, which keeps you guessing till the end – at first the cage is 'something made of wire', then 'an oblong wire cage' and finally Winston is told that, 'The mask will fit over your head, leaving no exit.'

Concave is the shape of the inside of a sphere, the shape that you see when you look inside a globe or a ball. **Convex** is the shape of the outside of a ball or globe.

ACTIVITY 2

(a) Work alone to answer these questions in brief note form.

(1) What two familiar types of object does Orwell combine in this passage?

(2) Identify the one simile used by Orwell. What does it enable him to explain?

(3) Do you think a thing such as this really exists? Explain your answer.

(4) What are the steps that Orwell takes to describe it?

(5) Why is this way of describing it so important here?

(b) Now compare your answers in class.

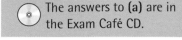 The answers to (a) are in the Exam Café CD.

What should come up in your discussion is whether or not O'Brien intends to carry out his threat and what is it that Winston believes is about to happen to him?

EXERCISE 2

Choose two items from the following list. For one of the items you have chosen, write a description in which it is presented as something to be ridiculed or laughed at. In the second description, present the item as something sinister or mysterious.

hairdryer	box of tools
mobile phone	small animal
address book	book
packet of sweets	remote control
plastic box	handbag
electric kettle	purse
reel of sticky tape	pocket calculator
bunch of keys	pencil
doll	roll of kitchen foil
toy car	tin opener

In these descriptions remember to consider using the different approaches used by Orwell in *1984*.

Descriptive nouns and other powerful words

Sometimes single words alone allow us to convey a great deal and we can use them in ways that are very powerful. For example, the names of animals are sometimes used in this way as insults, 'dog' and 'bitch', for example. Another example is 'excruciating' which is used to describe intense pain and, by extension, other intense feelings such as 'excruciating embarrassment'. The word means 'from the cross' and originates in the Latin *crux* (cross and crucifixion), the most painful means of execution that the Romans could devise. In English we use a Greek word *hippopotamus* to name a large African mammal that is found in or near water. In Greek the word literally means 'water horse'. In Afrikaans the word for hippopotamus is *zeekoei* which literally means 'sea cow'. In German the word for bat is *fledermaus,* a mouse that flutters.

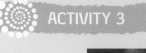

Work in pairs or small groups to respond to these questions with short written answers.

(a) How else might you describe a hippopotamus?

(b) Describe a camel to people who live near the Arctic Circle and have never seen one.

(c) Describe a polar bear to people who live near the Equator and have never seen any bear.

(d) Invent descriptive names for ten other creatures.

The following text is from the back cover of the book *And The Sirens Still Wail* by Nancy Burke.

It wasn't the volcano's increasingly violent fiery explosions that drove Nancy and Richard out of their beloved Montserrat. It wasn't the swift, incinerating pyroclastic flows, rapidly moving gas and lava that killed every living thing in their path. It wasn't even the hot rocks hurtling onto the roof of their house. It was the ash. It was the thick blanket of ash that covered everything inches deep, it was the film that grimed every surface, it was the powder that crept through every crack, squeezed into each sealed plastic bag, burrowed down to the skin of each bedraggled furry creature.

EXERCISE 3

Working on your own, respond to the following:

(a) List the unpleasant aspects of life on Montserrat that did not drive Nancy and Richard from the island.

(b) Explain how each of the first three sentences help build up to the revelation of just what it was that drove them away.

(c) With what is the ash compared when the author uses these words: 'covered', 'grimed', 'crept', 'squeezed' and 'burrowed'?

(d) List the things beside ash that are described. For each thing write one sentence explaining the descriptions.

(e) List the individual words that add to the power of the descriptions, words like the adjective 'beloved'. For each word that you list indicate what the word suggests about Montserrat and its volcano.

Challenge

(f) Explain the difference between the powerful descriptive words in the first half of the paragraph and those used in the second.

Concepts, pictures and words

Watership Down is the title of a classic piece of literature, first published in 1972 at a time when concern for the environment was growing. The novel is well-known as a story about rabbits, even to people who have not actually read it. It concerns a colony of rabbits and their struggles when confronted by human beings and other enemies. Watership Down is also the name of a real place in England. An Ordinance Survey map showing it follows, as well as a photograph of the location.

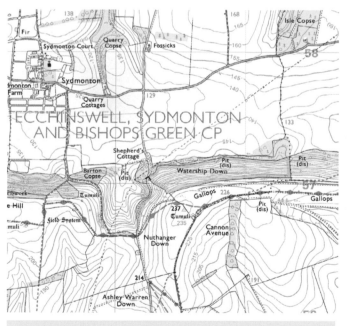

▲ A conceptual view of Watership Down on a map.

▲ A photographer's art – a view of Watership Down.

The extract that follows from *Watership Down* by Richard Adams also provides a description of the place – but simply, in words, and in rather a different way from the picture and map above.

It was the evening of the following day. The north-facing escarpment of Watership Down, in shadow since early morning, now caught the western sun for an hour before twilight. Three hundred feet the down rose vertically in a stretch of no more than six hundred – a precipitous wall, from the thin belt of trees at the foot to the ridge where the steep flattened out. The light, full and smooth, lay like a bold rind over the turf, the furze and yew bushes, the few wind-stunted thorn trees. From the ridge, the light seemed to cover all the slope below, frowsy and still. But down in the grass itself, between the bushes, in that thick forest trodden by the beetle, the spider and the hunting shrew, the moving light was like a wind that danced among them to set them scurrying and weaving. The red rays flickered in and out of the grass stems, flashing minutely on membranous wings, casting long shadows behind the flimsiest of filamentary legs, breaking each patch of bare soil into a myriad of individual grains. The insects buzzed, whined, hummed, stridulated (made shrill, rasping sounds) and droned as the air grew warmer in the sunset. Louder yet calmer than they among the trees, sounded the yellow-hammer, the linnet and greenfinch. The larks went up, twittering in the scented air above the down. From the summit, the apparent immobility of the vast, blue distance was broken, here and there, by wisps of smoke and tiny, momentary flashes of glass. Far below lay the fields green with wheat, the flat pastures grazed by horses, the darker greens of the woods. They too, like the hillside jungle, were tumultuous with evening, but from the remote height turned to stillness, their fierceness tempered by the air that lay between.

When we look at the map or the picture we are confronted with everything that the draftsman, the photographer or artist has to give us. Then we begin the business of understanding and appreciating it. Perhaps we step back to try to take it all in, or step forwards to search closely for some particular detail that might interest us. We can choose what we will look at first.

A passage of descriptive writing is different; a writer controls our attention in the way that an artist or photographer cannot for we have to follow the order of the words and absorb things in the order and manner in which they are presented by the writer.

Adams engages two of our senses – sight and sound – to describe the landscape. At the end of the passage there is a return to the starting point which gives the impression that we have looked around from a vantage point and taken in all that Adams wants us to take in. It is a rounded passage in which there is a sense of a journey, a tour around a landscape, and a sense of achievement, that we have absorbed the appearance and feel of the place. Adams has set the stage for the next scene in his story.

ACTIVITY 4

Work in groups or as a class.

(a) Can you find Watership Down on the map?

(b) Can you locate the place from which the picture of Watership Down was taken, either on the map or at a place in the text?

(c) Does Adams begin his description of the down close up or from afar?

(d) Can you find on the map the place where 'the down rose vertically'?

(e) Can you find 'the few wind-stunted thorn trees' in the picture?

(f) Which of our senses does Adams engage initially?

(g) To what quality of the view does he draw our attention in the first half of the passage?

(h) Which word signals a change of sense? What kind of word is it?

(i) Which words signal a shift in the writer's focus?

(j) What are the words and expressions used in the last three sentences that shift the focus of the passage once again? Which of our senses is engaged here?

(k) Draw a picture or diagram, or a series of them, to show your journey through Adams' description of Watership Down indicating the shifts in focus, the objects to which our attention is directed and the particular senses which are engaged.

EXERCISE 4

(a) Describe any landscape. Choose rural, suburban or city, or choose a seascape or cloudscape. The landscape could be real or imaginary. Try to engage more than one sense and to vary your focus as you describe the scene. Write between 300 and 400 words.

(b) From any of the preceding passages in this chapter, select four similes or metaphors and explain what you appreciate about the effect of each one. Make clear whether you find the comparison in each case to be effective.

Summary

You have examined descriptions of an industrial process, an instrument of torture, some animals, an active volcano on a small island and a rural landscape. You have looked at the way that these descriptions have been written and the purposes for which they were written.

You have also considered ways of describing things, other than in words, using conceptual images like a map and photographs. Interestingly, we found that sometimes a writer has more power to draw a picture for his readers and guide them through a landscape than a cartographer, photographer or artist might. You have been able to bring these new understandings to your own writing.

Chapter 18

Advertising and description

Getting started

In this chapter you will see that the business of description becomes rather more complicated when used in advertising. You will be involved in analysing the language used in advertising and then trying to understand and use it for yourselves.

Finally, you will be invited to write about things that you don't believe in, in order to sell a product!

What is advertising?

Advertising is the means by which companies and commercial interests attempt to persuade us to buy things that we might not purchase unless they were at least brought to our attention. Description is an important part of informing us about products and services that advertisers wish to provide. Think of health and beauty products which many of us would not even know about if we did not see them advertised. Advertisers hope that, once we've seen these things, we will suddenly feel that we need them. What we do need to remember is that there is a particular purpose behind the descriptions in advertising. We are going to see how advertisers use descriptions to help persuade us that we want things.

Look at these words which could well have been found in an advertisement for furniture.

> Such is the quality incorporated into Produits Georges Haricots that no enquiry will reveal its totality. You may ask about the touch of our craftsmen and women. You may seek to learn how we match inherent skill and innate prowess. How, you may ask, do we blend the softness of our touch with the durability of our products? Do not trouble yourself with such questions; trust time to tell the truth in all things.

You can imagine words such as these incorporated into advertisements for all sorts of products: perfume, shoes, clothing, furniture and crockery. It is familiar enough, but just what is being said?

ACTIVITY 1

(a) Collect and bring to the class magazines from which you can select advertisements for discussion. Look at the words that accompany the visual material and consider whether they convey information, suggestions or opinions.

(b) Discuss the language used in the advertisement on the previous page. Consider in particular what is suggested by words such as 'incorporated', 'inherent' or 'blend'.

> Start with the verbs in each sentence, not just the main verbs, but any verbs, words that suggest action.

(c) Now work in pairs to produce similar statements of a maximum of 40 words each to introduce:

(1) sausages

(2) medicine to counter indigestion

(3) a set of coloured pencils

(4) an apple

(5) a set of garden tools

(6) disposable nappies

(7) the latest mobile phone.

(d) Share and discuss your advertisements with the rest of the class.

Advertising and suggestion

Some advertising is more subtle and we have to look harder to distinguish between what we are told and what is suggested.

Date Listed	05/09/2010
Price	**$489,000.00**
Address	4 Ocean View, Bunbury, Australia
	View map
For Sale By	Owner
Bedrooms (#)	4 bedrooms
Dwelling Type	House
Size (sqm)	890
Bathrooms (#)	2 bathrooms
Parking	Double garage

Located in a quiet area, 3 min walk shops & 2 primary schools, 6 min drive high schools, train, major shopping centre, pool, gym & leisure centre, 1 min walk bus. Only 3 min to M2 & a few more mins to M4 & M7. Substantial kitchen with a walk-in pantry, well-lit atrium, traditional dining area. All four bedrooms have built-in cupboards with ensuite to main. Double garage. Beautiful outdoor entertainment area, with attractive rockeries & built-in natural gas bbq, area covered by shade sails. Simply requires you to move in.

The first part of the advertisement deals with factual matters, such as the price asked or the number of bedrooms. In the second part a number of items are mentioned and many of them are described in a particular way; why do you think we are told that the atrium is well-lit and that the outdoor entertaining area is beautiful?

Attributes are the characteristics or qualities of something. Physical fitness is an attribute of a professional sportsman or woman. Slipperiness is an attribute of ice.

The answer to (a) (1) is in the Exam Café CD.

EXERCISE 1

(a) Read the advertisement for the house for sale.
  (1) This advertisement of a house for sale draws our attention to a number of attributes. List the attributes **then** list the ways in which the advertisement is used to suggest the desirability of the property.

  (2) Write a description of a brick, or a plank of wood, or a similar item in which you use a similar technique to persuade your reader to make a purchase.

  (3) Comment on the information about the schools. What does this suggest about the people in this area?

Challenge

(b) Choose ONE of the following assignments. Plan and write between 200 and 300 words.

  • Write the beginning or ending of a short story, set in the house described in the advertisement.

  • Write an imaginary diary for a week in the life of someone who lives in this house.

(c) A friend has been in touch with you, offering to buy this house for you. Write a letter thanking the friend and explaining that it's not the sort of place where you would like to live. Describe the sort of place that you would prefer.

Challenge

Words with bounce

Have you ever thought about the music that is played in some shops? What sort of music would you expect to hear in a formal menswear shop, a dress shop or a sports shop?

Notice the short bursts of words in the next item and compare the flow of words here with the first advertisement considered in this chapter. Can you imagine particular types of music for each situation?

Look at this item for sale on a South African website.

Treat the kids this summer. Let them dance the night away on Wheelie Heelies – they'll brighten the floor with their dancing and skating all night. It takes only seconds to fit Wheelie Heelies onto your feet. No external power is required and they come in a range of sizes. Walk or run effortlessly on you Wheelie Heelies. Authentic, exciting and electric. Suggested maximum weight 75 kg. Comes with carrybag and tools. **Price: R149.00**

ACTIVITY 2

Work in pairs.

(a) Devise a name for this piece of equipment. Remember *zeekoei* (hippopotamus) and *fledermaus* (bat) from the previous chapter?

(b) Decide whether these Wheelie Heelies are something that would interest you. Explain why.

(c) Examine the use of words in this advertisement. How are the words organised? What do you think is meant by the word 'Authentic'? Does it tell us something or suggest something? Explain. What about the rest of the words?

(d) Compare the information provided in the three advertisements presented so far – the advertisements for furniture, the Australian house and the Wheelie Heelies. For each advertisement, set out in one sentence what you think the advertiser regards as the main attribute of the item for sale.

EXERCISE 2

(a) Write a paragraph describing someone's first attempt to use the Wheelie Heelies advertised on the South African website.

(b) Write a paragraph describing the performance of someone who has used them for a long time.

(c) Write a paragraph describing their appearance, construction and function, based on the information in the advertisement.

Other tactics advertisers use

Advertisers use many kinds of tactics, including appealing to people's vanity, their 'peace of mind' and their concerns about safety and security .

The Australian house would require no work on your part and the South African wheels would be great fun. In the advertisement below, there are two other tactics employed to encourage you to buy shampoo. Look at the words used by this advertiser.

Introducing A Safe, All Natural Way To Instantly Make Your Hair Soft, Shiny And Easier To Detangle, And With Just One Use Of This Powerful All Natural Herbal Shampoo You Will:

Get Silkier Shinier Hair, Put A Dead Stop To Frizzy And Unmanageable Hair, Moisturize Your Scalp With All Natural Nutrients And Essential Oils, Strengthen Your Hair From The Inside Out With All Powerful Rare Herbal Extracts, Banish Split Ends, Bullet Proof Your Scalp And Hair Against Heat And Humidity And Other Environmental Factors And Do It All Naturally And Absolutely Free From All The Harsh Chemicals Usually Found In Store And Salon Bought Conditioning Products.

This powerful all natural hair shampoo contains powerful herbal extracts and is especially good for the hair. They work both from the inside and the outside to keep your hair healthy and lustrous. Restore natural sheen and moisture balance.

Use Mira Herbals Natural Shampoo
to make your hair shinier, healthier and easier to manage!

Wouldn't You Love to Have a Glowing Head of Hair That Would Turn Every Man's Head for a Long Admiring Glance and Freeze Other Women in Their Tracks with Envy?

ACTIVITY 3

Work in small groups.

(a) What information is presented in this advertisement? Is it to do with facts which can be checked; with opinions which have to be explained or justified; or with suggestions that have to be considered? Make lists of these three types of writing in the advertisement.

(b) List the problems that can be experienced with hair. Why do you think these are mentioned in the advertisement?

(c) How many times are the words 'natural' or 'naturally' used? What is the importance of nature here?

(d) In the last sentence that begins 'Wouldn't you love', a different emotion is appealed to. What is it? What is its significance here?

Challenge

(e) Much of the advertisement seems to form a long statement. Examine the punctuation used and comment on the way that it works. To start with, look at the verbs in the advertisement.

(f) Identify the two instructions in the advertisement. Are they effective? Explain briefly.

These are statements of fact: 'We make this product.' 'Our production line is hundreds of years old.' 'All our executives give up their time for charities.' These facts can be verified by evidence such as a visit to the factory, photographic and documentary records, verification from the charities concerned and statements from witnesses.

Statements of opinion, on the other hand, reflect what people believe or claim to believe. They cannot be verified. They can be tested or challenged. If someone claims that their product is best we can test this by asking questions: How do you know? For what purpose is it best? What does *best* mean in this context? What about claims that contradict this opinion? Can we trust the person expressing this opinion?

> **Sentences** do one of three things.
> - Indicative sentences tell us things; they make statements of fact or opinion.
> - Interrogative sentences ask us things; they form questions.
> - Imperative sentences tell us to do things; they form instructions.

EXERCISE 3

(a) What is described in the shampoo advertisement? What are we told about each item? Write about 100 words.

(b) Sum up in another 100 words what the advertiser seems to think about the people at whom this advertisement is aimed? Is there a dialogue involved?

Challenge

(c) Comment on the use of words to involve the reader's emotions in a paragraph of no more than 100 words.

Advertisements for services

So far we have considered advertisements for things, tangible items that can be seen and handled. Services are also sold and consequently we find them advertised. Look on the internet and in newspapers and magazines and you will find advertisements for banks, insurance companies, veterinary services, online job hunting and gymnasiums. These are all services that can be provided, that can be purchased, rather than products and just as we have to ask questions about products that are advertised, so we have to ask questions about services, such as travel.

> The word **tangible** is from the Latin *tangere*, which means to touch. Hence a tangent is a line which touches a circle.

The travel advertisement below is from the travelmalaysiaguide.com website.

Sipadan Island is the only oceanic island in Malaysia. It is well-known in the international diving fraternity as one of the world's five best dive sites. Rising 600 meters from the seabed, Sipadan Island is located in the Celebes Sea east of the major town of Tawau and off the coast of East Malaysia on the Island of Borneo. This beautiful oceanic island was formed by living corals growing on top of an extinct volcanic cone that took thousands of years to develop.

Sipadan Island is located in the centre of the richest marine habitat in the world, the heart of the Indo-Pacific basin. In this ecosystem, over 3,000 species of fish and hundreds of coral species have been classified.

In the waters around Sipadan, rare diving scenes are frequently seen such as schools of green and hawksbill turtles nesting and mating, schools of barracuda and big-eye trevally in tornado-like formations, pelagic species such as manta rays, eagle rays, scalloped hammerhead sharks and whale sharks. Therefore, Sipadan is popular with its unusually large numbers of green and hawksbill turtles which gather there to mate and nest. And it is not really rare for a diver to see more than seventy turtles on each dive.

Besides that, there is a mysterious turtle tomb that lies underneath the column of the Sipadan Island. The turtle tomb was formed by an underwater limestone cave with a labyrinth of tunnels and chambers that contain many skeletal remains of turtles that have become lost and drown before finding the surface.

Why Go?

The name of Sipadan is a legend in the diving circles, conjuring the images of patrolling hammerhead sharks, millions of colorful reef fish and, above all, dozens of sea turtles swimming peacefully everywhere. As one of the five top diving destinations in the world, Sipadan, the small rainforest-covered tropical island rising from a 700 meter abyss in the Celebes Sea, is an ultimate diving spot that a committed diver cannot miss.

Diving at Sipadan is certainly world class, so this place has attracted many diving lovers. It is well-known that divers are able to see about 150 species of butterfly fish within a single dive in Sipadan. Utilized by marine biologists as the indicators of coral reef health, a great number and species diversity of butterfly fish implies the abundance and diversity of corals. Pristine coral reefs are also landlord to other reef dwellers such as angelfish, snappers, wrasse, sweet lips, and parrotfish as well as the larger pelagic, barracudas, mantas, whales, dolphins and schools of hammerhead sharks.

Besides that, Sipadan Island is well-known with its vast numbers of Green and Hawksbill turtles which feed and breed within its waters before the females climb ashore to lay their eggs in the white sandy beaches. Other than that, diving near the coral reefs surprises you with incredible phenomena like thousands of schooling chevron barracuda and big-eye trevally or 'Jacks'. Moreover, floating inside such a tornado of fish is a truly breath-taking experience that is hard to beat.

The article below is from the newzealand.com website which promotes travel to New Zealand.

Award-winning Whale Watching

Whale tail – off Kaikoura, New Zealand

If you believe tourism should make a positive contribution to the world, there are few better destinations than New Zealand for you to visit.

Hot on the heels of the country's win at last year's Virgin Responsible Tourism Awards, a New Zealand wildlife experience has now won the 2009 Supreme Award.

This year's winner, Whale Watch Kaikoura, offers close encounters with marine animals in their natural environment, including giant Sperm whales, fur seals, pods of Dusky dolphins, and the endangered Wandering albatross.

But it wasn't just the company's success on the water that won them the Supreme Award – it was the operator's commitment to the local community. The company is 100% Maori owned, and creating employment and opportunities for local Maori was a driving force behind its creation. Whale Watch Kaikoura now operates as a charitable organisation for the indigenous Ngati Kuri Maori tribe and four local founding families. Over 5% of profits are distributed throughout the Kaikoura community and used for education, employment, poverty relief, and to protect the environment...

Kaikoura was also the first place in New Zealand and the second in the world to be green globe accredited, affirming the community's commitment to the environment.

 **ACTIVITY 4**

Work in pairs.

(a) What is meant by the following expressions in the first advertisement?

- [1] 'international diving fraternity'
- [2] 'tornado-like formations'
- [3] 'a labyrinth of tunnels and chambers'
- [4] 'conjuring the images of patrolling hammerhead sharks'
- [5] 'a truly breath-taking experience that is hard to beat'

(b) What is meant by the following expressions in the second advertisement?

(1) 'a positive contribution'

(2) 'Hot on the heels of'

(3) 'close encounters with marine animals in their natural environment'

(4) 'a driving force behind its creation'

(5) 'affirming the company's commitment to the environment'.

Advertisers have to present products and services in a positive light if they are to engage interest in them. We are all targets for advertising. Normally we are passive when we encounter advertising but in the next exercise you will need to be mentally active as you examine how advertising works.

EXERCISE 4

(a) Compare the target customers of the two travel advertisements and the way that each advertiser targets them.

(b) From each advertisement, select three sentences that you find particularly persuasive and explain how each one has its effect or effects. Point out the extent to which each sentence uses facts and appeals to the emotions. What does each of these sentences actually describe?

(c) Write the words of an advertisement to encourage visitors to the place where you live. State in a preliminary sentence the kind of visitor you want to attract. Write a maximum of 150 words.

Challenge

(d) The first advertisement is 503 words long, and the second contains 203 words. Comment on this difference.

Breaking our rules

We're always taught to be honest, but let's take a look at how this rule is sometimes broken in the world of advertising. We often assume that advertisers really believe in the products and services that they encourage us to buy. Do you remember when, at the end of **Chapter 6**, we said that writing about something that really matters to you or you believe in is much easier than writing about something that you do not care about? In Exercise 5 you will be asked to write about something that you don't believe in. It is rather like running with weights carried on your back. If you can manage this assignment – which has the added difficulty of promoting something you dislike – then you will be much more able to write effectively. You will be a 'fitter' writer.

 **EXERCISE 5**

Think of something or some activity that you particularly dislike that could be described in an advertisement. It could be a type of food, a style of clothes or a particular kind of music.

Start by writing one sentence in which you explain your dislike, then set out the words you would use in an advertisement to advertise this thing positively.

Aim to write a maximum of 200 words.

Summary

Having used and played with the sort of language advertisements use, you will now understand it better and appreciate that there is more to advertising than merely describing things. Few, if any, other types of communication are projected at us as aggressively and with as much expense as the advertising we are bombarded with daily, from the television to billboards, from buses to the internet – most of us can't even check our inboxes without having to learn about the latest products. If we are going to understand and use our language to good effect, we must understand how it is used in the world of advertising.

In this chapter we have dealt with different ways in which the basic structure of the language, the sentence, is used to persuade us to want things. What, you should now ask yourselves, are advertisers really trying to tell us?

Chapter 19

Using empathy

Getting started

When a friend says, 'I've got a headache,' we say how sorry we are, but how can we know that we understand what they are suffering? How do we get under somebody's skin?

We cannot begin to understand them unless we have an idea of how they feel. We cannot feel another person's feelings directly but, using our imaginations, we can identify what it is that they feel and empathise with it. To help their readers do this, writers need to describe things in a way that readers can relate to and identify with so that they can get a real idea of what someone else might know and feel.

In the extracts in this chapter, we are going to meet three characters, or groups of characters, with whom we are expected to sympathise: a boy who doesn't understand his mother's emotional entanglements with a series of boyfriends; two sailors in wartime returning home to face the unthinkable; and a family of children who are amazed by the outrageous conduct of an uncle.

Describing and revealing bewilderment

According to the *Oxford English Dictionary*, bewilderment means to be utterly perplexed or confused. A few words from a dictionary make a definition easy but it takes more than a definition to enable us to appreciate another person's bewilderment.

The author of this passage is conveying a feeling of bewilderment to us. In Nick Hornby's book, *About a Boy*, the main character, Marcus, is an intelligent child who is bewildered by the relationships between his mother and her boyfriends. He is at an emotional age when he has yet to see relationships between adults as anything more than an extension of childhood friendship.

Marcus wasn't surprised that she couldn't explain what had happened. He'd more or less heard the whole argument, and he hadn't understood a word of it; there seemed to be a piece missing somewhere. When Marcus and his mum argued, you could hear the important bits; too much, too expensive, too late, too young, bad for your teeth, the other channel, homework, fruit. But when his mum and her boyfriends argued, you could listen for hours and still miss the point, the thing, the fruit and homework part of it. It was like they'd been told to argue and just came out with anything they could think of.

"Did he have another girlfriend?"

"I don't think so."

"Have you got another boyfriend?"

She laughed. "Who would that be? The guy who took the pizza orders? No Marcus, I haven't got another boyfriend. That's not how it works. Not when you're a thirty-eight-year-old working mother. There's a time problem. Ha! There's an everything problem. Why? Does it bother you?"

"I dunno."

And he didn't know. His mum was sad, he knew that – she cried a lot now, more than she did before they moved to London – but he had no idea whether that was anything to do with boyfriends. He kind of hoped it was, because then it would all get sorted out. She would meet someone, and he would make her happy. Why not? His mum was pretty, he thought, and nice, and funny sometimes, and he reckoned there must be loads of blokes like Roger around. If it wasn't boyfriends, though, he didn't know what it could be, apart from something bad.

EXERCISE 1

(a) Write out in your own words what you understand by these words:

    (1) 'more or less heard the whole argument'

    (2) 'hadn't understood a word of it'

    (3) 'still miss the point'

    (4) 'That's not how it works'

    (5) 'a piece missing somewhere'

    (6) 'the fruit and homework part of it'

(b) Look at the third sentence of the passage, and at the words 'important bits'. Explain, in a brief paragraph, what the important bits are for Marcus. Look at the next sentence. What do you think this piece of description helps us to understand?

Challenge

(c) Summarise what Marcus understood and what he did not. Contribute your responses to a class discussion and compare your ideas.

> Ask what it is that is happening with Marcus's mother and her boyfriends, and then you will find it easier to understand Marcus's bewilderment and frustration.
>
> 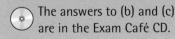 The answers to (b) and (c) are in the Exam Café CD.

Describing and revealing grief

Grief is defined in the *Oxford English Dictionary* as 'deep or intense sorrow or mourning'.

The Cruel Sea by Nicholas Monsarrat is regarded as one of the best novels to have come out of World War Two. In this extract from the book, two shipmates return to Liverpool only to find the area where Tallow lived with his widowed sister smashed by air raids. On a previous visit, Watts had persuaded Tallow's sister to marry him.

"They might have damaged the telephone wires," said Watts after a pause. Tallow nodded again. "It might be that."

But the nearer they got to the house, after crossing the river by ferry-boat, the more they knew that it was not that. From the landing stage they walked uphill towards Dock Road, slowly because of the blocked roads and the rubble and glass and smashed woodwork which was strewn over the streets; the trail of wrecked houses and the smell of newly extinguished fires was a terrible accompaniment to their journey. They did not talk to each other, because the cruel destruction was saying it all for them: there was no need to speculate on what they were going to find, when the odds mounted with every pace they took, with every shop and little house which had been blasted to ruins. Presently, walking in step, side by side, smart and seamanlike in their square-cut uniforms, they turned the last corner, or the place where the last corner should have been and looked down Dock Road.

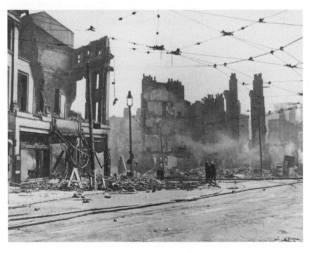

In this extract, Monsarrat describes the actions of the two men in a way that also leads us towards what they are feeling. He does not tell us directly that the two men are beginning to grieve. Instead he tells us what Watts said, that Tallow nodded, that they crossed the river on the ferry, that they walked slowly because of the debris in the roads and that they eventually came to Dock Road. The destruction along the path is described, but not their feelings.

We are not told what the 'cruel destruction was saying' to them. The 'cruel destruction' is described to us so that we can feel for ourselves what it is saying and thus sympathise with them. If we need to be told what the 'cruel destruction' was saying, then the writer has not succeeded with his description of the destruction. If we can imagine something of what the two men must be feeling, then the description of the destruction has done its work.

 **EXERCISE 2**

(a) Write down what you understand by these phrases and sentences from the passage:

    (1) 'strewn over the streets'

    (2) 'the trail of wrecked houses'

    (3) 'a terrible accompaniment to their journey'

    (4) 'there was no need to speculate on what they were going to find'

    (5) 'the odds mounted with every pace they took'

    (6) 'the place where the last corner should have been'.

(b) What is the significance of Watt's words at the start of the extract? In other words, what is important about his words and what do they suggest?

(c) What is the implication of Tallow's reply? In other words, what are we led to conclude about Tallow's view of things? Does he really believe that damaged telephone wires are the cause of Watt's concern?

Challenge

(d) What are the two journeys depicted here?

> The answers to (b) and (c) are in the Exam Café

> One is physical. The other had started last time the two men were home on leave.

There are as many ways to reveal grief as there are people and sources of grief and words to describe grief. In writing, it could be depicted in a distorted face, sounds out of the mouths of the parents of a dead child, or suggested by actions that we would not expect in happy times – there are many ways to help an outsider in to understand a little of someone else's suffering.

Describing and revealing delight

Delight is defined in the Oxford English Dictionary as 'to please Greatly'. In the extract from *Cider with Rosie* that follows the author Laurie Lee conveys a sense of delight caused by the imagined terrors of a neigbour's goat. Jones's goat was usually chained to a stake that had been driven five feet (1.5 metres) into the ground.

    The first time I actually saw him myself had a salt-taste I still remember. It was a frost-bright, moon-cold night of winter, and we were sitting in the kitchen as usual. The fire boiled softly, the candles quivered, the girls were drowsily gossiping. I had fallen half-asleep across the table, when Marjorie suddenly said, 'Ssssh!....'

    She had heard something of course, somebody was always hearing something, so I woke up and listened vaguely. The others were in attitudes of painful attention; they would listen at the drop of a feather. I heard nothing at first. An owl cried in the yew trees and was answered from another wood. Then Dorothy said, Hark!' and Mother said, 'Hush!' and the alarm had us all in its grip.

Like a stagless herd of hinds and young our heads all went up together. We heard it then, faraway down the lane, still faint and unmistakable – the drag of metal on frosty ground and an intermittent rattle of chains.

The girls exchanged looks of awful knowledge, their bright eyes large with doom.

'It's him!' they whispered in shaky voices. 'He's broke out again! It's him!'

It was him all right. Mother bolted the door and blew out the lamps and candles. Then we huddled together in the fire-flushed darkness to await his ominous coming.

The drag of the chains grew louder and nearer rattling along the night, sliding towards us up the distant lane to his remorseless, moonlit tread. The girls squirmed in their chairs and began giggling horrible: they appeared to have gone off their heads.

'Hush,' warned out Mother. 'Keep quiet. Don't move....' Her face was screwed in alarm.

The girls hung their heads and waited, shivering. The chains rattled nearer and nearer. Up the lane, round the corner, along the top of the bank – then with a drumming of feet, he was here....Frantic, the girls could hold out no longer, they leapt up with curious cries, stumbled their way across the firelit kitchen, and clawed the dark curtains back....

Proud in the night the beast passed by, head crowned by royal horns, his milk eyes split by strokes of moonlit, his great frame shaggy with hair. He moved with stiff and stilted strides, swinging his silvered beard, and from the tangled strength of his thighs and shoulders trailed the heavy chains he'd broken.'

EXERCISE 3

(a) What do you understand by:
 (1) 'the candles quivered'
 (2) 'attitudes of painful attention'
 (3) 'the alarm had us all in its grip'
 (4) 'looks of awful knowledge'
 (5) 'the fire-flushed darkness'
 (6) 'stiff and stilted strides'

How is the author showing us his sister' delight?

(b) What is the first indication in this extract of the children's reactions to the goat? What is said that indicates a state of excitement?

(c) List the images given in this third extract. Write them out. (the first one is done for you) 'a frost-bright, moon-cold night of winter' How many sentences in the extract do not contain images?

(d) Find a word or short phrase that sums up the reactions to this episode, of the writer, of his mother and of the girls.

(e) In one sentence for each individual or group, explain why the words you identified in (d) above are appropriate.

(f) What do the actions of the girls suggest about their real reaction to the goat?

(g) How does Lee, the author, keep our attention on the goat while describing his mother and his sisters?

None of our attempts to convey someone's emotions will succeed, except with people who can empathise with other people. Think of very young children who whine and moan without realising that their parents are even more tired or hungry than they are. They are not yet aware of any other person's feelings – only their own.

We can attempt to analyse and explain emotions but, unless we understand and accept that other people have feelings just like our own, we will find it very difficult to cope with the idea of other people's emotions. The ability to understand others' feelings comes with emotional maturity. Our capacity to empathise is recognised as a sign of emotional maturity which has established itself in most of us by the time we are about twelve years old.

◀ Learning to empathise with others' feelings is part of growing up.

An image is usually an impression of the outward appearance of something. An image can also represent the inner characteristics associated with that thing. For example, a commemorative statue of a sportsman or woman could be a physical likeness of the person; a representation of the sport he or she played; or of an ideal of such sportsmanship with its notions of fair play, honour and hard work. A word image can work in the same way. Think of the simple word image 'a dark cloud'. This could literally mean a cloud which is a dark colour or it could suggest a foreboding (a warning of bad things to come).

ACTIVITY 1

Discuss these comments and questions in pairs or groups initially and then as a class.

(a) In one passage the author reveals external things, in one passage, internal things and in one passage both inward and outward things. Identify the three passages.

(b) Compare the images used in the three passages. How important are the images in each passage? Does each author use similar images or varied images? Can you suggest why?

(c) For each passage decide which is the most striking or memorable image in it. Explain your view briefly to the class.

EXERCISE 4

(a) Summarise the situation of the main character(s) in each passage and describe their reactions to their situations. Aim to write about 150 words in total.

(b) Choose one of the main characters from these extracts and write a brief character sketch. Remember that you can describe external features or internal features or both. Aim to write no more than 150 words.

(c) Describe an exciting moment in your life. Aim to write between 300 and 400 words.

Challenge

(d) Write a brief narrative in which someone has to come to terms with a disappointment or loss. Choose an appropriate setting and decide whether other characters will be of importance in describing the response of your main character. Maximum is 400 words.

Summary

You have learnt how characters' feelings can be conveyed in words in ways which will engage our sympathies. To do this, writers have to appeal to our imaginations and the way to engage our imaginations is to describe actions, speech, appearance and thought so that we can relate to how others feel and so begin to understand other people and what they think and feel.

We looked at some examples of the feelings that authors sometimes need to convey. They were bewilderment, grief and delight. Now you have tackled this chapter you will better understand and appreciate the business of describing feelings.

Dealing with ideas and opinions

Getting started

In **Section Four** we will be working on handling opinions and ideas, both in verbal discussions and in written work. Reflecting, pondering, considering, thinking, thinking aloud, discussing, arguing, disputing, debating, exhorting, persuading, convincing, choosing, deciding, reasoning and explaining ideas are what we'll be thinking about.

An idea can be defined as a plan, a mental impression or a concept. In this chapter we are going to practise putting ideas into words and look at the different ways that this can be done. We will see a range of discursive writing in which ideas may be simply mentioned or persuasive writing in which opinions are more tightly argued. We'll also look at being part of the national debate, even at a young age, and consider the different ways in which people express their opinions – calm and measured, or heated and passionate.

Debating ideas

How do we encourage people to discuss ideas? Who do we allow to join in the national and local political debates? Who should be allowed to vote?

In the news

Glarus decides to grant vote from 16

The people of Glarus debate matters before taking decisions.

Glarus, the central Swiss canton, has narrowly voted to extend the franchise, the right to vote, to young people from the age of 16. For the first time they will have their say in cantonal and communal affairs. At the canton's annual Landsgemeinde or open-air assembly, voters supported a proposal by young Socialists on the issue, which is also being discussed elsewhere in the country.

The Landsgemeinde, an open-air assembly in which citizens take keypolitical decisions by raising their hands, is a unique Swiss institution, thought to have been established here in Glarus by 1387. Women were granted the right to vote in 1972.

The Landsgemeinde meets in Glarus, ▶ Switzerland.

For local citizens, Denise Marx and her husband Nick, the Landsgemeinde is an excellent way to get young people interested in politics and the couple have brought their children to enjoy the occasion.

From Germany, Peter Neumann, director of the Institute for Direct Democracy in Dresden, has come with his students to see for himself; he is impressed by the idea of voting by a show of hands. "You see direct democracy in action," Neumann said. "It's an awe-inspiring event for us. You can see that people take it seriously and show respect for their fellow citizens by listening to what the various speakers in the open-air assembly have to say."

Fritz Schiesser, a member of the Glarus parliament and senator for his canton in the federal parliament, shares this opinion. Schiesser has always been aware of the Landsgemeinde's significance which involves more than making political decisions. In his eyes the high point is the moment when citizens who participate in the annual assembly are required to raise their arms and swear an oath to abide by the law and pledge allegiance to the state.

There are restraints in an open-air assembly where votes are cast openly and where every citizen can speak out and submit their own ideas. Here majority decisions are based on estimates, rather than accurately counted votes, and require a much greater length of time.

Despite these shortcomings however, the Landsgemeinde's future is safe. This is the view of Silvano Möckli, professor at the Institute for Political Science in St Gallen. "The Landsgemeinde is a very special trademark and key to the cohesion of society, especially in a rural or remote region. It is crucial to safeguard things that distinguish your community from the rest in a globalised world."

ACTIVITY 1

(a) Working alone, list as briefly as you can the ideas that you find in this article. Look out for matters that people would want to discuss, argue about, consider, reflect upon and about which they might become passionate. If you find ten you will have done very well indeed.

The answers are in the Exam Café CD.

(b) Working in pairs or small groups, make sure that you understand the following words and expressions from the passage:

   (1) 'has narrowly voted'

   (2) 'supported a proposal'

   (3) 'estimates, rather than accurately counted votes'

   (4) 'Despite the shortcomings'

   (5) 'the cohesion of society'.

> Think of *adhesion* and *adhesive*.

(c) What does Peter Neumann particularly appreciate about the Landsgemeinde?

(d) What is implied by: 'It is thought to have been established in Glarus by 1387. Women were granted the right to vote in 1972.'

(e) Compare the lists of ideas that each of you drew up in **(a)** and form one agreed list.

(f) Were your original lists different? If they were, how did you manage to agree on one list? Did one of you decide arbitrarily? Did you discuss your lists?

> The word **arbitrarily** comes from the French *arbitre*, which means a referee.

(g) Adjacent to each item on your group's list of ideas, write what your own personal views are on that issue. You might agree or disagree with what was said in the article, and your views may differ from some of the others in your group. Make these opinions, and differences of opinion, on these ideas clear in your notes. Keep your notes safe as you will use them at a later stage.

EXERCISE 1

Would you like to have a say in the running of the town or community where you live? Would you like to see it organised along the lines of the Landsgemeinde in Glarus? If you could have a say, how would you change things in your town or community?

Plan and set out your views in writing in a maximum of 300 words.

Discussion

In less formal settings a rapid exchange of ideas is possible, as long as people are prepared to listen carefully as well as speak. Sometimes all that is required is an exchange of ideas, for people to come to the best option and agree together what to do. There does not have to be a vote or a decision. As we listen to facts, reasons and opinions we need to make up our minds about them and consider whether our own views have been challenged.

The notes you wrote in Activity 1 (e) should help you remember key points. Remember to write single words, or possibly short phrases, to remind you of something that is important. Sometimes you can re-order the points in your notes by numbering them or cutting them out into separate pieces of paper and then rearranging them as you think about how best to use them. You must decide how to order your material in ways that are appropriate and effective.

Discursive writing discusses an issue or situation, presenting it in a more balanced way than argumentative and persuasive writing does. It should cover the arguments both for and against a given position. After having assessed and evaluated all arguments, the writer usually states his or her opinion at the end.

ACTIVITY 2

This activity is a class discussion. The best arrangement would be for the same groups or pairs who worked together in Activity 1 to sit together again, facing a focal or central point, behind desks or tables on which they can keep notes and write. Everyone should keep very brief notes of the discussion, noting important points and ideas with a few, well-chosen words to serve as reminders.

(a) One member of each group explains again briefly to their group the ideas that were jointly identified in the one agreed list in Activity 1(e). It might be a good idea to list these points again on a board.

(b) Choose one of the ideas to discuss as a class. Allow no more than five minutes discussion on that idea. Appoint a chairperson to direct the discussion, largely by deciding fairly who is to speak next. Then vote on the idea discussed – whether you agree with it or not.

(c) Choose a second topic to discuss and so on, as long as time permits.

EXERCISE 2

You can do this discursive writing exercise for homework. Plan and write a report of the discussion held in Activity 2, indicating the topic or topics discussed and the views expressed. Include your own views, either in the main part of the essay or as a final paragraph. Aim to write between 350 and 450 words.

Expressing views

When a person has the opportunity to set out their ideas more formally, without interruption, it usually requires the person to write out their ideas in continuous writing. This can then be read aloud as a speech (or be memorised and recited with brief notes or key words as pointers) or be read, privately, by individuals.

The most common image of someone doing this is a member of parliament explaining his or her political party's views on an issue. But these skills, the ability to set out one's views, play a more common role in the life of our society. Think about times when you might need to write a letter of complaint explaining your grievance about something or when you could write a letter to the editor about a problem in your community. About writing to the newspapers, remember that this can make a difference to what happens in your community and country because it is the common view of politicians and newspaper editors that the view of that one letter represents many people (maybe even hundreds) who share that view but who haven't written in. So get writing. You might have a much bigger impact than you anticipate.

This next piece appeared in *The Paper,* a British newspaper run by young people.

Terror Down Under

Australian correspondent Mike Baines discusses the reaction of his nation's people to the terrorist attack in Bali.

If you've spent much time with Australians, there's a good chance you've heard the expression, "She'll be 'right, mate." This phrase is just our way of saying that our problems will sort themselves out; everything will be okay. It's not surprising that Australians have developed this carefree attitude. We are comparatively unaffected by many of the troubles that plague the rest of the world such as famine, disease and war. Another problem that the Australian people have not had to worry about is the threat of a terrorist attack... until now.

On 12th October 2002, two bombs exploded in the town of Kuta on the island of Bali, killing at least 180 people and injuring many more. The rest of the world may simply see the attack as another of the enemy's moves in the global war on terror, but for Australia this attack meant much more for three reasons.

The first is the death of so many Australians (30 and rising). While Australians are occasionally victims of terrorist attacks overseas (four Australians, for example, were killed when the World Trade Centre was destroyed) it is uncommon that Australians are the target of such attacks, as we are coming to believe was the case in Bali.

The second reason is the popularity of Bali as a holiday destination for Australians. Bali has been a popular target for young Australian travellers for more than 40 years, and this has a lot to do with the low cost of flying to and staying there. Now, however, budget-minded Australian holidaymakers might stick to their own island.

The third reason is the proximity of Bali to Australia. If you pull out an atlas you'll see; the island of Bali is just a skip and a jump north-west of the land down under. It is this reason that has fuelled the reaction of Australia to this incident; our people are beginning to realise that acts of terrorism are not exclusive to lands distant, they can happen in the country next door. And if they can happen in the country next door, maybe they can happen here.

Reactions amongst the Australian people range from indifference to strong anger. The reaction of Michael, 20, from the Sydney suburb of Belrose is an example of the latter; "It makes you want to join up with the army and kill..." Others are less angry but no less disturbed, like Dee Why resident Matthew, 21, who simply said, "It's sad." Macquarie University student Karl, 20, has put some thought into the reasons behind the attack, speculating that Australians may now be a target because of their latest foreign policies; "Many would suggest that Australia has been too vocal in supporting the US." This notion was more or less confirmed in the latest report from ASIO (the Australian Security Intelligence Organisation), who believe Australia's support of the United States in their anti-terrorism campaign may, understandably, have landed us in the bad-books of terrorist organisations such as al-Qaeda.

The bombings in Bali have not affected the Australian people anywhere near as strongly as September 11 affected the Americans. This is understandable, as the attacks on the people of the United States happened on American soil and thousands of Americans were killed or injured. In comparison, the Bali bombing, which may or may not have been an attack on the Australian people, happened overseas and nowhere near as many people were killed or injured. While many of us are disturbed by this incident, many others are largely indifferent to it all. Nevertheless, the one thing the Bali bombing has left with most of us is that in regard to the "War on Terror", we might not always be able to say "She'll be 'right, mate."

Mark Baines contrasts the easy-going approach to life of most Australians with the shock of this terrorist outrage. A relaxed way of encountering difficulties is regarded by some of his countrymen as their trade-mark, something of which they are proud.

The answers to **(a)**, **(b)** and **(c)** are in the Exam Café CD.

ACTIVITY 3

Work in pairs.

(a) Identify the main concern of the writer of this article, Mike Baines.

(b) What is the writer trying to convey in each of the first two paragraphs? Identify key words and expressions.

(c) Explain, in your own words, the reactions recounted in the penultimate paragraph and the writer's conclusion in the final paragraph.

(d) Mike Baines numbers three of his points. Why do you think he does this? What effect does it have on the article?

(e) Which of his points seems most important to you? Why?

Measured or moved

Ideas are exchanged or communicated in a variety of places and for a variety of purposes – in the media and on the internet, in parliaments (the word means the place where people talk), in the courts, in places where people meet socially, on trains, buses and planes, in schools and in our own homes.

The way we communicate an idea depends on a number of factors, such as:

- its importance or significance
- the people to whom we are communicating it – do they share our view of the matter or do we need to approach them with care?
- what we are trying to achieve – to persuade someone to join us or to change someone's opposition to our views?

Sometimes we need to present ideas in a measured manner, and sometimes it is best to allow ourselves to be more moved.

Measured	**Moved**
Tends to be:	*Tends to be:*
ordered and connected	spontaneous and disconnected
judges, advocates, editors, medics	columnists, orators, friends, neighbours
often written	usually spoken
formal, complete sentences	casual, snatched phrases
cold, clinical, dispassionate	heated, passionate, unconstrained
wary in response	eager in response
planned with great care	scribbled
formal – debated	shouted back
thoughtful	excited
a school report	gossip
detached – a sentence, a diagnosis.	engaged to the end.

A school report is unlikely to begin with the words, 'Oh, by the way...' Similarly, a friend is unlikely to get you to listen to their new favourite song with the words, 'My considered opinion is...'. If they used these words, they would probably fail. Deciding just how formal and correct you are going to be, how measured or moved, is a matter of judgement on a sliding scale. There are no hard and fast rules. Good comedy in which ideas and conversation are handled inappropriately – too informally or formally – shows this very effectively.

Lawyers' letters, on the one hand, and comments shouted across the playground, on the other, represent the ends of this scale, but in the middle, for much of the time, we have to make judgements about how best to communicate. Our way of judging these things becomes part of our character; you will know which members of your class will respond immediately and noisily to ideas and those who will choose another approach.

EXERCISE 3

Think back to your discussion in Activity 2. In groups you discussed the ideas raised in the article about the Landsgemeinde in Glarus. Write a brief report about the conduct of your classmates in the class discussion that took place. Use the words in the two columns on the previous page and any other words that you find helpful. Write a maximum of 300 words.

Libby Purves' article which follows is a good example of combining the very best of both approaches – measured and moved. Follow the steps in her argument in this newspaper article. Consider the comments that accompany each paragraph.

> Was the debate conducted calmly or were some people very eager to share their opposing views? How did these different ways of expressing opinions contribute to the discussion? You might find that in some groups, the discussion was more passionate than in others. Was that because of personality or maybe even cultural differences? How can we use our differences in positive ways?

Nocturnal adventurers scale Blackpool Tower

The Times

Libby Purves berates a boring, safety-first culture and turns to a website that cheeringly tells of an adventure; not safe, not belt-and-braces, not even legal.

This is the chronicle, of the dark Friday night when two young men calling themselves Scott and Stepping Lightly completed the climb of the 518ft (158m) Blackpool Tower. They used climbing ropes, helmets, carabiner clips. They trained for weeks, scaling a 300ft mill chimney in Oldham the night before, for practice. Nobody knew, nobody saw, nobody in the bright-lit throbbing summer city was disturbed.

> The first paragraph focusses on it being an impressive climb. The emphasis is on the fact that it was professionally done and no one was troubled by it.

The writer mocks and exaggerates the comments from the critics in order to undermine their arguments.

Here the emphasis is on the scale of the achievement and the climbers' modest view of it. The writer says that they are not interested in promoting themselves – this further undermines their critics.

Admiring the achievement, the writer dismisses concerns about its legality. She holds the opposite view of the critics of this stunt, describing it as 'a good example of training and professionalism'.

She mocks the critics, saying 'fill in your own (negative) words' and says how brilliant the climbers are.

She mocks herself and the man in the street in order to get sympathy for their mundane lives in urban squalor which so contrast with the brave acts of the climbers.

The conclusion is that this is a triumph of the human spirit.

The final challenge is the writer's confidence – do we dare to disagree?

The first the authorities knew of it was through pictures on the internet. Police are, of course, furious. They have to be. It's their job. Irresponsible! Trespass! An "ill-advised stunt" undertaken "without permission or supervision". Oh, and the owners add, suppose they had injured "innocent people" by falling? (Not very likely, given the carabiner lines and that they'd most likely have fallen on to the roof of the building below.) It was trespass, it was illegal, criminal. The only other time the tower was topped, in 1963, there were two arrests. One of the first internet responses to The Times report piously deplored the fact that the "taxpayer" would have had to clear them up if they'd fallen.

And yet somehow, the heart sings. What they did was crazy, but only as a piece of carefully crafted original art is crazy. It has a quality of defiant freedom, of unmercenary and anonymous endeavour. These unofficial boys wanted to reach the flagpole, and they did so soon after midnight. The diary says: "The tension's on. The temperature has dropped, talk about illuminations – the ambient light is intense... Don't look down... That's it. The top, the tip. Lost for words. But with a view like that... Incredible. Time to abseil the rope into the abyss."

It is a kind of art, braver and harder work than much of what we are served as such. It is also a kind of crime, but less damaging than any other I can think of. It will be excoriated as a Bad Example, encouraging teenagers into silly stunts: but they do those anyway, and the main extra example they get from this one is a fierce emphasis on long training and professional safety gear.

These adventurers (all right, criminals, illegals, fill in your own words) do something special and consoling for our urban landscapes. They are an extreme version of the leaping, flying skateboarders on the concrete wastelands, or those wonderful young practitioners of "parkour" free-running who vault from bollard to railing, run vertically up walls to execute the "équilibre de chat", and do elegant handsprings off street furniture.

For the rest of us, earthbound and plodding off to sign up timidly for the padded weight-machines and 15ft climbing-wall at the leisure centre, these people offer something important. In an urban world of vast brutalist buildings and heartless machines, bossy signage and pedestrians forced into dank underpasses for cars' convenience, such unregulated climbs and leaps teach a lesson.

Fragile bodies, transient and mortal, soft and vulnerable, throw a playful, defiant challenge to harsh immensities of concrete and steel. They celebrate human simplicity and human grandeur. Even the mild criminality of it intensifies the glow.

Can't you see that it's beautiful?

ACTIVITY 4

Each of you should spend a few minutes thinking about which of the words found in the two columns on page 154 (Measured and Moved) you would apply to this article.

Then discuss your conclusions in groups or as a class. Remember to use the distinction between *measure*d and *moved* especially if you have to write an extended piece of coursework

> Support your answer with evidence from the text. For example, the opening words of the article, 'This is the chronicle...' are <u>ordered</u>, <u>planned</u> and <u>measured</u>.

Expressing your opinions

Ask yourself, if the argument is that important to you, why risk losing it by avoiding a few minutes of preparation? However anxious you are to tell your audience exactly what you think, a few minutes spent planning or reflecting about your ideas before you express yourself is crucially important.

- List your points. The one you thought of first might not be the most important so decide in which order you are going to present them.
- Decide whether you are going to start or finish with the strongest point; you may wish to shock with a dramatic revelation at the start to get people's attention or to finish with a memorable conclusion to which you have led your reader or your audience. Some people say that you should put the most important points first so that if people stop listening after a few minutes, at least they will have heard the most crucial points. This is how news items in newspaper articles are written; journalists expect their readers to tail off toward the end. But then you also want to make sure that you finish on something really memorable so that it sticks in their minds even after you've stopped speaking.
- You may have points which would help strengthen your ideas, for example, a short explanation of what caused you to hold this particular view. That might be a personal experience or a powerful story about someone else's experiences. Some research cannot go amiss; people are often convinced by statistics and figures. Use these kinds of points sparingly because you need to remain focussed on your topic. Decide carefully where and how you'll fit them into your piece.

EXERCISE 4

(a) Choose ONE of these topics for a composition. Aim to write between 300 and 400 words.

- Set out your ideas for improving your school, or the provision of education in the area where you live.

- What are the best ways that people from your country can get along with people from other countries? Are there things that make it easy or difficult for people in your country to do this?
- What future is there for the family?
- What do you think is the most important issue facing your generation?

(b) You have been offered a guest spot in a newspaper or magazine, or on a website, to write about any topic about which you have strong views. The editor has told you that the article should be very provocative because he wants to challenge his readers and get them thinking and discussing. The article must be about 300 words long. Plan and write the article.

(c) Once your teacher has seen the work written for (a) or (b) try to develop your ideas further into a piece of 500–800 words. Bear in mind the advice earlier in the chapter about *measured* and *moved*.

Summary

In this chapter you looked at how ideas can be debated and discussed. Glarus and its Landsgemeinde encouraged you to think about the role all of us should play in sharing opinions and discussing our views to make our communities a better place. You then practised discussing views. You also looked at the different ways in which people discuss issues, comparing a more measured style of debate with one that is more based on being moved in the moment. Once again, you were reminded of the importance of planning and organising your work.

Chapter 21

Dealing with questions

Getting started

Questions are important starting points when we want to find out things; whether that be information, opinions, reasons, justifications, feelings or beliefs. Questions form an important part of discussion. Sometimes, before we try to answer them, they deserve closer scrutiny.

Open and closed questions

If you asked someone to tell you what they preferred to eat and they replied, 'Wednesday', you might ask whether they understood English. If they persisted with this answer to your question, you would wonder whether they realised that your question required a matching answer.

ACTIVITY 1

(a) Imagine that you have arrived in class without some homework. Which of these questions would you find easiest to answer? Why?

(1) Have you forgotten your homework?

(2) You haven't forgotten your homework, have you?

(3) Why haven't you done your homework?

(4) Why do you think I set that homework?

(5) Where is your homework?

(6) Do you know what happens to people who don't do their homework?

(7) Why should I bother to teach you if you can't be bothered to do your homework?

(8) Why should I excuse you for not doing your homework?

(9) Do you want to pass your exams?

(10) Don't you want to pass your exams?

(b) Working in groups, discuss where or when you would expect to be asked questions like these:

    (1) Which flavour would you like?

    (2) Who do you expect to win?

    (3) Why are you home early?

    (4) Why did you take that money from the table?

    (5) What is it like now that you're on your own?

    (6) Why on earth do you believe all that?

Your answers will show that you know how to *interpret* questions.

(c) Now look at some more questions:

    (1) Do you like strawberries?

    (2) Will the home side win?

    (3) Has there been another fire at school?

    (4) Have you got any business taking my money?

    (5) Are things any better now?

    (6) Do you really believe all that?

What choice of answer do you have with this second group of questions? Are you more limited in your answers with this set of questions, or with the former?

(d) Explain the times when you would rather answer the first sort of question and the times when you would rather answer the second?

Questions can be divided into two categories – open questions and closed questions.

In Activity 1, the first set of questions (b) are open and the second questions (c) are closed.

Open questions allow us to provide substantial answers. We have considerable control over our responses. For example, think of the question: *Why haven't you brought your homework?* There are many different answers that you can give to this question. You might try one that went something like this:

Well I was just getting ready for school when I noticed that our dog, who is always hungry (he's always eating the tennis balls that come over from next door), was sniffing around my bag. Before I could stop him, he grabbed my homework book and ran off with it to the bottom of the garden. By the time I'd caught him, he'd chewed it all up.

There is no reason why you should stop at this point. You could add even more to your answer. The reason is that the question is an open one.

However, if the question had been something along the lines of: *Have you forgotten your homework again?* Then you would have to choose between three short possibilities: *Yes, No,* or *Don't know* to answer the question. This closed question gives us little room to manoeuvre.

When we need information quickly, we usually ask closed questions such as, 'Is this the road to Birmingham?' We simply need a yes or no answer. Other examples are 'Does she like chocolate?' or 'Can I go home, please?' Once a reply has been given, the questioner keeps control of the conversation, unless the person answering the question interjects with a comment or question of their own. Closed questions such as these are often used by lawyers, teachers and parents to control conversations or discussions and usually to help 'get to the bottom of things'.

In these types of discussions, people can also use open questions such as, 'Why did you do this?' or 'What happened next?' These kinds of open questions usually hand the initiative to the person being questioned, but of course the information given by way of reply again hands back ideas and information to be scrutinised and enables the questioner to ask yet more questions such as, 'Why did you think it was a good idea to do this?' or 'Once the crash had happened, why did you not summon help?'

If someone working in a shop asks you a closed question such as, 'Can I help?' it is easy to say, 'No, thank you,' and walk away. If they ask, 'What can I interest you in?' you are more inclined to stop and think about what might provide an answer or something that you might be interested in, rather than asking yourself whether you want to be questioned. Shop workers dealing with the public are often trained to ask open, rather than closed, questions to get the customer talking and thereby make it easier to sell something to him or her.

▲ Shop workers are often trained to ask open questions to engage a customer in conversation.

EXERCISE 1

You are going to write 12 short pieces of dialogue, each between four and ten lines.

Each piece will start with a question from the lists of questions in Activity 1 (b) and (c). Deal with the questions in pairs so that you start with (b)(1) then (c)(1) then (b)(2) then (c)(2) and so on. Remember to show the difference between open and closed questions in your writing.

Responses to questions

When we ask a question, we need to be aware of whether it has been answered directly or if the person has skirted around the question and given us a different response. We'll look more closely at that in the exercise that follows.

When might interviewees not want to answer questions directly? Think about the kinds of difficult questions some people might wish to avoid if they were being interviewed. Examples include a sportsman being asked about his affairs outside of marriage or a politician being asked about money that has been squandered.

This activity requires you to undertake some research. It may take you a week to get all the information together. You need to watch or listen to interviews. Television and radio talk shows and interviews would be good. Otherwise you could trying visiting the website www.youtube.com and searching for 'interview' – that would bring up literally thousands of very interesting interviews.

Make a list of six questions that you have heard in interviews, noting what was asked. Decide whether the person being interviewed (the interviewee) actually answered the questions.

Challenge

If you can note responses from the interviewee that are not actually answers then that will be a real bonus. When you have collected your material, discuss what you have found in small groups before presenting the most striking or amusing examples to the rest of the class.

Your **constituency** is the people you represent following an election.

Here is an example of the sort of question and reply that you might hear in the interviews that you listened to in Exercise 2 above.

> *Interviewer:* 'Tell me, should your constituency/clients/patients/ students trust you after what you have done?'

> *Interviewee:* 'Well, let me tell you that in our political party/ company/hospital/school we have learnt lessons and put in place procedures to ensure that nothing like this ever happens again.'

What sort of question was asked? It was a closed one. The only direct answers that can be given to that question are 'yes', 'no' or 'don't know'.

The response that this interviewee has given is not an answer to the question which was asked. A good interviewer will ignore the answer and insist on repeating the question, 'Should your constituency/clients/ patients/students trust you?' until he or she gets a direct answer.

A similar open question, possibly to follow the previous one, could also attract a 'non-answer'.

> *Interviewer:* 'Tell me, if you were the electorate/clients/patients/ students, what would you do in this situation?'

> *Interviewee:* 'As an organisation we have learned important lessons and so have retrained most of our staff and set out new guidelines for dealing with this kind of situation.'

The interviewee does not answer the question and tell us what he or she would do. Instead, the interviewee has simply stated some facts designed to turn our attention away from an unpleasant truth, that trust has been lost.

If you asked your teacher whether you had failed or passed an examination, which answer would you rather be given?
'I'm sorry, you've failed,' or 'I'm afraid that you have not indicated sufficient understanding to reach the target grade.'

Good answers

Now that you have looked at the connections between questions and answers, you can now look more closely at what makes a good answer. We use questions to communicate our need for: information, opinions, reasons, justifications, reassurance, sympathy and support. Good answers provide these things.

Non-answers masquerade as answers and are really used to smuggle in whatever the responder hopes to get away with, like the story of the dog that ran off with the homework (page 160).

 **ACTIVITY 2**

(a) Working in pairs, look at the questions that follow. Identify in them any key words that indicate what is expected in an answer. Make any additional observations that you can about the sort of ideas that you would expect to find in an answer.

(1) Who are you?

(2) How long will it take my friend to get well again?

(3) Why did the alarm go off?

(4) Why should criminals go to prison?

(5) What was it like after the impact?

(6) What is the most important part of your faith?

Remember that you don't have to answer the questions, just consider what would be required in an answer.

(b) Working on your own, look at some more questions and again make a brief note or list of the key words that indicate what one would need to include in each answer.

(1) What two reasons are given in the passage to explain why the children could not control the fire?

(2) Why do you think the writer describes the boys as looking on in 'horrid fascination'?

(3) What do you understand by the words, 'still continuing a tradition'?

(4) Why do you think the writer uses the word 'mythology' in the final paragraph?

These are proper questions from sample examination papers. Some 'questions' are really invitations to show that you understand or appreciate something.

Challenge

An example is: Why did the boys cry out? The word *why* is a reminder that a reason is required in the answer. The answer is: They were frightened. That is a reason for someone to cry out; it is an answer to the question.

Examination questions

Examination 'questions' are not questions in the ordinary sense. Sometimes they are requests for information which you are expected to know, as a way of testing your knowledge, but more often they are instructions, directing you as a candidate.

Here is an example of an examination 'question' that invites you to do several things. In the question, you are first asked to read a passage about two young people who have been entered for a young citizen of the year award. The 'question' that follows this passage is:

Write a letter to the organiser of the award explaining carefully your reasons for nominating one of the young people for winner over the other. Make clear how far each of them reflects your values and beliefs. You may develop the information with details of your own.

How should you examine the question? Let us look at it sentence by sentence. There are three sentences.

In the first sentence there are five pieces of information:

- what to do – write
- what to write – a letter
- to whom – the organiser
- what to write – an explanation
- what to explain – the reasons for your nomination.

In the second sentence there are two pieces of information:

- what you are to do – make clear – in other words, explain
- what you are to explain – how far each of the young people reflects *your* values and beliefs.

In the third sentence there are three pieces of information and a **warning**:

- you may develop – this is an invitation to take your ideas further
- what you should develop – the information (already given)
- how you should develop this – with details of your own
- the **warning** – the 'invitation' in this sentence that 'you may' is really a strong hint that you **should** bring ideas of your own to your response to show your writing in the best possible light.

This way of analysing an examination question is very full and is intended to ensure that you omit nothing of importance when planning your answer. An easier and quicker way when you take an exam is to mark up the question in some way to make sure that you have left nothing out. Here is the question that we have just analysed, highlighted to show just how you can do that quickly and easily.

▲ Examine questions thoroughly before you start writing.

Write a letter to the organiser of the award explaining carefully your reasons for nominating one of the young people for winner over the other. Make clear how far each of them reflects your values and beliefs. You may develop the information with details of your own.

You may well have your own way of responding to examination questions. That is fine. The essential thing is to have an approach that you can fully rely on to ensure that all aspects of the question are dealt with and responded to.

EXERCISE 3

Choose ONE of the following essay titles. Draw up a brief plan of no more than 50 words or four lines of the page, before you start. Aim to write about 400 words in your essay.

- 'To hate people is always wrong.' Argue a case for or against this view.
- 'The most untidy place I know.' Describe it.
- Write a story, or part of a story, in which someone stands up for his or her beliefs.

Summary

In this chapter we have examined questions and answers so that you can respond more effectively to questions. You looked at the different kinds of questions there are – open and closed questions – and the kind of response each one calls for. This made you more aware of people's attempts to avoid answering questions and made you think about what a good answer is.

You have begun to apply your greater understanding of questions to those encountered in examinations, looking at how to pick examination questions apart to ensure that you deal with and respond to every part of the question.

Chapter 22

Making the most of your words

Getting started

When we write about our opinions and ideas we need to make our words work as well as possible. To do that we've got to choose carefully the words that we are going to use and then combine them in the best possible way. To help you see the effect of these choices, we'll do some editing. This will help you to see how passages that you and others have written can be improved by a more careful choice of words and expression. We also look at two pieces of classic literature to see the interesting ways of presenting ideas and opinions that these authors use.

Editing to develop writing skills

The first and most important way to learn to write well is to take in, immerse yourself in and understand, what other people have written well. Listening and reading are primary skills, essential for learning the secondary skills of speaking and writing. That means that you should listen before you learn to speak and you should learn to read before you learn to write. Speaking and writing are performance skills which demand more from you than listening and reading. In **Chapter 3** you may remember we looked at how much longer it takes a person to write than to read.

Later in this chapter we are going to read an extract from a work of fiction by the novelist, Kenneth Grahame, and a poem by the poet, John Keats, to see what they can show us. Both these works are examples of the use of highly effective language. However, first you are going to do some editing, to identify the kinds of errors that creep into written work.

ACTIVITY 1

For this activity you will need some samples of your own writing. They will need to be between 100 and 500 words long. Earlier assignments in English, or other subjects, will be suitable. Photocopy them so that you do not work on the originals. Work with a partner or in a group of three.

(a) Exchange a piece of writing with your partner(s). Read through the piece that your partner gives you and make sure that you understand it. Ask questions if necessary. Then try to find ways to improve what has been written. You may find words that are more suitable and you may find ways of re-organising the words better. You might even find some errors. Make your alterations in pencil.

(b) When you have finished, return the work to its owner and take it in turns to discuss and explain the alterations you have made.

Editing a piece of work that someone else has written is often easier than checking and improving your own work. When you've worked on a piece of writing for a long time, especially if it is long, you can easily become 'blind' to the errors in it (and that is a reason why we suggested reading your work aloud earlier in the book). Working on other people's work is a good way of improving your own writing skills too. It makes you think about how to improve written work.

 **EXERCISE 1**

Do this for homework. Take home a photocopy of a piece of work written by one of your classmates. Attempt to improve the passage, making your alterations in pencil. When you have finished, rewrite the passage in its entirety. Later, it could be marked by or discussed with its original writer.

To write well we must focus on choosing the best words, and then combine them in the best way possible. Remember these pointers:

Choosing words

- Choose words that are simple and clear, yet descriptive: *Sticky toffee pudding* rather than *chef's recommended dessert.*
- Think about the sounds of words: *bang, pop, hiss.*
- When appropriate, choose words with double meanings or which hint at other meanings. An example is cow which is *a source of milk* but, sometimes, *a disagreeable female.*

Combining words

- Place important words carefully: *The piano – that was what he had always wanted to play.* Or, *He had always wanted to play the piano.* In both sentences the word piano is emphasised, by a pause in the first sentence and by its location in the second sentence, at the end of the sentence. The version that follows gives the word piano little prominence: *The piano was what he had always wanted to play.*
- Build up arguments or drama. *She noticed the movement, reached for her camera, checked the switch and, as it rounded the corner, pressed the button.*
  Here there is also a sense of rhythm to move the words and the sense along; it is caused by a pulse or push on each of the verbs.
- Striking or unusual words or expressions can 'catch' the reader's eye. *The storm hovered over its victims before striking them down with a hail of icy stones.*

Once you start writing using a word processor on a computer, you will find that it gives you a great deal of flexibility when you are playing with words and developing your written work. Many people find that they can manipulate the text much more easily, moving phrases and sentences around and trying out new words. It is a good idea to learn to type properly – with the correct fingers on the keys, and then to practise. This is a skill that will carry you through life. You don't want the search for keys impeding on your thought processes as you compose great literature.

Lessons from literature

A fictitious character in a story can have the same urgent need to inform, describe or argue as a journalist with a deadline to meet or a student sitting an examination. Fiction uses the very same language as non-fiction and is a worthy source of ideas and examples. Fiction and non-fiction writing can be judged in very much the same way. Whether the writing is a news article in a newspaper, or a short story in a book or on a website, the writing in itself can be considered, analysed and argued about in similar ways.

Writers of creative fiction need to be especially aware of the effects of the words they choose, particularly if they are writing poetry. In order to consider as closely as we can the effects of the words we choose to use – and there are over 200 000 to choose from in English – we are going to examine two short literary items. As a class, listen to the extract that follows from Kenneth Grahame's *Wind in the Willows*. Although the narrative seems to be aimed at young readers, the book is very much appreciated by adults for the quality of its writing.

Mole reflects upon his first summer on the river bank and appreciates all its drama.

And what a play it had been. Drowsy animals, snug in their holes while wind and rain were battering at their doors, recalled still keen mornings, an hour before sunrise, when the white mist, as yet undispersed, clung closely along the surface of the water; then the shock of the early plunge, the scamper along the bank, and the radiant transformation of earth, air, and water, when suddenly the sun was with them again, and grey was gold and colour was born and sprang out of the earth once more. They recalled the languorous siesta of hot midday, deep in green undergrowth, the sun striking through in tiny golden shafts and spots; the boating and bathing of the afternoon, the rambles along dusty lanes and through yellow cornfields; and the long cool evening at last, when so many threads were gathered up, so many friendships rounded, and so many adventures planned for the morrow.

Here is a summary of Grahame's passage: animals sheltering from winter remember the three other seasons when they are more active: the chill of early spring mornings, the glory of a summer full of life, and the harvest in autumn when, with friends, they plan to enjoy the next year.

- Now let's examine the writer's use of words. Look at the comments in the margin that relate to the highlighted text.

And what a play it had been. Drowsy animals, snug in their holes while wind and rain were battering at their doors, recalled still keen mornings, an hour before sunrise, when the white mist, as yet undispersed, clung closely along the surface of the water; then the shock of the early plunge, the scamper along the bank, and the radiant transformation of earth, air and water, when suddenly the sun was with them again, and grey was gold and colour was born and sprang out of the earth once more. They recalled the languorous siesta of hot midday, deep in green undergrowth, the sun striking through in tiny golden shafts and spots; the boating and bathing of the afternoon, the rambles along dusty lanes and through yellow cornfields; and the long cool evening at last, when so many threads were gathered up, so many friendships rounded, and so many adventures planned for the morrow.

contrasts the warmth indoors with the wet and cold outside

alliteration

the simple and complicated sounds and rhythms represent simple and complicated movements

refers to the four elements (the Sun represents fire)

striking ideas

another striking image

the three commas work as pauses to build up to tomorrow's anticipated delights

In this passage, the author also appeals to our senses:

- touch – 'the shock of the early plunge and languorous siesta of hot midday'
- sound – 'wind and rain were battering at their doors'
- sight – 'the white mist as yet undispersed'; 'grey was gold and colour was born'; and 'the sun striking through in tiny golden shafts'.

Now we are going to look at a second piece of creative writing. It is a poem, a sonnet called 'To a Cat' by John Keats. Along with Wordsworth, Byron and others, Keats wrote verse that encouraged the engagement of the emotions. This became part of what we now call the Romantic Movement.

This cat, described by Keats, is someone's favourite cat. He is past his best but is still a charmer – with an interesting past.

To a Cat

Cat! Who hast pass'd thy grand climacteric,
How many mice and rats hast in thy days
Destroyed? – How many tit bits stolen? Gaze
With those bright languid segments green, and prick
Those velvet ears – but pr'ythee do not stick
Thy latent talons in me – and upraise
Thy gently mew – and tell me all thy frays
Of fish and mice, and rats and tender chick.
Nay, look not down, nor lick thy dainty wrists –
For all thy tail's tip is nick'd off – and though the fists
Of many a maid have given thee many a maul,
Still is that fur as soft as when the lists
In youth thou enter'dst on glass bottled wall.

The cat has been a hunter, a thief and a fighter but now, in old age, he wants sympathy. The speaker in the poem teases the cat and reminds it that it has not really changed.

What is important here about the way the poet has used the language? Again, look at the comments in the margin that relate to the highlighted text.

we anticipate a verb, which then shocks with its power on the new line

a striking image which suggests light, and slow, relaxed movement, then narrow, squinting shapes as well as colour

those claws are held back till the cat strikes with them

double alliteration here – repeated initial sounds (n/l n/l) which emphasise three negative words

alliterations (repeated initial sound) and assonance (repeated vowel sounds) combined to emphasise a loss that does not trouble the cat

there is a contrast between the soft fur and the sharp glass; the phrase 'enter'dst on glass bottled wall' uses *s* and *t* sounds for a sense of sharpness

Cat! Who hast passed thy grand climacteric,
How many mice and rats hast in thy days
Destroyed? – How many tit bits stolen? Gaze
With those bright languid segments green, and prick
Those velvet ears – but pr'ythee do not stick
Thy latent talons in me – and upraise
Thy gently mew – and tell me all thy frays
Of fish and mice, and rats and tender chick.
Nay, look not down, nor lick thy dainty wrists –
For all thy tail's tip is nicked off – and though the fists
Of many a maid have given thee many a maul,
Still is that fur as soft as when the lists
In youth thou enter'dst on glass bottled wall.

Look too at how the poet uses senses to describe the encounter:

- sight – 'gaze' – to look beyond the speaker as if ignoring him or her
- sound – 'mew' – to utter a pleading sound, like a small kitten
- touch – 'latent talons' – powerful weapons that can be deployed at will, a contrast with the sound.

The poet likes the cat but addresses it as if delivering a reprimand.

The manner in which he does this combines the lofty formality of 'grand climacteric' with the quick informality of 'tit bits'.

The formal language of a judge is combined with casual expressions used in everyday speech.

(a) Working in pairs, answer these questions about the extract from *Wind in the Willows*.

   (1) Why do the animals welcome summer?

   (2) List, for each of the four seasons, a word or phrase used in the extract that reminds us of it.

(b) Still in pairs, answer these questions about the extract from *To a Cat*.

   (1) List the main points made in Keats' poem.

   (2) What two things does Keats tell the cat not to do?

   (3) What do you imagine a 'glass bottled wall' to be?

   (4) How does Keats indicate that his criticisms of the cat are not serious?

Challenge

(c) For both the extract and the poem, list three words or phrases which help the reader to imagine what is going on.

EXERCISE 2

In this exercise you are going to use the lists of the main points of the poem and the words used in the extract that you drew up in Activity 2 (a)(1) and (b)(1) as the basis for brief passages of writing. Each passage should be no more than 60 words.

(a) Tell, in your own words, the story of the encounter with the cat.

(b) Describe in your own words what the animals in *Wind in the Willows* recall of their busy times.

(c) Comment on the ease or difficulty of doing this exercise. For example, did you find that 60 were enough words to write what you needed to, or was it too many words?

(d) Write a summary, of one paragraph each, of Grahame's extract and of Keats' poem. In the first one try to sum up Mole's view of his new life and, in the second one, set out Keats' opinion of the cat.

Challenge

ACTIVITY 3

(a) Listen to the extract from *Wind in the Willows* and the poem *To a Cat* read again by a member of the class.

(b) Compare your experience of hearing the readings now with your first hearing of them. Did doing Activity 2 and Exercise 2 help you to understand and enjoy the passages more?

Summary

You have considered the need to select and combine words as thoughtfully as you can in order to communicate effectively. You practised editing passages so that you could apply these skills and so improve your writing.

You then looked closely at how two highly-regarded authors, Kenneth Grahame and John Keats, used the qualities of the language, especially imagery, to convey so much more than a simple narrative. In your particular way, and for your particular purposes, you need to choose the best possible words and arrange them in the best possible order.

Diction – Keat's choice of words

A particular characteristic of this poem is the use of words that are rich in meaning:

- 'Destroyed' suggests overwhelming damage as compared with the alternative *killed*.

- 'talons' are associated with larger animals and here Keats mockingly reminds the cat that it is relatively small, a pet with claws.

- 'velvet' provides a tactile image of something unspoilt; blemishes are easily seen on velvet. Words such as *neat* are less precise and would not suggest what it is like to touch or fondle the cat's ears.

- 'segments' are part of the circles formed by a cat's eyes, only part because they are almost closed as if the cat is not really taking any notice of what is being said. *Eyes* would suggest circles (eyes wide open) and the effect would be lost.

- 'lists' rather than the possible alternative *fighting* allows further mockery of the cat. Lists were the areas in which knights in armour fought on horseback following the complex rules of aristocratic conflict. Nothing could be further from the sort of desperate struggle in which two cats attempt to tear each other apart and which would account for this cat's damaged condition. By pretending that the cat's way of fighting is somehow noble, Keats emphasises its unprincipled viciousness.

Chapter 23

Narrative, descriptive and discursive writing

Getting started

How do we decide what to write about and where do we find inspiration for our writing? It is all around us – in the lives of the heroic and in the everyday. Sometimes it just requires us to take a new angle on an old topic.

In **Section Two** of this book we looked at narrative writing, that is, how writers craft storylines – the plot of the story. In **Section Three**, we looked at powerful descriptive writing such as Charles Dickens and considered how we as writers can create 'word pictures', called images. In **Section Four**, we've looked at presenting our ideas and opinions. The aim of this chapter is to see how we can bring these types of writing together – narration, description and writing about our ideas and opinions. Now, we'll consider why this is important, and then give some thought to the future.

Inspiration for writing

The briefest of incidents can have the most unimaginable of consequences – and provide the inspiration we need for some really good writing. Remember to look at events and people from different angles.

The first meeting of Desmond Tutu and Trevor Huddleston and its consequences could be told in different ways – described, told as a short story or have its significance explained.

When he was a young boy, Tutu watched as his mother, a domestic servant, answered the door of the house where she worked. The caller, a white man, was Trevor Huddleston, an Anglican priest. Huddleston was wearing a broad-brimmed hat which he removed

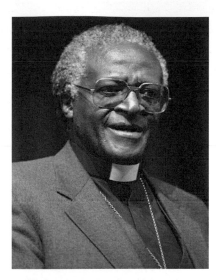

Desmond Tutu, former archbishop of Cape Town, is best known for his work to reconcile former opponents in post-apartheid South Africa.

The late Bishop Trevor Huddleston fought apartheid during his time in South Africa and afterwards.

as soon as he found himself speaking to a woman. From behind his mother's skirts, Desmond Tutu watched and realised, for the first time, that whites and blacks could treat each other with kindness, courtesy and respect.

 **ACTIVITY 1**

Working in groups of three, reread the account above of Desmond Tutu's first sight of Trevor Huddleston. Three versions of this story are required from each group, with each member of the group getting a different version of the story to write:

(1) one in which the end of the story is told at the start of the narrative

(2) one in which the end of the story is told in the middle of the narrative

(3) one in which the end of the story is told at the end of the narrative.

Each person should write no more than 150 words. Read the pieces written by the other members in your group.

When you're looking for inspiration and topics to write on, you can look at the great and the good, the big things and events in life, but you can also look for inspiration in the smaller everyday activities that we all take part in. You'll be surprised at what you can find in yourself when you are looking for story ideas.

(a) Think of ten things that happened to you in the last week, however mundane or boring they might seem. What seems to be the humdrum of your life might be very interesting to other people – teenagers in other parts of the world, youth workers and yes, even your parents.

(b) Think of ten significant things that have happened to you in your life. Some of the ideas you come up with might be the circumstances of your birth, sad events that you have experienced, moving home, holidays you've been on, the first time you had romantic feelings for someone or special moments you've had with a family member.

(c) Think of ten things that you feel strongly about. They might be things that you have personal experience of or that you are worried about. Sometimes we have strong feelings about things that we think won't be important to other people. Put them on your list too. You can also add issues that are part of the national debate such as animal cruelty, abortion or recycling.

Many of the items that you have put in these three lists would provide very good material for stories and essays.

ACTIVITY 2

Work in pairs or groups.

(a) In pairs, list ten stories that you each know. They could be historical, mythological, national, local, personal or connected with your family. Give each story a descriptive title.

(b) Let your partner choose one title from your list for you. Take the title chosen by your partner and turn it into a written passage of between 300 and 400 words.

Using all three types of writing

In the exercise above we looked at different ways to approach the storyline and the presentation of the events in Tutu and Huddleston's meeting. So far we have considered the plot and the storyline which form a narrative. Their meeting also provides wonderful opportunities for descriptive writing – when you focus on describing the characters and other elements in the story in order to bring them alive for your reader; and discursive writing – when you share different ideas and opinions about their meeting.

 **EXERCISE 2**

Write three paragraphs.

(a) Give a chronology of the basic events in this story.

(b) Describe the meeting in your own words, focussing on a description of the characters and their actions.

(c) Share your opinions and ideas about the importance and significance of this event in a short story that ends with the words, 'Oh, I see.'

> In each of these passages you will mainly use one of the elements of writing that we have worked with in this book. In (a) you'll write a primarily narrative piece, in (b) a descriptive piece and in (c) you'll express opinions and ideas. While each of these paragraphs focusses on using one type of writing, you may also use the other types of writing.

Good writing usually uses all three types of writing. The passage that follows is a good example of this. In a section of his autobiography, *Slide Rule,* the novelist Neville Shute tells of the death of his brother in the trenches of the First World War. Shute was sixteen at the time of his brother's death.

In the trench warfare of those days the curious operation of mining was common on both sides. Where the trenches were frequently within a hundred yards of each other you would collect a party of miners, coal miners in civil life, perhaps, and dig a tunnel underground till the end of it was beneath the enemy trench. The enemy was well aware of what was going on, because he could hear the men digging underground, but he was generally powerless to do anything about it. I doubt if such a thing could happen nowadays with the increased fire power of the infantry but in that war it was a common tactic. The climax, of course, was that you filled the end of the tunnel with high explosive, fired it with a fuse at a suitable moment, and blew up the enemy trench; in the confusion you then assaulted with infantry and gained a few yards. In these days of mobile warfare it seems a great deal of effort for very little advantage, but that is the way things were in 1915.

Fred's bit of trench was mined by the Germans and everyone knew it. The only things that could be done about it were retreat or counter-attack, and the local position permitted neither. Those last days after the noise of tunnelling had stopped, waiting for the balloon to go up, must have been very trying for Fred; he wrote home a couple of jocular letters about it to my parents. It went up on June 13th and twenty-four of Fred's platoon were killed or wounded by the explosion; at the same moment the Germans put down an artillery barrage. Fred was unhurt, but his sergeant and several men were buried by the debris. No doubt, having survived the explosion, he had the strengthening feeling that I know so well – "This can't happen to me" – for he led a party of men out from the remains of the trench to dig out his sergeant. There the shell got him.

> **Jocular** means deliberately light-hearted or jovial.

In these days of sulphur drugs, blood plasma, and penicillin nobody would die of the wounds Fred got, extensive though they were. He was evacuated down to the base hospital at Wimereux and for ten days or so he made good progress. Then gangrene set in and became uncontrollable, in itself an indication of the march of medical science, because the medical attention that he got was very good. My mother and father crossed to France to be with him as was common in those days of gentler war, and he died about three weeks after he was wounded with my mother by his side. If Fred had lived we might have had some real books one day, not the sort of stuff I turn out, for he had more literature in his little finger than I have in my whole body. He was only nineteen when he died, and after nearly forty years it still seems strange to me that I should be older than Fred.

ACTIVITY 3

(a) Working in pairs, identify in this passage:

(1) things that are explained

(2) things that are described

(3) things that are dramatised

(4) what Shute reflects upon (his reactions to elements of this story)

(5) places in the passage where explanation, description and drama work together.

(b) Does it matter that this is a true story, that it really happened to someone? Do you think that readers would feel differently about the story if they thought that it was just that, a piece of fiction? Explain your view.

(c) Report your findings in a class discussion.

Try to approach any writing task with a clear idea of what is expected and consider carefully how you will set about the task. This is why planning a composition is so important. Know exactly what the examination question is asking – does it require descriptive or narrative writing, or is it asking you to give your opinion and ideas? Or can you use a combination of two or three types of writing?

It is best to feel confident about undertaking any kind of writing so that you know that you can make a good job of whatever question you are faced with. You may well have a preference for one type of writing (be it narrative, descriptive or explaining ideas and opinions), but you may have to make choices in the examinations when a particular title of a different type is attractive to you in terms of the topic.

Think, what sort of writing do you prefer to do?
What sort of writing do you do best?
How can you combine different types of writing effectively?

ACTIVITY 4

In groups or pairs, examine these topics for compositions. Allocate each title to a member of the group. Spend no more than ten minutes planning a composition based on the title allocated to you. Then explain your plan to the group.

(a) Narrative writing
Write a story (or part of a story) in which two people meet unexpectedly.

OR

'His/her finger hovered over the button while he made up his mind.'
Continue the story.

(b) Descriptive writing
Describe a day in which confusion and uncertainty are resolved.

OR

'He, or she knew that the shock of all this would remain for some time.'

Describe a shock experienced by you or by someone you know.

(c) Discursive writing
'Should people be encouraged to take up hazardous sports such as base jumping and pot-holing? Set out your views.

OR

At what age should people take on the rights and responsibilities of adulthood?

Pointers to the future

Have you ever been asked to predict the exciting changes to our lives that science and technology will bring during your lifetime? In particular, have you ever considered the way we communicate with recorded versions of the language? Chinese is still written in pictograms and educated Chinese people have to learn about 30 000 of them to be literate, whereas in English we use only 26 letters to represent all the sounds of the language. Will people discover an easier way to record and communicate the things that they want to say?

If the future of communications interests you, you should read the article written by Ben Macintyre called 'The internet is killing storytelling' which is used in the Sample Paper 2 in **Section Five** (pages 184 to 185).

Also with the future in mind, do you think that you could write something for a newspaper or another publication? If you have something to say and can say it clearly and bring it to the attention of a newspaper editor, you might appear on the nation's newsstands. You'll be surprised to find out how eager many people are to hear from the younger generation – and how many editors would be happy to publish their ideas and opinions on newsworthy topics and events. Of course, you could also blog your ideas and see what effect they have.

◀ Writing an article for a newspaper or blogging your ideas allows you to share your thoughts and opinions with others.

This is a passage written by two Australian teenagers that was featured in the *Sydney Morning Herald*.

Fashion icon offers young women a retouch of sanity

October 28, 2009

Sarah Murdoch should be applauded for challenging the false images presented to teenagers. With so much at stake, it's time others followed her lead, write Clare Sibthorpe and Albona Osmani.

Skinny waists, perfect curves and flawless skin. These are what we teenagers see in magazines and aspire to attain.

But why has it become such a high priority? Why are young people obsessed with body image?

We all know the women on magazine covers are airbrushed and edited to perfection, yet all we think when we see them is, "I want to look like her".

A digitally slimmed and altered bone structured image of US singer Kelly Clarkson was recently published on the cover of *Self* magazine. When readers expressed their disappointment and outrage, the magazine's reported defence was the image was "only to make her look her personal best" and it had created a "picture of confidence".

In fact, it encourages the exact opposite. A false image creates false hope for teenagers.

Society should be encouraging us to understand that everyone is made differently, everyone's body is unique, and every teenager changes as they age. Instead, we are constantly faced with the unrealistic expectation we can be perfect, and that we need to be perfect in order to feel confident.

These unrealistic images are now widely perceived as realistic and children in primary school believe them to be true reflections. A friend's 10-year-old sister, for example, recently said she thought she looked much prettier wearing make-up.

There is not enough awareness about the effect false images of unrealistic and often superficial role models have on young people. That is why high profile women like Sarah Murdoch, who has had natural and unedited shots taken for a magazine cover, are positive influences on the model industry and more broadly.

Negative images and false perceptions of beauty are challenges teenagers have always faced, so why is it only now that some action has been taken?

One person taking action is not enough.

So much is gained by the advertising industry and modelling agencies from creating false images because they rely on them to be financially successful.

And when a magazine editor is drastically altering a photograph, we suspect they don't often consider enough the effect this will have on the teenagers who see their final product, but rather see it as doing a job.

Things need to change. The public already knows this.

More people need to follow Murdoch's example. She says: "I hope that my unique perspective can in some way help develop national strategies that promote healthy body image, especially in girls and young women."

While there is a growing awareness that body image is a serious issue, we need to use this information to take more positive action to help our generation.

Clare Sibthorpe and Albona Osmani are year 10 students at Canberra High School.

ACTIVITY 5

Discuss in small groups the girls' story and consider these questions.

(a) What is the central event which drives the story; what is recounted at the start? To what use then do the authors put their story?

(b) Do you think that the story will remain relevant for any length of time? Why?

(c) This story is particularly aimed at other girls. Are boys subject to similar pressures?

(d) What other topics might concern teenagers, especially things that may affect their lives in the future?

EXERCISE 3

Select ONE of the following. The last topic is a little more challenging.

- Choose a topic that concerns you. Write a piece of about 400 to 500 words for a newspaper. Bear in mind the people who read this newspaper and the need to attract their interest from the start.
- Describe the way in which you expect to receive and send information in twenty years' time.
- Explain any scientific or technological achievement in sending and receiving information, or reading and writing, that has impressed you.
- A breath of fresh air. Are there questions that trouble the adult world for which young people are more likely to have an answer? Identify one of them and explain how your generation might show adults a way forward.

Summary

In this chapter you've looked at where you can find inspiration for your writing. We read the story of Desmond Tutu and Trevor Huddleston's meeting and considered it from different points of view. You then thought of your own topics and material for stories and hopefully found that you already have a lot more ideas in you than you expected.

We examined the ways that narrative, descriptive and discursive writing can work together. You then considered your own preferences for and strengths in different types of writing – bearing in mind that the more writing styles you are practised and confident in, the more choice you'll have when it comes to choosing examination questions. We considered how interested many people are in the views of young people and looked at an article written by two young people which was published in an Australian newspaper.

Section Five: Ready for the exam

Getting started

In **Section Five** we are going to look closely at the Cambridge IGCSE English First Language examination. We will look closely at a sample of each paper and at the coursework. There are several routes through the examination which are set out here.

1. You will have to take either:

   Paper 1 (Core) – which is based on one reading passage or

   Paper 2 (Extended) – which is based on two reading passages.

2. For both the Core and Extended courses, you will also have to take:

   Paper 3 (directed writing and composition) OR submit **Written Coursework** (a coursework portfolio of written work).

3. You have the option of completing the Speaking or Listening part of the course. If you take this option, you either have to have **an assessment of your speaking and listening** OR submit a **coursework folder of your work in speaking and listening**.

The section that follows will provide you with guidance on the compulsory and optional assessments. In it you will find:

- information and guidance related to what the examiners look for when they mark your work

- advice from an examiner (your author) who has followed the marking of the thousands of scripts

- detailed analysis of sample examination papers

- links back to relevant sections of this student book to help you revise

- a brief section about handwriting – poor handwriting often makes it difficult for examiners to award marks as generously as they would like.

Compulsory assessment

A complete set of sample examination papers follows. These match those used for the Cambridge International Examinations IGCSE English First Language examination.

These sample examination papers have been annotated in accordance with the marks scheme used by examiners when they mark the papers and with the Principal Examiners' report on students' responses to these papers, provided by the examination board.

We'll deal with the **Written Coursework** (the alternative to **Paper Three**) later in the chapter.

When you sit an examination, remember these points:
- Read all the material, the questions and the commentaries.
- Be prepared to spend more time on questions that carry more marks.
- Ensure that you understand the comments and advice that are given in the paper.
- Seek further help if you are not sure about what you are expected to do. You can ask the invigilators about the instructions you have been given.

Sample Paper 1

Sample Paper 1 Reading Passage (Core),
1 hour 45 minutes
Answer all questions.

Dictionaries are not permitted.

The number of marks is given in brackets [ ] at the end of each question or part question.

A Year in a Golden Cage
Our children sent us away to boarding school

When the author's children left university, he and his wife set off to teach in an international boarding school and left the children in charge of the family home. This extract is from an unpublished novel by the author and records his first lesson with a class of students from all over the world.

"So you are?"

"José, sir."

"And you think it doesn't matter if you arrive late for class then?"

"I er, er, I didn't say that, sir."

"You must forgive our friend here, sir." A Russian boy had got to his feet and was standing protectively in from of the Spaniard who towered over him. "You see, sir, he's not had time to acclimatise himself to La Clem. I will instruct him before our next class, sir." 5

Misha had moved to one side of the taller boy and was grinning at the class. Paul had not taught him before but knew of him, knew the sound of his voice and his reputation. The voice, with its rolling Russian letter r and the boy's obvious love of words, stayed with him for a moment. 10

"You know sir, in Russia, we always give new people a chance to settle.

You must be kind to him sir. He's only a lonely Spanish."

"Right then, Misha, I will hold you responsible for José until he's settled. Now, sit down please."

Sir, I promise...."

"Sit down Misha." The boy's last words were lost in the scraping of chair legs on the hard floor. Misha's new friend sat next to him, having moved past other students with a minimum of fuss. You could sense his urge to apologise for his new companion.

"You'll just need paper and a pen today. I should have a couple of text books for you next lesson. Today I want you to make a few notes about the first part of the course and then you are going to prepare some writing, something simple, just so that I can get to know something about you." Paul looked over to the corner where the two boys had settled. The girls in front had turned round and Misha was haranguing one of them.

"What's the matter ladies?" Before either of the girls could answer, Misha had anticipated the direction of his question.

"I'm trying to negotiate some paper for my new friend here."

"Don't you have any to lend him?"

"No sir. I will have to supply myself from whatever I can get for him. It is an easy Capitalist trick, to help your friend and take the percentage."

The class laughed. Paul put aside his annoyance – at least there was some easy discussion started. He remembered Hyung-mi, one of the girls; what was her English like now? He glared at Misha and set about coaxing some words from the girl who was trying very hard to ignore the Russian.

Later in the lesson, he realised that Michael was missing and wondered whether the class would know anything. There had been rumours about a visit to their home by a colleague who had left under a cloud.

"Michael, sir? Haven't you heard – no chance of him coming back."

"No sir, he said he couldn't stand the idea of catching up with all that work, or repeating the year."

"Someone told him he'd have the same English teacher again this year." There was laughter, then a small cheer went up.

"But why isn't he coming back? He's not done anything wrong. He seemed happy so long as I didn't push him for work." Some of the class remembered Michael's record number of detentions – he had been teased about it during several assemblies and had squirmed. He was a clever boy and the reminder about an uncomfortable truth had hurt, especially as, in the circumstances, sitting on the gym floor, he had not been in a position to challenge the tall figure of the director who had known that the students appreciated the truth of what he was saying and would laugh down any protest from the floor.

Consider impressions as well as facts.

1. (a) What differences are revealed between José and Misha? [2]

Two very different things are involved here.

    (b) What two things does the teacher want to find out? (lines 30 and 43) [2]

(c) What does Misha explain about borrowing from friends? What does he try to achieve when he borrows from friends? [4]

Compare what the boy says with what he actually aims to achieve.

(d) What does the expression 'a colleague who had left under a cloud' suggest? (line 45) [2]

A number of possibilities can be found here.

(e) Does the author give the impression that the lesson really has got under way? Explain your view. [3]

Ask yourself what you think the purpose of the lesson is.

(f) From the last section of the passage, explain three reasons for Michael's failure to return. [6]

It might help you to consider how you would use the quotations in explanations which start like this: 'She told him an uncomfortable truth which...' 'This easy Capitalist trick allowed him to...'

(g) Explain, using your own words, what the author means by:

  (i) 'an uncomfortable truth' (line 55)

  (ii) 'an easy Capitalist trick'. (line 38) [4]

(h) Write a summary of Paul's view of Michael and his situation in a paragraph of about 50 words. [7]

[Total: 30]

Make a short list of the items of information that you can find – use just one or two words for each item. Rearrange the order of the items if you think it would help, then aim to write one sentence for each point, in one paragraph.

2. You have been commissioned to write the first episode for a television 'soap' set in a classroom in an international school. Use the passage above as your starting point, setting out the script with the identity of each speaker shown clearly and stage directions written in brackets.

You should base your ideas on what you have read in the passage without copying from it. You should write about 1 to 1$\frac{1}{2}$ sides, allowing for the size of the handwriting.

Up to 10 marks are available for the content of your answer, and 10 for the quality of your writing. [Total: 20]

As regards the content of your answer to 2, good answers will:
- use and develop <u>several</u> ideas
- make use of factual ideas, ones that are stated clearly, such as Paul's familiarity with Misha's voice and reputation
- make use of ideas that can be drawn from the passage, such as Paul's measured response to Misha's joke about a Capitalist trick
- elaborate and develop details persuasively – you should be thinking all the time about the effect your ideas are likely to have on your reader, for example, the helplessness of the students sitting on the gym floor, challenged by the imposing figure of the director.

As regards the quality of your writing, good answers will contain:
- fluent sentences properly sequenced – check this by imagining that you are reading aloud (hear the words in your head)
- a wide range of vocabulary – use the right word or words
- an effective structure – organise and order your points as you plan your writing
- an appropriate register (level of formality) – remember who it is you are addressing and why.

Sample Paper 2

Sample Paper 2 Reading Passage (Extended),
2 hours

Answer all questions.

Dictionaries are not permitted.

The number of marks is given in brackets [ ] at the end of each question or part question.

Part 1

Read Passage A carefully, and then answer Questions 1 and 2.

Passage A

Narratives have long been a staple of every culture the world over. Now there are fears that they are disappearing in an online blizzard of tiny bytes of information.

The internet is killing storytelling

The Times, November 2009

By BEN MACINTYRE

1   Click, tweet, e-mail, twitter, skim, browse, scan, blog, text: the jargon of the digital age describes how we now read, reflecting the way that the very act of reading, and the nature of literacy itself, is changing.

2   Addicted to the BlackBerry, hectored and heckled by the next blog alert, web link or text message, we are in a state of Continual Partial Attention, too bombarded by snippets and gobbets of information to focus on anything for very long. Microsoft researchers have found that someone distracted by an e-mail message alert takes an average of 24 minutes to return to the same level of concentration.

3   The internet has evolved a new species of magpie reader, gathering bright little buttons of knowledge, before hopping on to the next shiny thing.

4   It was inevitable that more than a decade of digital reading would change the way we do it. In a remarkable recent essay in the *Atlantic Monthly* Nicholas Carr admitted that he can no longer immerse himself in substantial books and longer articles in the way he once did. "What the net seems to be doing is chipping away at my capacity for concentration and contemplation," he wrote. "My mind now expects to take in information the way the net distributes it: in a swift-moving stream of particles."

5   If the culprit is obvious, so is the primary victim of this radically reduced attention span: the narrative, the long-form story, the tale.

6   Last year Hollywood veterans and scientists from the Massachusetts Institute of Technology teamed up to create a laboratory aimed at protecting the traditional tale from oblivion: the Centre for Future Storytelling. However ludicrous that may sound, they have a point. Storytelling is the bedrock of civilisation whether the stories are true or imaginary.

7   Stories however demand time and concentration; the narrative does not simply transmit information, but invites the reader or listener to witness the unfolding of events. Stories introduce us to situations, people and dilemmas beyond our experience, in a way that is contemplative and gradual: it is the oldest and best form of virtual reality.

8   The internet, while it communicates so much information so very effectively, does not really "do" narrative. The blog is a soap box, not a story. Facebook is a place for tell-tales perhaps, but not for telling tales.

9   Meanwhile, a generation is tuned, increasingly and sometimes exclusively, to the cacophony of interactive chatter and noise, exciting and fast moving but plethoric and ephemeral. The internet is there for snacking, grazing and tasting, not for the full, six-course feast that is nourishing narrative. The consequence is an anorexic form of culture.

10   Plot lies at the heart of great narrative: but today, we are in danger of losing the plot. Paradoxically, there has never been a greater hunger for narrative, for stories that give shape and meaning to experience. Barack Obama was elected, in large measure, on the basis of his story, the extraordinary odyssey that begins in Hawaii and ends in the White House, taking in Chicago and Kenya along the way.

11   The news stories that compel us are not the blunt shards of information, but those with narrative: the tragic mystery of Madeleine McCann; the enraging saga of parliamentary scandal; the strange decay of a premiership. Reality television, *The X Factor*, *Strictly Come Dancing*, all are driven by personal narratives as much as individual talent.

12   Our fascination with other people's stories is as great, if not greater, than any time in history. This year I am judging the Costa biography of the year award. The astonishing range of biographical writing is testament to our appetite for narrative. Reading several dozen lives, one after the other, has been fascinating, but also unfamiliar, and exhausting. Like Carr and, I suspect, many others, I too have become used to absorbing lives in Wikipedia-shaped chunks.

13   What is needed is a machine that can combine the ease and speed of digital technology with the immersive pleasures of narrative. It may not be far off. Japan has recently seen an explosion in the popularity of thumb novels, *keitai shosetsu*, book-length sagas that can be uploaded to the screen of your mobile phone, one page at a time.

14   These mobile telephone tales are written in the language of the net: scraps of text-speak, slang and emoticons, but these are still unmistakably narratives, stories with a protagonist, a beginning and an end. They are also hugely popular, proof that the ancient need for narrative, hardwired into human nature, can sit comfortably with the wiring of the newest technology.

15   Narrative is not dead, merely obscured by a blizzard of byte-sized information. A story, God knows, is still the most powerful way to understand. In the beginning was the Word, and the Word, in the great narrative that is the Bible, was not written as twitter.

copyright © The Times, 05.11.2009 www.nisyndication.com

1. Write a report for primary school teachers, explaining the importance of stories.

    Write approximately two sides allowing for the size of your handwriting.

    Up to 15 marks will be available for the content of your answer, and up to 5 marks for the quality of your writing.   *[Total: 20]*

2. Re-read the descriptions of:
    (a) changes brought to our reading habits by the internet in paragraphs 1–3;
    (b) *Keitai shosetsu* in paragraph 13 and 14.

    Selecting words and phrases from these paragraphs to support your answer, explain the effects the writer creates in using these descriptions. Base what you write on what you have read in Passage A.   *[Total: 10]*

Using Language

The two passages here in Sample Paper Two differ markedly.

Ben Macintyre jostles us with evidence at the start of his first sentence: 'Click, tweet, e-mail...' Then explains its importance: this is 'the jargon', the new terminology that describes the way we read. He softens us up with the first nine words so that we are anxious to learn what all this is about.

Biola Olatunde allows herself something more poetic at the start. Notice the stresses on the words 'old', 'Africa', 'taught', 'values' and 'stories'. These are important words; the others simply serve to connect them. It is the gentleness in this passage that makes it easy for us to read on. One writer shakes us with words so that we have to hold on and the other writes smoothly so that we do not, as it were, fall off.

Olatunde starts with 'In the old days', words which provide us with a sure starting point. Then, as we become familiar with her subject, the sentences become longer and more complex. It is as if the author does this because she is confident that we, the readers, can follow.

Macintyre too finds a use for the qualities of words: Facebook is 'a place for tell-tales perhaps, but not for telling tales'. We are forced to pause here to consider the slight difference between the two expressions and accept the enormous differences in their meanings.

Both writers want us to think about the story; one drags us along, the other beckons.

List or identify the main ideas in the passage by highlighting or underlining key words and phrases. The examiners are looking for the use of ideas from the article which you have adapted appropriately for this particular task. The best answers will distinguish between information, explanations and conclusions and will incorporate them carefully into the report.

The key thing here is the skill with which you select words that are particularly effective or unusual and explain their effects. Are we impressed, amazed or convinced about something, for example? Show how the words you refer to bring about these effects.

Make a list of the items of information that you need for each part of Question 3, (a) and (b). Just write one or two words for each item on your list.

Rearrange the order of the items within each list if you think it would help to write better summaries. Aim to write one sentence for each item on your list in each answer. Make sure that you make each point as clearly and concisely as possible.

Remember that good answers will contain:
- fluent sentences properly sequenced – check this by imagining that you are reading aloud
- a wide range of vocabulary – use the right word or words
- an effective structure – organise and order your points as you plan your writing
- an appropriate register (level of formality) – remember who it is you are addressing and why.

Part 2

Question 3 is based on Passage A and Passage B.
Read Passage B and re-read Passage A.

Passage B

African Story Telling - Lessons and Entertainment

By Biola Olatunde

In the old days in Africa, we taught ourselves values through stories. We had quite a lot of stories. We used all the methods we could then. Some stories were songs that spoke of the heroic battles of our heroes. We had heroes that everyone in the community could identify with. We had stories of animals through which we told our children the virtues of life like honesty, honour, loyalty and courage. Animals represented different things and concepts. For instance from my part of the world, we had stories of tortoise being shown as wily, cunning, sometimes hilarious but always with an underlying lesson for us. It was natural every evening after the day's work to sit by the fireplace, or under a big tree and hear of the escapades of the tortoise. However in all these stories of the tortoise, a thread of a code of ethics was woven for us. It was usual at the end of each story for the story teller to ask us the listening children, what was the lesson of the story.

In the broader sense at the government level, we had festivals, that were used to teach the leaders the essence of honour and integrity. Such festivals were usually some kind of masque in which erring leaders were lampooned in songs, drama and such devices that sent the message home. It was understood that the actors of any masque could not be punished. The victim who felt very bad at being lampooned would naturally keep to his farm for a few days and weeks depending on the severity of the satire. He returned to the larger community after a time hoping everyone had forgiven or forgotten that misdemeanor. You however notice that in his anxiety not to have the same experience the following year, he would amend his ways.

Society was friendly, knew its place and governance was at most times benevolent and inclusive. Story telling had its uses and was a simple form of entertainment as well as instrument of instruction. Sadly however, the story is radically different today in my part of the world. The only viable story telling we can tell each other these days are of poverty, disease,(some really strange ones our forefathers never heard of) and of our insensitivity to each other. In those golden yesteryears, a thief could not find succor in any place unless he changed his ways. His family disowned him. His community would reject him and no matter how wealthy he became, he was never given a chieftaincy title. The community will watch him in derision if he even attempted to contribute to the common wealth of the people.

Today, there is no more story telling. There is no more sitting by the big tree to watch the moon, sing to the moon or tell stories of the escapades of the tortoise. There are no more moonlit games or wrestling or folksongs or beauty pageants in which we show off our African hairdos. What we have now is the television that has made apes out of the dignified African, the fashion that has stripped us naked and left us naked. The thieves get chieftaincy titles now and sometimes decided the course of a people that was once proud and self sustaining.

We can still go back to the story telling days. We can still use stories to change our concepts to something noble and uplifting. We may not be able to physically sit by the big tree, but we can still tell stories about honour and integrity for these stories are as timeless as the virtues they preach. It is the essence of real civilization. Do we still have good story tellers?

3. Summarise:

   (a) what Biola Olatude appreciates about storytelling in Passage B.

   (b) the effect that the writer claims electronic media has on the narrative in Passage A.

Use your own words as far as possible.
You should write about 250 words (roughly one page).

Up to 15 marks will be available for the content of your answer, and up to 5 marks for the quality of your writing.   *[Total: 20]*

Sections One to Four of this student book provides specific links, exercises and guidance to answering Papers 1 and 2. The chapters that you will find them in are **2, 3, 5, 7, 8, 10, 11, 14, 15** and **17–23**.

Sample Paper 3

Both students doing Core *and* Extended either do Paper 3 OR submit a coursework portfolio of written work. We'll look at the coursework option later in this section.

Sample Paper 3 Directed Writing and Composition,
2 hours

In this paper you will have to answer two questions:

Question 1 (Section 1) and one question from Section 2.

Dictionaries are not permitted.

All questions in this paper carry equal marks.

Section 1 (Directed Writing)

1. You are looking for a summer job. A company has decided to provide activity days for local children in your town during the long school holiday. They are advertising for teenagers to work as junior leaders, to help with the children and activities. See the advertisement on the next page. Anyone interested must apply in writing.

   Write an appropriate letter of application to the organisers in which you present yourself as someone who would be a good junior leader. In your letter you should:

   • show that you understand what the job requires
   • make clear that you are confident that you have the necessary skills and qualities for the job as a junior leader.

   Your letter should be based on the promotional leaflet that follows. Your attempts to demonstrate your suitability must be related to this promotional material.

   You are expected to write between $1\frac{1}{2}$ and 2 sides, allowing for the size of your handwriting. Use these words to start your letter:

   Dear Organisers

   I would like to apply for the position of junior leader on the activity days you are providing.

   Up to 10 marks will be given for the content of your answer and up to 15 marks for the quality of your writing.   *[Total: 25]*

HOLIDAY FUN FOR EVERYONE!
Are your children bored?
Are they missing their friends?
Are you worried that they never get any exercise?

Let them come to our activity days and they'll have no more to complain about.

We offer a full day activity programme starting at 07.30 and finishing at 18.00.

Where are the activities?
We base our activity days at a local High School, using all the facilities, indoor and out. Day trips are also arranged to places of interest.

What can my child do there?
Children can choose between four types of activity:
• Art and Craft
• Sport
• Music
• Adventure
In addition we offer swimming daily and a 'chill out' session (quizzes, videos and relaxation).

What about food and drink?
Breakfast and lunch are included. We also offer unlimited healthy drinks and snacks.

Will they be happy?
We divide children into three groups: 6–8, 9–11 and 12–13 years old, to ensure all activities are just right for their age and ability level.

Each group is led by a qualified adult staff member assisted by a number of junior leaders from the local community. These young adults are hand-picked to ensure that your daughter or son has the best possible time with us.

Just look at what past participants have had to say:

"I first came on one of these days two years ago. I was shy at first but quickly met others thanks to my junior leader, Ash, who introduced me to everyone."
Katja (8)

"I loved the adventure stuff. I went abseiling and canoeing. There were two older boys helping with the

group and they both belonged to a local climbing club so they helped me a lot, explaining what the instructors said and keeping me going when I was a bit nervous."*
Sam (12)

"I made a jewellery box in a craft session. I'd never even picked up a hammer before but Saskia, our junior leader, said that she'd have a go so I thought I would too. It took me ages, but I did it."
Suzannah (10)

"My favourite part of camp was the music. Mital, our junior leader, could play the guitar and he suggested we form a rock band. We played in one of the 'chill out' sessions and everyone loved it!"
Krisstof (11)

"Every day each group did different duties like camp clean up and cooking. I liked making lunch because we got to have second helpings. Our young leader was firm but he showed us how to make sweet and sour sandwiches which were a bit odd!"
Deepak (9)

Will they be safe?
All our staff are security checked and have been through a rigorous selection procedure.

All staff assisting with water sports must have a swimming qualification and/or a life-saving certificate.

All staff assisting with sporting activities have had at least two years' experience in the sport and have attended a special training day prior to the start of the programme.

So what do I have to do?
Just drop your children off at the school from 07.15 and collect them again at 18.00.

All booking details can be obtained from our help line: 012 345-678 or visit the school office.

Adapted from Cambridge International Examination, IGCSE English – First Language 0500/03 Paper 3 Q1 Oct/Nov 2007

You have been told how to start the letter, and there is a clear indication of what the examiners expect you to do: show that you understand what will be required of you if you get the job and convince the organisers of the activity days that you really are the person they need.

Remember these points:
• Use a final sentence or short paragraph to draw the letter to a close and to indicate that you have said all you need to say and to indicate what you expect or would like to happen next.
• Focus on the information in the text and develop ideas and responses from the text. Make the best use that you can of the information in the leaflet.
• To gain high marks you must ensure that your letter is carefully planned and directed clearly at the target audience, the people from whom you want a job.

You might loathe letter writing and the thought of working with younger children might appal you. This is, however, a compulsory part of the paper and you want to do your best. So, keep your own likes and dislikes out of the exercise and use storytelling skills if necessary. You don't need to write about yourself – you can invent a character who is keen to get a job such as this one. Take on the persona of this character and write the best letter you can on your character's behalf. In this way your ability to read information and to convey it accurately and effectively will be shown to best effect.

Sign the letter with your own name.

Section 2 (Composition)

Write about 350 to 450 words on ONE of the following:

Argumentative/discursive writing

2 **(a)** 'Too many of the role models presented to young people by the media lead lives that are nothing like those enjoyed by most of us. They should be ignored.' Do you agree? *[25]*

OR

(b) 'University is not for everyone. Many successful adults have never been near one.' What do you think? *[25]*

Descriptive writing

3 **(a)** Describe the most exciting or enjoyable day of your life. *[25]*

OR

(b) Your best friend has been excluded from school and asks you to go home with him or her to face their angry parents. Describe your journey there and the atmosphere indoors once your friend has explained what has happened. *[25]*

Narrative writing

4 **(a)** 'The Floods': You have watched the news then gone to bed. Write a story in which you dream that you are involved in a flood. *[25]*

OR

(b) Write a section of a story in which a character believes that someone, or something, is following her. You could build the story into something frightening or comic. *[25]*

Sections One to Four of this student book provide specific links, exercises and guidance to answering Paper 3. The chapters that you will find them in are **3, 4, 5, 6, 7, 8, 10, 11, 13–17, 19, 20** and **23**.

Choosing examination questions

You *can* afford to spend at least five minutes studying the questions, deciding what would be required of each one, considering your own preferences and strengths and making a choice. This is time well spent because the rest of your planning and writing will be much easier and much more effective as a result.

Be aware that the examiners find that questions such as **2(a)** and **2(b)** are usually tackled less effectively than the other four choices. Argumentative/discursive writing (writing in which you need to express your opinions) is usually the most difficult to undertake. However, if you are attracted to the question, have clear views about the topic, develop and order your ideas and look at the question from more than one point of view, then you could choose one of these titles with confidence.

Keep in mind the kind of writing that you have chosen to do. If you include writing of another genre, a piece of description perhaps, to dramatise a narrative or to strengthen an argument in discursive writing, remember that you are doing so in support of your particular title. You must always keep in mind the main purpose of your writing.

Checking your work

When you think you have finished, read through your work **at least twice**. Make sure that you have included all the ideas that you intended to include, that they make sense and are in the right order. Try to imagine that you are reading someone else's work to check the sense of what they have written. Imagine the sound of your voice reading the piece aloud to help check punctuation and sentence structure.

If you are running out of time, in an emergency, circle and number completed paragraphs and indicate clearly where you intend to change the order in which they should be read. When you make changes, strike out words calmly with a single diagonal line.

Written Coursework (the alternative to Paper 3)

This is the alternative to doing the written examination paper. You are required to submit a portfolio of three assignments, each of about 500 to 800 words:

- one assignment that is informative, analytical and/or argumentative
- one assignment that is imaginative, descriptive and/or narrative
- one assignment that is a response to a text or texts chosen by the school.

The object of your coursework option is to improve your writing skills by developing and extending your ideas through editing, revising and correcting. Essentially it requires a return to ideas and a re-consideration of material. It is important that you have a detailed discussion about the work with your teacher who will have further details of the coursework requirements.

Assignment 1 (informative, analytical and/or argumentative)

A number of the assignments in **Section Four** of this book would provide suitable material for Assignment 1. Look, for example, at Activity 4 and Exercise 4 in **Chapter 20**. Extending the questions, or combining them, would provide a substantial basis for a coursework assignment. For example, you could write about the most pressing problem for people of your age and then extend your work to explain and justify what you would do to address this problem.

Another opportunity could be provided by extending the idea of a newspaper article in Exercise 2 of **Chapter 20** by reporting on other people's views as well as your own and arguing for your own position. As an indication as to how much you should write, Libby Purves' article 'Nocturnal adventurers scale Blackpool Tower' is 500 words long, the minimum length that is required for this type of assignment. Lively expression of your own versions is sought here so consider: writing in the first person, writing a speech, choosing a subject with which you are familiar and addressing a particular audience.

Assignment 2 (imaginative, descriptive and/or narrative)

Sections Two and **Three** contain a number of exercises which would provide a sound basis of this type of assignment. For example, Exercise 3 (b) in **Chapter 7** provides three suitable topics for this assignment and the guidance in this chapter would be very helpful.

In **Chapter 14** (Exercises 2 and 3) and **Chapter 15** (Exercises 1–3) for example, there is much advice about descriptive writing and there are a number of topics from which to choose, many of which could easily be developed as coursework material. Whether your topic is factual or imagined, your work can be enhanced by the way you include descriptions, reactions, emotions and characterisations to help your reader.

Assignment 3 (a response to a text or texts chosen by the school)

In this assignment be aware that your ability to engage with ideas and opinions for yourself will be tested. Your teacher may allow you to choose your own text and will provide help and guidance. Rather than wait to be told what to do next, you should be asking yourself what needs to be done next.

Choose one article rather than several, one that is approximately one side of A4 and which involves a controversial topic with strong opinions. Avoid plagiarism – copying other people's ideas and be prepared to speak out boldly.

Look again at earlier sections of the book; in particular, look at the discussions about the way that texts are written and at writers' purposes in writing. Chapter 11 includes a discussion of two literary extracts (*The Day of the Triffids* and *The Handmaid's Tale*) and Chapter 4 contains a non-fiction text, the article about the kidnapping of a train crew in India, with guided discussion which indicates the way to approach the task of commenting on texts. Much of the material, the activities and the exercises in Chapters 1 to 4 will help you with setting out your ideas as clearly as possible and also with the business of checking your work for errors, as well as the business of proof-reading. See Chapter 1 (Exercises 1 and 2), Chapter 2 (Exercise 2) and Chapter 4 (Exercise 3).

Examiners report that candidates who achieve high marks with coursework:
- read and think for themselves
- make good use of drafts to edit and revise their work
- demonstrate their personal interest and enthusiasm
- proof read their work.

Remember, you will be expected to show that you can read and understand opinions and ideas and can organise and express your response clearly and effectively. Whatever the text you find yourself addressing for Assignment 3, aim to proceed along these lines:

- Establish a clear understanding of the text. Could you easily summarise it?
- Ask yourself why the text was written; what is it that the writer concentrates on?
- Look at the way the ideas are ordered and presented
- Consider how successful or otherwise the writer is in communicating ideas and opinions
- Set out your responses, including your own ideas and opinions
- Re-consider, check and amend if necessary what you have written, several times.

Speaking and Listening

This is an optional addition to the English language course. It enables students to demonstrate clearly their ability to communicate in speech. This ability is important in itself and as the means to consider and prepare written material. A considerable amount of the activity in **Sections One to Four** provides useful practice for the speaking and listening assessment. Some of the chapters to look at are **1, 6, 9, 11, 13, 14, 15** and **20–23**.

Your teacher will have detailed information about this optional aspect of the course. Essentially, you may approach this aspect of the examination either through:

A Speaking and Listening test involving an individual task and a group discussion.

OR

Speaking and Listening coursework: an individual activity, a pair-based activity and a group activity. This would comprise the coursework folder of your work in speaking and listening that you would need to submit.

In both the test and coursework you will be expected to:
- handle facts, ideas and opinions
- convey experience, ideas and feelings
- speak clearly and fluently
- take into account your audience and the context of what you are saying
- show regard for the contributions of others.

The Speaking and Listening test

There are two parts to the test. Firstly, an individual task lasting three to four minutes, for example, a presentation, a talk, a speech or a monologue (a monologue is a brief talk that you give about a topic such as an encounter with someone who is well-known, music that you enjoy or a hobby that you pursue).

This is followed by a conversation with the teacher/examiner about your chosen topic which can be further developed at this stage.

Speaking and Listening coursework

Candidates are assessed on their performance during the course in three different speaking and listening tasks:

Task 1 – an individual activity, as in the test above

Task 2 – a pair-based activity, such a dramatised reading from a novel

Task 3 – a group activity, such as a discussion about work experience.

Tasks 2 and 3 are similar to the pair and group activities you did in **Sections One to Four** when a passage or topic was discussed.

Examiners report that candidates who achieve the highest possible marks in the Speaking and Listening part of the course:

- are prepared to explore and challenge ideas and are creative
- listen carefully to others' ideas then help to develop them further.

Handwriting

In their report provided by the examination board, the examiners referred twice to the problems caused by poor handwriting.

Here is an easy way for you to analyse and improve your handwriting. Write out this sentence three times on ordinary lined paper with a pen:

The quick brown fox jumps over the lazy dog.

Leave two lines blank after each of the lines on which you write.

When you write, remember the four S.s – Shape, Size, Slope and Space.

Now pencil in over each line of your handwriting:

line 1: a line 3 mm above the base to indicate how well the letters are <u>shaped</u> and <u>sized</u>

line 2: lines extending parts of letters that should be formed with straight lines

line 3: as many o.s as you can between the words.

Now check whether you have written clearly:

line 1: the main body of your letters should touch both the base line and the 3 mm line above it. The letters should also be recognisably shaped, for example, g or p

line 2: the extended lines should be vertical to the base line and parallel to one another

line 3: spaces that can accommodate only one o.

In your fourth blank line, draw a construction line in pencil 3 mm above the base line, as in line 4, write the sentence in pen and then erase the construction line.

Practise your handwriting little and often. Don't expect sudden or dramatic results. In time you can modify bad habits and form a handwriting style that examiners and others can read clearly.

Index